Supply
Chain
Optimization

Supply Chain Optimization

Building the Strongest Total Business Network

CHARLES C. POIRIER

&

STEPHEN E. REITER

Berrett-Koehler Publishers
San Francisco

Berrett-Koehler Publishers, Inc.
155 Montgomery Street
San Francisco, CA 94104-4109
Tel: (415) 288-0260   Fax: (415) 362-2512

ORDERING INFORMATION

Individual sales. Berrett-Koehler publications are available through most bookstores. They can also be ordered direct from Berrett-Koehler at the address above.

Quantity sales. Special discounts are available on quantity purchases by corporations, associations, and others. For details, contact the "Special Sales Department" at the Berrett-Koehler address above.

Orders for college textbook/course adoption use. Please contact Berrett-Koehler Publishers at the address above.

Orders by U.S. trade bookstores and wholesalers. Please contact Publishers Group West, 4065 Hollis Street, Box 8843, Emeryville, CA 94662. Tel: (510) 658-3453; 1-800-788-3123. Fax: (510) 658-1834.

Printed in the United States of America

 Printed on acid-free and recycled paper that is composed of 85% recycled fiber, including 15% postconsumer waste.

Library of Congress Cataloging-in-Publication Data

Poirier, Charles C., 1936–
   Supply chain optimization : building the strongest total business
network / Charles C. Poirier and Stephen E. Reiter. — 1st ed.
     p.   cm.
   Includes bibliographical references and index.
   ISBN 1-881052-93-1 (alk. paper)
   1. Business logistics—Cost effectiveness.   2. Business networks.
I. Reiter, Stephen E., 1952–   . II. Title.
HD38.5.P64   1996
658.5—dc20   96-7814
                                            CIP

First Edition

99 98 97 96   10 9 8 7 6 5 4 3 2 1

Book Production: Pleasant Run Publishing Services
Composition: Classic Typography

Dedication

To Charles Jones,
for his patient support of
two recruits as they made a
transition into a new profession

Contents

Preface

．．．．．．．．．．．．．．．．．．．．．．．．．

In today's fiercely competitive business environment, certain factors have become characteristic of those who survive and prosper. It is essential, for example, for some form of continuous improvement process to be functioning at high levels of effectiveness. Only by incessantly chasing every possible avenue of process improvement and seeking any beneficial enhancement to quality, productivity, cost, and customer satisfaction can companies hope to survive into the next century. To do otherwise is to abdicate the future to more effective competitors, who will find the enhancements needed to take market share regardless of historical positions or personal relationships.

The ability to generate double-digit savings on an annual basis and to constantly improve satisfaction ratings with customers has become a normal ownership expectation. No matter what the previous record of earnings has been or how effective customer performance has been rated in the past, today further, substantial gains have to be made in earnings and customer satisfaction. With an eye to success and survival, management has made these factors top priorities. However, the factors fall into a preferred order.

Firms that place their attention on generating high levels of customer satisfaction before concentrating on achieving profits are
the exception rather than the rule. Although the customer is the
key ingredient for success, so much pressure exists to achieve
short-term financial results that profit enhancement is the primary measure of performance in the current business environment.
Any cursory glance at how most senior executives are chosen will
reveal a preference for those who have generated a turnaround situation or have been hard-nosed about cutting costs.

The world is changing, even for organizations that are accustomed to having good market conditions. The opportunity, for
example, to raise prices on nationally advertised products that are
in constant, heavy demand on an annual basis has been replaced
by the requirement to reduce costs each year and to sustain and
build on whatever operating margins used to exist. Pricing moves
inexorably toward the consumer, and with it the need to find the
maximum savings in the system that delivers products and services to those consumers, at ever-higher levels of satisfaction. To
do otherwise is to watch as earnings are relinquished.

It is also necessary to have an extremely effective total quality
process in effect, to protect against losing customers because of
nonperformance. Organizations that attempted to create such a
culture and failed must rethink and reactivate their efforts. The
ultimate customers do not concern themselves with corporate
earnings, which they assume are obscenely high. They do put
quality at the top of their list of important factors. They presume
that quality is present; if it is not, they will return purchases. The
new customer demands are measured in terms of product and service qualifications, including ease of return, and they include the
expectation that they will receive the highest possible levels of performance from their purchased products. In a service environment, this means that if they are not treated in a helpful, courte-
ous manner, without complications in the transaction, they will
go elsewhere.

Providing a suitable level of responsiveness in this environment
mandates the deployment of information technology–based systems that ensure the highest level of practical development, with
features that meet or exceed the wants of the most difficult cus-

tomer. This condition guarantees the minimum amount of redundancy and eliminates all unnecessary forms of interaction by
automating manual processes that might slow the flow of information and lengthen the cycle time from production to consumption. Electronic solutions, based on the growing amount of
useful data-base information, have become the methodology for
securing an advantage over slower, less agile competitors who are
constrained by poor data communication systems. These solutions also lead to the elimination of extra, nonvalue-adding work
that places a burden on the speed and accuracy of the supply
chain.

Finally, the pressure for lowest-cost leadership throughout a
business network demands elimination of unnecessary inventories designed to cover system inadequacies. For the leading firms,
the just-in-time concept has been extended to the point where
delivery of necessary materials, products, or services at the precise time of need, in the correct amounts to meet consumer needs,
is becoming the expected norm. The traditional practice of foisting safety inventories onto suppliers to keep high fill rates and
maintain on-time deliveries has been replaced with systems that
make the need for these inventories go away. This removes the cost
of the inventories from the network, creating a more effective supply chain. In the service environment, the parallel technique is to
have the correct number of trained and customer-oriented personnel available for all customer demands.

With these conditions satisfied, a firm is prepared to become a
market leader in the current business environment. To reach the
level of greatest advantage, however, the firm must see that these
conditions are extended across the full supply chain system, from
initial raw materials, through manufacture and distribution, to the
retail outlets and the ultimate consumer. In the service arena, they
are extended from beginning facilities and supplies, through service creation and distribution, to receipt of customer feedback.
We call this system of supply the *interenterprise network;* it consists
of the chain of alliances that exists to satisfy the ultimate consumer with highest-quality, reasonably priced products and services at the moment of demand. It is the system used by any
business firm that receives incoming supplies or services for the

purpose of transforming them into a usable product, or into a sub-part for distribution and sale by a customer that in turn provides products and services to the ultimate consumer.

Our Research

We have visited and worked with over a hundred business organizations in the last five years, attempting to develop a supply chain model that would lead to optimized conditions for such business networks. Our intention was to gather as much information as possible on what was being practiced, what had worked and not worked, where opportunities still existed for further improvement, and how a total supply chain system could be developed that removed all extraneous costs.

As we conducted our research, we found that virtually every company we contacted was chasing the same imperatives—continuous improvement, total quality, shortest cycle time, smallest supporting inventories, and highest possible customer satisfaction—while continuing to maximize earnings. What we did not find was a single organization that had developed an optimized *total* enterprise network. For all the effort and good work expended, we did not see any company that had accomplished significant success across the entire supply chain.

We did find islands of impressive progress. Some of the firms that will be mentioned in this book have had outstanding accomplishments in areas that pertain to supply chain management. But no single company had extended its gains across an entire horizontally linked chain from original supply to final consumption. Thus it became our quest to find how the various pieces of the optimization puzzle could be fitted together to make a collage that would deliver today's supply necessities: the shortest cycle times, the smallest inventories that would meet consumption demands, the lowest delivered unit cost, the best error-free system to avoid the need for replacements caused by failures within the system, and pricing that satisfied the consumer and allowed the constituents within the chain to make a reasonable profit for their effort as well.

As we persevered in this quest, we began to find partners who wanted to chase the same objectives. With the help of these organizations, which will be duly noted, we were able to bring the concept into test conditions. Under these circumstances, it was possible to fit together the work done by many groups into an optimization model for supply chains. After going through many iterations, this model resulted in a format for developing the most effective manufacturing, service, and delivery system possible with today's technology.

We found that as enabling and enhancing information technology was brought to the front edge of supply chain needs, we could save significant amounts to support our business plan. We also found other savings that helped our partners and their customers. As we combined resources and worked together on pilot projects, we uncovered savings that were shared across the networks we were building. With these savings, our partners were able to self-fund efforts that led to meeting goals and objectives related to their business plans and strategies. In brief, we found that chasing supply chain optimization enabled us and our partners to meet current financial requirements and to sustain the improvements that are necessary for survival in the future.

The purpose of this book is to share these discoveries with the reader, and to outline and develop a model that can lead to meeting today's business imperatives through the development of the most effective supply chain system possible.

Intended Audience

This book is intended for those who are interested in learning how to build on what they have already done to create a more effective supply chain system. It is based on the concept that no one organization has a lock on all of the best improvement ideas and is intended to illustrate how existing initiatives can be enhanced by combining resources that are usually overlooked or avoided in the supply system, in order to build additional improvements into the supply network. Our intended audience includes those people in business who are never satisfied that they have found the ultimate solution.

We do not recommend throwing away whatever effort has been developed to improve supply chain efficiencies. Rather, we advise building on to that work, in much the same way that a large jigsaw puzzle would be constructed, adding pieces that make sense to frame a more complete network and system for delivering what the customer wants to consume. We have found that most practitioners have viable supply chain solutions under way. Indeed, many have leading-edge practices at work. What they lack is the application of those practices across the full supply network. It is for those in search of the solution to the complete puzzle that we present this book

Overview of the Contents

The book has ten chapters. In the first chapter, we establish what a supply chain is all about and how it is used to bring goods and services into today's markets. We also discuss the concept of building an optimized supply network by using electronic technology and sound principles of partnering. The idea is not to use partnering for leveraging buying positions, but rather to find the scarce, talented resources that can be applied to a joint improvement effort.

In Chapter Two we present a historical perspective, illustrating how the supply chain network has evolved and how it has led to such ideas as efficient consumer response (ECR), continuous replenishment process (CRP), electronic data interchange (EDI), and other replenishment and quick-response methodologies. We also consider why these soundly based concepts have received slow implementation, and what it will take for them to have more universal application.

In Chapter Three we present the interenterprise model, a four-step sequential model that turns the traditional "push" system of supply into a "pull" system based on actual consumption. With this model, we illustrate how the great potential for improvement within supply chains can be tapped.

Chapter Four positions business partnering across the four-step model as the catalyst that makes the system work for all the constituents. We redefine this much-abused and often-misunderstood concept in terms that are useful for making supply chain optimization a reality.

Chapter Five outlines the obstacles that will prevent success with the model if they are not identified and overcome. Organizations have tolerated too many of these obstacles, causing incessant and unnecessary delays in achieving the full potential of supply chain optimization.

Reengineering is the theme of Chapter Six, in which we consider where to apply this new and powerful tool. Too often, the tool is misapplied, leading to a success rate of less than 50 percent. Applied properly, it becomes one of the most powerful of the modern process improvement techniques.

In Chapter Seven we move into the arena of advanced partnering, discussing actual examples of successful application of the ideas and methods that make the interenterprise model work. We also describe the importance of developing the enabling and enhancing information technology and tell how to link this critical element with business objectives related to supply chain improvement.

In Chapter Eight we position the vital area of logistics, under the demands created by today's conditions, as the enabler for achieving the short cycle times with minimal handling, inventory, and warehousing and maximum accuracy of deliveries that are so important to optimization.

We take a future look at supply chains in Chapter Nine. Here we explore where the trends of today will lead and draw a picture of the next century's network of supply systems.

Finally, in Chapter Ten, we draw together the concepts that have been presented and summarize our argument and the implementation model. Supply chain optimization is a worthy quest and a feasible concept. This book should prove useful for anyone interested in moving in that important direction.

Acknowledgments

Many people have been extremely helpful to us as we developed our model of optimization across a full supply network. Nicholas Ciaccio of Dominick's Finer Foods became our first true sponsor, and we thank him and salute his foresight. Dan Baumgartner, Cate Boeth, David Livingston, Donald Madsen, and Toni Wilson of IBM were extremely helpful and cooperative as we developed the model that was to become the guide to optimizing a supply chain. Gregg Granberg offered invaluable assistance and helped immensely, with Frank Babel, in transferring our expertise to clients within the Electronic Data Systems Corporation (EDS) network.

Many people within EDS provided valuable support and critiques, particularly Jack Barry, Mike Bauer, Todd Harbison, Charles Jones, and Larry Menefee. Bill Markham and Jim Morehouse, with A. T. Kearney, contributed their editing skills to enhance the contents, and we gratefully recognize their help. Barbara Santeler and Cecelia Toepfer had the patience to prepare the many early versions of the manuscript. John Rivard, Sue Brosnan, and Gerrie Urbanek assumed the task of bringing the final document into prepared form and patiently helped with the arduous task of editing. Steven Piersanti and the staff at Berrett-Koehler were, as usual, most helpful with ideas and comments on development and publication. Without their support, there would be no manuscript. Mary Garrett and, particularly, Stanley Bass gave us the editorial comment required to finalize our manuscript. Many others helped in the concept and implementation, and we have endeavored to mention them at the appropriate positions in the book.

Chicago, Illinois   Charles C. Poirier
May 1996   Stephen E. Reiter

Chapter One

The Supply Chain

Business organizations today face unrelenting pressure to find new and more effective means to bring their products and services from concept and creation through delivery, on to the outlets of their customers, and then into the hands of the ultimate consumers. The demands of today's fiercely competitive environment have made it imperative that companies not only target every ounce of inefficiency that exists within their system of delivery but also redefine and reengineer how supply chains should function, in order to establish an error-free, totally efficient network from original supply to final consumption.

Several schools of thought have developed on how to accomplish this purpose. One group of improvement technologists argues for developments that seek maximum efficiency with the shortest cycle times. For this group, such a system will foster a stream of innovative products that can be brought to market faster than any competitive network. Unfortunately, the track record for many of these new introductions is less than exciting. Fewer than a hundred new products survive from the thousands introduced each year. But the consumer's desire for a stream of innovation

2
• • • • •

must be satisfied, and this group is in the forefront of that response.

Another group advocates extracting every possible savings to reduce the already attractive "everyday low price" (EDLP) that exists at certain retail outlets. If they do this, they can tell consumers that there is no need for special discounts or promotions. The everyday pricing will be as low as possible at all times. For this group, the intention is to maximize market position. However, for the consumer to become loyal to EDLP firms, these groups must face unyielding pressure for cost improvement by quickly delivering the fruits of their efficiency to the store shelves.

A third camp would use leading-edge information technology to link the members of a supply chain to the network, which would then become a model of effectiveness. This network would eliminate all duplicated effort and reduce paperwork to an absolute minimum in a virtually errorless system. For this group, success comes from knowing that their network cannot be matched in terms of efficiency. Low cost is presumed to exist in this type of supply chain.

A fourth group seeks the means to turn the traditional "push" of the product toward the retail customer into one that would "pull" the product through the network in response to consumer purchases. For scores of years, supply chains were oriented around the concept of manufacturing goods in demand, at the lowest unit cost, for movement (push) toward the consumer. Improvements were generally focused on faster speeds or on the unit-to-time ratio, so item costs would steadily decline. As profits were generated, a portion always went to increasing capacity, causing more units to be produced at ever-lower costs. The sales concept was to push this volume toward the consumer. Inventories that built up between manufacturing and consumption were conveniently stored in warehouses or distribution centers so that the push would be uninterrupted.

The emerging concept is to eliminate the significant costs embedded in those inventories and warehouses by developing closer links between actual consumption and production. Using ever-increasing data bases containing information on what has been purchased by specific categorized customers, it is now possible to pull products and services in direct response to what has been consumed. This network will function with the lowest inventories, damage, and obsolescence. Quick response is the motto for this group, which strives to build a system that pulls through only the products that are in actual demand, using a methodology that concentrates on the transactions taking place at the cash registers and checkout counters.

Growing armies of specialists chasing supply chain improvement are considering, testing, and developing these and many more approaches, focusing attention on the manufacture, conversion, storage, and logistic distribution of products and services. We see a great opportunity to combine the energy of these schools into a unified effort that seeks what each group ultimately craves: an optimized supply chain network that generates shared savings for all constituents, while establishing a competitive advantage in the market of choice. The savings extracted from such a system could be shared in part with the ultimate consumers, but a portion would create the funding to develop further network enhancements on a continuous basis. Only in this way will the network keep pace with the ever-changing patterns of consumption to sustain the coveted competitive advantage. To develop such an optimized scenario, we need first to understand the supply chain and the factors that are affecting the drive for improvement. This knowledge begins with a consideration of exactly what constitutes a supply chain.

The Supply Chain Illustrated

A supply chain is a system through which organizations deliver their products and services to their customers. For our purposes we will illustrate this chain as a network of interlinked organizations, or *constituencies,* that have as a common purpose the best possible means of affecting that delivery.

Suppliers

The network begins with sources that can provide the basic ingredients to start a chain of supply—raw materials, ingredients, commodities, subassemblies, and so forth. We will call these sources

4
• • • • •

suppliers. In the truest sense, we could include suppliers' suppliers, but that only makes a simple process more complex than it has to be and places constraints on achieving success. If we consider that virtually any business has a limited number of primary sources that provide 70 to 80 percent of the incoming raw materials from which the finished product or service is generated, we see that a supply chain can be started with this limited group of suppliers.

These key suppliers provide the metal for stamping; the vegetables and cans for soups; the sand and labels for bottles; the subassemblies for manufacture and assembly of automobile components; the flour, sugar, and other ingredients for baking; and so forth. This first link is sufficient to start the process without making the chain of supply an endless connection.

Suppliers ➧ Manufacturer

The second linkage is with the manufacturer, converter, or processor who builds, assembles, converts, or furnishes a product or service that is clearly identified as the consumable in the network. For our purposes, we will call that link the *manufacturer,* although an easy transition to a service environment can be made with the same model. This simple, primary connection already contains ample opportunity to begin the drive for savings. The inventory of raw materials that resides somewhere between the supplier and the manufacturer is an obvious target. In our experience, reductions of 40 to 60 percent or more are possible in most situations. By applying the concept of supplier partnering in this arena, we have eliminated paperwork in the form of purchase orders and acknowledgments. With the help of people from both constituencies, we were able to effect beneficial changes to specifications and pricing and to expedite information transfer and billings. More important, we succeeded in finding value enhancements in these primary couplings that ran to millions of dollars, often at single manufacturing sites.

Suppliers ➧ Manufacturer ➧ Distribution

The chain now needs a means to get the product to the consumer. Although many alternatives are available, we will examine a *dis-*

tribution system because it fits the requirements of most supply chains. This system transports the finished product from manufacture through a warehouse or distribution center, if necessary, and delivers the appropriate amounts to the retail outlet at the time of request. In some networks, a wholesaler will be part of the chain. This constituent will take responsibility for breaking down larger loads and delivering the product to small outlets.

Wholesalers typically operate their own warehouses, but they may use public facilities to stage the product before delivery to their customers. Again, we find ample opportunity to cut inventories and warehouse space and to reduce costs and cycle times as we analyze the traditional distribution systems and redesign them for greater effectiveness. Within virtually every network that we studied, opportunities were uncovered that led to space and inventory reductions.

Suppliers ➧ Manufacturer ➧ Distribution ➧ Retail Outlets ➧ Consumers

From their shelves or floors, *retail outlets* then offer the product to would-be purchasers. These outlets include the grocery stores, department stores, deep discount outlets, club stores, superstores, and mass merchandisers from which the final purchase is made. Although the chain of physical distribution is concluded at this point, the model would be incomplete if we did not include one final element. *Consumers* have the final decision in selecting their products of choice and making purchases that conclude the chain. For simplicity, we will stop the illustrated chain at this point.

The Supply Chain Model

A more elaborate model, developed by A. T. Kearney (Kearney, 1994), is depicted in Figure 1.1. In this illustration, suppliers' suppliers have been included to show the complete linkage of groups of enterprises that come together to acquire, convert, and distribute goods and services to ultimate consumers. This depiction also highlights the need to distribute new designs throughout the network in order to anticipate and respond to the requirements of the markets being served. The key factors in achieving optimization are the creation of a flow of information that moves easily and accurately among the network constituents and an efficient and effective product transition with resulting high levels of ultimate consumer satisfaction. A similar model can be developed for service organizations. A financial firm would start with supplies and facilities and progress with an intellectual conversion, rather than a manufacturing step. Distribution would then take place through branch offices, taking the actual financial service to a consuming entity.

Most organizations must seek enhancements to their own version of this chain of supply, to induce the appropriate consumer response and to develop optimized techniques and systems that will allow them to sustain or improve their margins as they strive to meet changing customer demands. Organizations on the leading edge of this effort are also seeking the means to enhance the entire chain, to make their network as efficient and effective as possible. It is the combination of these competing efforts that creates the enormous pressures organizations now feel to make enhancements all along the supply chain, from raw materials to consumption or from initial input to final service. Those who are not in the midst of such an improvement effort risk being left out of future competition.

This search for optimization begins with the consideration that any supply chain starts with a certain amount of incoming materials and supplies. For products with as many components as an

FIGURE 1.1. Supply Chain Model.

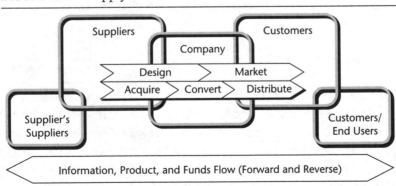

Source: Kearney, 1994. Used with permission.

automobile or airplane, the number of suppliers is large, but current efforts are under way by virtually every manufacturer to reduce that number and to remove levels of complexity from the system. The basic concept in the late 1980s was to prune the supply base to reduce variability and to cut the costs of negotiating and tracking. In the 1990s, these efforts include developing a core group of select or strategic suppliers who have met criteria that set them apart in terms of quality and value. The idea is to align the firm with those organizations that will be the winners in the twenty-first century. Supply chain optimization efforts should begin with this core group. We will refer to this cadre of important entities as *key suppliers* or *strategic sources.* For manufacturers, the initial key group should be the select sources that represent the bulk of the incoming elements or ingredients that are crucial for strategic purposes, and from which the final conversion is made. For service organizations, the key group can be developed with similar sourcing efforts focused on finding the cadre of important suppliers that will help enhance future viability.

Managing the Flow in a Supply Chain

To achieve the optimum conditions of supply, it is then necessary to have a picture that is representative of the chain of links that begins with these logical sources. For paper products, the chain could start with the forest of trees or the storehouse of recycled products that initiates the process. It can more simply be the block of suppliers that constitute 70 to 80 percent of the ingredients that end as a salable paper product. For a bakery item, the same chain could start with wheat, sugar, eggs, milk, and flavoring suppliers. A furniture manufacturer might start with steel, plastic, fixtures, and fabric sources. A bank's chain could begin with suppliers of forms, computers, and software and a reliable placement bureau. The resulting picture would be a depiction of how these materials and resources are ordered, assured of quality, received, and processed.

The steps that link manufacturers to ultimate consumption should similarly be illustrated, so that those who would do the optimizing can clearly see how the product is moved to the consumer. If wholesalers are necessary in the chain, they should be depicted. If direct store deliveries are made, the picture should reflect that condition. Again, we prefer simplicity for the sake of focused effort, rather than the complexity that usually accompanies an overly ambitious depiction. With this illustration, which is quite simply a full system flowchart of interactive processes, we can move to consider how the current circumstances of consumption in the chain under analysis are having an impact on the need for enhancing the network.

Flowcharts are an essential element of supply chain optimization because they depict the current state of interactions, allowing improvement redesign to be initiated. Many texts on flowcharting are available from reference and business sources. General Electric Company is a particularly good resource because of its extensive use and success with flowcharting as an improvement technique. For our purposes, we have found success using simple block diagrams that plot the flow of product or service creation and delivery to the consumer. Detail is reserved for later steps in the analysis, as the focus shifts to specific processes that show up on the flowchart and are identified as candidates for redesign. Figure 1.2 is an example of a flowchart for an order fulfillment process.

Emerging Consumer Demands

With the current steps in a supply network illustrated, the attention on improvement begins at the consumption side of the flowchart. Too many firms have wasted too much effort by improving the front end, or upstream side, of the flowchart and not introducing the change elements that meet the real needs of the final consumer. Changes in the habits of consumers have dramatically altered patterns of consumption, casting the consumers as the ultimate controllers of most supply chain systems. They are the individuals who really determine how supply chains should function. Today's consumers want a pleasant shopping experience; they will avoid returning to retail outlets or institutions that disappoint them. This alteration in buying habits is swift and final.

FIGURE 1.2. Sample Flowchart.

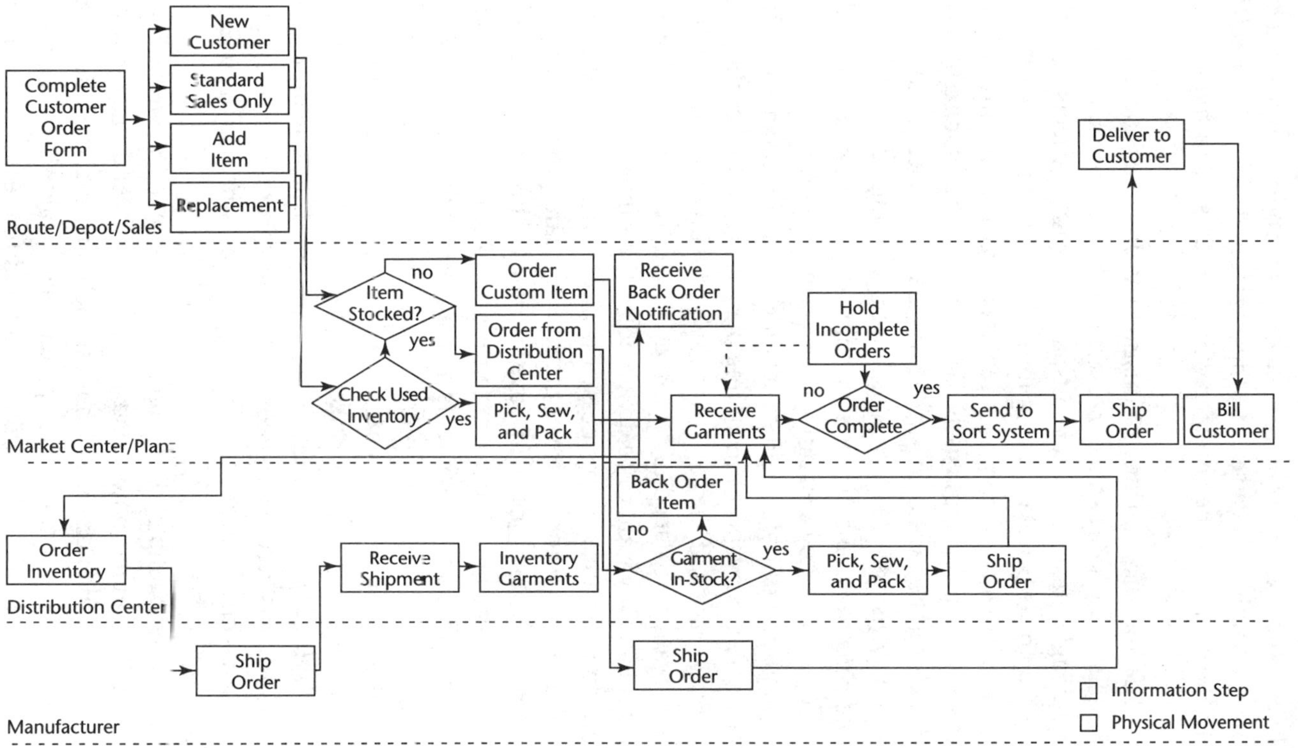

Route/Depot/Sales

Complete Customer Order Form → New Customer / Standard Sales Only / Add Item / Replacement

Item Stocked? — no → Order Custom Item / Order from Distribution Center
Item Stocked? — yes
Check Used Inventory — yes → Pick, Sew, and Pack

Receive Back Order Notification

Receive Garments

Order Complete — no → Hold Incomplete Orders
Order Complete — yes → Send to Sort System → Ship Order → Deliver to Customer → Bill Customer

Market Center/Plant

Back Order Item
Garment In-Stock? — no
Garment In-Stock? — yes → Pick, Sew, and Pack → Ship Order
Receive Shipment → Inventory Garments → Ship Order

Distribution Center

Order Inventory → Ship Order

Manufacturer

☐ Information Step
☐ Physical Movement

Consumers want creative sales approaches, the height of friend-liness, and the appearance of innovative products and services—all at what they perceive to be the lowest price for every purchase. The exception is the shopper who is interested in high-prestige items.

The modern consumer consistently demands more for less. Families may have two income sources, but they are under pressure from higher taxes, medical costs, and interest payments, as well as having the expense of caring for children while they work. Con-sumers, other than the rich, have less disposable income and want to spend their earnings wisely. With time constraints also having an impact on their willingness to shop, they spend less time in stores and only visit selected locations, looking for immediate satisfaction and perceived value. In this environment, a store's nonvalue-adding functions have to be eliminated or it will disappear.

Consumers look for products that are environmentally correct and safe in all aspects, including packaging, but what they value most is service. If they are not delighted with what they purchase, they want it replaced or repaired, hassle-free. In a service envi-ronment, they want to be delighted by their interaction with peo-ple. In most areas of business, it is now widely accepted that the voice of the customer drives the supply chain process. Only with infusions of high levels of advertising can this voice be directed toward particular sources, or to the purchase of specific products. The supply chain constituents who answer to that voice now must focus on it with greater intensity. The characteristics of consum-ers' fluctuating patterns are what create responses at the retail level. Value and service rank near the top of the list of require-ments, followed by savings in time and innovative features. Con-venience has become a byword in this new world of easy selection backed with a radically new concept: friendly help in the selection process.

As one example of changing patterns that have to be recog-nized, consumers now spend 43 percent of their dollars in restau-rants, convenience stores, and fast-food outlets rather than in tra-ditional grocery stores. This pattern has established a new set of criteria for retail outlets, which have had to create new processes to meet these changing demands. Today's grocery store now contains an ever-increasing amount of floor space dedicated to specialty departments such as in-house baking and delicatessens as well as to a variety of fresh products and items prepared on-site. McDonald's, Little Caesars Pizza, and Starbucks Coffee are among the specialties moving onto supermarket floors. The emerging superstores offer restaurants, pharmacies, department store shopping, and groceries. Their size continues to grow in an effort to create the one-stop shopping center that they believe will capture nearly all household purchases in a single visit. Fresh America, an alliance formed with Wal-Mart Stores, now operates the fresh produce department in the Sam's Wholesale Club outlets and has experienced over 80 percent annual growth.

Alternatively, a new type of retailer has emerged to meet the needs of consumers who do not care for one-stop shopping for all of their needs. Termed "category killers," these retailers focus on a specific area, or category, of consumption. Pet stores, automobile supply stores, sports centers, linen outlets, and others represent the idea of building specific-focus outlets. At these centers, the consumer is greeted with a bewildering array of products that are specific to the category of interest. Revenue growth at these outlets has initially been very impressive, often exceeding 20 percent per year.

Another cause of alterations in retail outlets is the increasing ethnic diversity of some neighborhoods, which has given rise to micromarketing strategies. The need to meet this desire for local options has caused many stores to trim some national-brand goods and allocate more space for specialty items that better match local ethnic preferences. Most grocery stores now have sections dedicated to the buying wants of the ethnic groups in surrounding neighborhoods; portion sizes have also changed to match family sizes in those areas. Clothing retailers also make adjustments in stock and floor space to meet local demands.

Recognizing that the buyer is the controller, some organizations are attempting to create the shopping experience of the future. In Chicago, Jewel Food Stores has introduced interactive shopping via computer networks. After subscribing to the service, called Peapod, the buyer doesn't have to leave home to buy groceries. Using a personal computer and a modem, he or she can "walk" into the Jewel store, go down any aisle, and make whatever selections are desired. Jewel delivers these selections to the house within hours. We will revisit this concept in Chapter Nine as we look at the shopping experience of the future.

Business networks engaged in meeting these changing consumer patterns must form alliances that are oriented toward the ultimate consumer, for if they fail to do so, they might not survive. Those who want not only to survive but also to perpetuate a competitive lead must first meet, then exceed, those consumer expectations. This means that organizations have to set aside the traditional power struggles that pervade most supply chains. It is not enough to wring the last concession from a supplier; instead, the most efficient supply network must be created, from the initial source to the cashier in the store. Inherent in this requirement is the redesign of existing networks by tapping the imagination and accessing the best thinking from all the network constituents to create the preferred system of the future. As we develop our argument in the ensuing pages, we will synthesize our position into a compelling thesis that meets this system need: we believe that adversarial self-interest can be changed to cooperative, mutually beneficial relationships that actually work for all network participants.

Rising Power of the Retailer

If consumers are the major element of control in the new supply chain, then their chief agent is the retail outlet or service organization from which their purchases are made. Retailers and service providers have indeed responded to this new and more powerful voice of consumption by revamping their stores, offices, personnel, and techniques. Consolidation of firms in nearly every consumable area is concurrently creating new ownership, larger entities, and the spawning of larger individual stores. In the process, retailers are finding a new sense of power that, if it is not controlled, could weaken the very supply chains on which they depend to meet these ultimate consumer demands. If their power goes unchecked and they overly concentrate on their buying power to force unrealistic concessions from their upstream sup-

pliers, gaining these concessions could ultimately force manufacturers to develop a direct linkage with consumers.

B
•••••

No force can stop the drive by retailers to try to extract every
potential saving from the supply system. The nature of their existence is to get the products in demand at the lowest possible cost.
And little can be done to keep most of those savings from the
hands of their customers. A glance at historical profit levels reveals
generally low overall margins for this sector of business—1 to 2
percent net profit is common. It is traditional for most of the savings to be passed on to the consumers. The complication of this
time-honored process is that the current power position of the
retailers sometimes drives costs down faster than the suppliers can
find the means to maintain their margins. Much of the savings has
come from process improvement, but a large portion has simply
consisted of cost concessions on the part of compliant suppliers.
This condition leaves the upstream players without a sufficient
portion of the savings to generate further improved processes and
does little to establish an incentive to dig out other enhancements.

In a time when organizations should be linked together in a
business network that functions to best meet consumers' interests
and desires, we see less talk about establishing such systems and
more about who will control the network. We find little conversation about the elements of sharing, trust, and partnering, but
much about the shift of power into the hands of the retail outlets.
This power shift has created a jaundiced view on the part of manufacturers, especially as they are approached for participation in
supply chain improvement activities.

The matter of control is important for those who are upstream in
the typical supply chain; they see this ramp toward the retailer
becoming the highway for shifting all the potential savings toward
one element in the network. Such a scenario briefly makes the retailer, and most likely the ultimate consumer, very happy, but it does
little to create the funding to continue the drive for future enhancements or to advance toward the ultimate target—an optimized supply network. In spite of the current stories that herald the savings
being generated by what appear to be cooperative supplier-retailer
efforts, we see a cloud of concern forming among manufacturers
who see margin erosion as the price to be paid for joint improvement

efforts, particularly with the largest retailers. This trend runs counter to our thesis that mutually beneficial relations actually work and can be the driver behind supply chain improvement.

We prefer a network built on the concept of partnering, in which a portion of the savings is shared across the supply network, with each constituent benefiting from what will surely be a major redesign effort. Otherwise, the network will never be optimized, because the upstream participants will lose the incentive to dig out the truly hard-to-find savings. Our experience with testing pilot models of such a network has demonstrated that logical sharing is not only feasible but essential in creating the lowest-cost network. Partnering becomes the catalyst that makes it work, but only after the players demonstrate a different level of trust than the one that exists in the typical relationships we see today. A new playing field has to be defined on which the constituents work together for mutual advantage and to provide the end results desired by the new consumers. Only in an atmosphere of cooperation will the greatest savings accrue to the network.

To us, this argument seems logical. It plays well with the firms and management with which it is discussed, but a survey of current practices definitely shows a shift in power toward the retailer. In analyzing why this condition is prevalent, we first see that the retailers have the information edge on their suppliers. They can now electronically scan the products moving through their stores and direct their flow of orders based on actual consumption. Whereas the national brands used to have an edge due to heavy investments in market research and after-the-fact buying analyses, up-to-date consumption information now gives the managers of local stores what they need to stock tomorrow's shelves. Stocking releases (the goods that are sent to the retail outlet to replace what has been purchased) are moving inexorably toward this most current of consumption information, and with it control of what is sent to the retail outlets.

Powerful retailers like Wal-Mart, Kmart, Home Depot, H-E-B Food Stores, and the warehouse clubs seem to be in the lead in using this important information. Their plan is to use point-of-sale (POS) data to create quick-response alliances with selected suppliers, who will take direct responsibility for replenishing stocks to store shelves and floors at predetermined levels. Wal-Mart has the largest satellite communication network in this industry, linking its headquarters, stores, and selected suppliers in a system that brings replenishment cycles to radically short times. Using a software system called Retail-Link, they have forged a precedent-setting alliance with the Procter & Gamble Company to stock and replenish selected items in as short a time as twenty-four hours.

Linda Perry reports that Troy, Michigan–based Kmart has also been doing well with this technique (Perry, 1992). Working with three hundred suppliers of nonclothing products participating in a program called "Partners in Merchandise Flow," Kmart has launched a system that shifts "the burden for managing stock from the giant retailer to its suppliers" (p. 61). With plans to add to the supplier base, the system already functions in the direction intended by its designers. Perry elaborates:

At 7 A.M. each day, Kmart transmits to its vendors via EDI (electronic data interchange) three categories of data on its current inventory levels: what's available in the distribution center, what's in transit, and what was sold the previous day at the retailer's 2,000-plus stores.

With that data in hand, suppliers determine how much to ship and when to ship it. Their performance is measured according to how often inventory is turned over at the stores and how often a customer is unable to buy an item because it's out of stock.

Clearly, Kmart is one organization that is moving aggressively forward to make its supply chain more efficient, using its data base and current purchase information as leverage. Kmart is also following the shift in power by directing those higher up in the supply chain to take responsibility for inventories and deliveries, a responsibility that had typically been borne at the retail level.

In this environment, the group that makes the most demands is the mass merchandisers—the retailers who offer discounted prices on a wide array of products, from soft goods to groceries and appliances. These outlets insist that those within their supply chain be fully able to offer error-free bar coding, direct store delivery, and custom packaging and to provide mixed-pallet loads (instead of the traditional one-item pallets). This retail group generates a growing list of demands for improvements that appear to the upstream participants to be more concessions than beneficial changes to the system. Typical of the items on the concession list is the transfer of inventory costs to the manufacturers, the need to place goods on consignment, elimination of distribution charges, charge-backs for nonconformance, and marketing support that is beyond normal levels. Missing from these relationships is the interactive working out of mutual improvements that benefit both parties.

As this particular group is upping the ante for using floor space in its outlets, grocers are also responding with new demands. As retailers find an opportunity for higher margins, private labels are encroaching on the space they formerly allotted to the national brands. At the same time, in spite of a trend toward EDLP by some national brands, many grocers are insisting on the maintenance of promotions and the advantage they create for "forward buying." This practice, which has long endured in the grocery system, affords the purchaser the opportunity to take advantage of a promotion by buying extra amounts that are subsequently sold at regular prices. (We will discuss these practices in greater detail in Chapter Two.) Grocers also are asking for special delivery conditions and are nearly universal in their insistence on the use of bar coding on all incoming orders.

The retail world suffers from the development of space that has outpaced the growth of consumer demand for goods and services. Because of this, retailers have created a battle for market share. One ultimate trend of this warfare is for the retailers to conduct their affairs as if they were in the business of leasing real estate. With this shift in focus, they provide their floor and shelf space as outlets for suitable manufacturers, while requiring all responsibility for replenishment to be passed up the supply chain to those manufacturers, leaving the retailers with the role of optimizing the use of the available space through increased sales. This shift means that all inventory and delivery costs must be shouldered by those upstream of the retailer. The manufacturer, in turn, has been looking upstream as well to find compliant suppliers to whom some of these replenishment costs can be transferred. All of this effort overlooks the possibility of working out improvements that benefit the total supply network, even though it certainly is a favorable trend for those in retailing.

As the emphasis shifts to bidding for floor space in the outlets, the retailers enhance their position of power. In a complementary vein, they are pushing another advantageous feature, demanding the added benefits that an electronic linkage can bring in terms of elimination of errors, quicker response, and reduction of paperwork. In sum, the general short-term future looks reasonably bright for the retailer, assuming that the firms can cope with changing consumer patterns and competition for the consumer dollar. This group would do well, however, to look more closely at the potential to optimize across the entire supply chain, rather than just in the local areas that favor their own short-term profitability and service. By doing so, they would help to develop a supply base that continually seeks further improvements. On the other hand, if they do not work hard in this area, they run the risk of promoting adversarial relationships that slow real progress and the discovery of total system savings.

From First Supply to Final Consumption

Looking across the total supply chain, we can see that the ultimate consumer provides the final determination of who will achieve success. In other words, customer satisfaction has to be viewed as the driving factor. With retailers functioning as the primary providers of that satisfaction, several questions take on importance for those upstream in the supply chain:

- How can the manufacturers and distribution organizations provide the enabling services and sustain their margins?
- How does the supply chain make certain that the best-selling or highest-margin items are always available and are not sidetracked somewhere in the delivery chain?
- How does the system ensure that the retail shelves or floors are stocked with items the customers want at any particular time or season?

- Where will the funding come from to support the necessary investment in new systems, software, hardware, and changes to current practices?
- Who will provide the resources to develop the needed process redesigns?

Our response is that more work needs to be done to pool the successes that have been achieved and to create an execution model that can be optimized, while leaving funds available to continue to find solutions for these problems and others that perplex those who are chasing supply chain improvement. To emphasize our position that this further work can lead to improvements that would otherwise be overlooked, let us relate an experience with a retailer who is operating in this new environment of greater control. In an interview with one of Chicago's largest retailers, we asked if the recent Christmas season had been a success. "One of our best," was the crisp reply. When we asked if their stores could have sold more, the retailer quickly answered, "Of course." When we persisted in asking why, the retailer said that the stores had gone out of stock on many key items. Hearing this from an organization that has taken a lead in forging new shorter-cycle, automated supply systems, we realized that supply chain optimization still has much to accomplish.

We asked this same source if he believed that the organization could avoid being out of stock with an effective supply chain system. He responded affirmatively, but quickly added that the effectiveness would have to begin at the start of the supply chain. This reply confirmed a key part of our argument. For want of a nail, a kingdom could be lost, and for want of a label, box, pallet, ingredient, or truck, a sale could be lost. The system is only optimized when all the links are functioning, so that whatever is needed to achieve total customer satisfaction is ready, is of the requisite quality, and is delivered in the most efficient manner possible to the point and at the time of need. Anything less puts at least one order at risk of being lost to the network.

Alternatively, a network may fall back on what most supply systems rely on: excessive inventories that allow goods to be pulled from stock to meet short-term demands. This concept is hopelessly flawed, however, since such systems frequently result in too much of the wrong inventory, outages in demanded goods, extra handling costs, damage, obsolescence, and heavy carrying costs that eventually are pushed on to the consumer. In one case, we worked with a well-established retail firm that had developed a five-year data base on actual sales. In spite of this knowledge, the firm constantly struggled with the question of what to stock for the new season and how to keep the inventory prime. A more effective system would work out the methods and processes that provide the goods and services needed without heavy doses of inventory. Inventory should be limited to sustaining high turnover levels and covering the slowest-turnover items in such a way that the cost of carrying these supplies is minimized.

What we are proposing is the development of the latest evolution of just-in-time delivery, in which the right amounts of the right products are delivered to the point of purchase at the right time, with inventories as close to zero as possible. This system is not only feasible but is becoming a key to long-term survival, because no one wants to pay for the costs of these inventories. Many organizations have achieved success in certain areas of their supply chain. What remains is to find the means to extend these successes across the total chain. The more successful leaders in this effort are busy reengineering their supply chain systems, putting their focus on such novel arrangements as:

- Building alliances with suppliers that bring them together to work out improvements to forecasting, order fulfillment, planning, scheduling, packaging, delivery, replenishment, billing, and inventory control
- Outsourcing arrangements that put certain necessary functions in the supply chain in the hands of the constituent who is most capable of performing them successfully
- Placing new emphasis on the logistics function, to ensure not just that the product gets to where it should be, but that all the inherent costs are minimized
- Designing radically different distribution strategies to enhance the network's position with the consumer and create the most efficient system of delivery

- Reducing cycle times between producers and stocking of stores from just under a week to one or two days, with an ultimate measurement target in hours
- Reducing supporting paperwork to the level necessary to satisfy financial reporting
- Shifting from a draw-from-inventory stocking system to a flow mentality that pulls product immediately into and through the system based on actual consumption
- Looking to the information technology function to provide links across the full supply chain, cutting manual redundancies and other nonvalue-adding functions

Achieving these objectives has proved to be elusive for some organizations but feasible for others, at least in some areas. What loom as the largest obstacles in achieving success are factors that are grounded in human nature and in the heavy reliance on tradition in the practices that pervade retail supply and selling.

The Dilemma of Achieving Optimization

The first step in building an optimized supply chain is to improve daily communication between suppliers, manufacturers, and distributors. With accurate information on consumption, the network will be able to respond to the demand without requiring large inventories. Permanent warehouse space and the carrying of safety stocks will move closer to minimization as this daily system includes the promotional and seasonal adjustment information that already exists within the retailers' data bases. Unfortunately, this need reflects the prevailing problem of the reluctance of retailers to share commercial information with those upstream in their network. A few retailers are offering this information at a charge; several organizations, such as Nielsen N.A. and IRI Logistics (a division of Information Resources, Inc.), collect and offer it as a service for a fee. In our experience, regardless of the format, as this information flows more freely, the need for supporting inventory shrinks dramatically.

In one of our pilot experiments, in an effort to demonstrate the value of shared data, we requested access to a manufacturer's shop floor information, a previously sacrosanct area. In this particular situation, our organization was upstream of our customer, the manufacturer. The purpose of the request was to enable us to make delivery closer to the time of need, rather than from built-up inventory. As we broke down the traditional wall of resistance by offering access to another sacrosanct area of our own, that of actual manufacturing costs, we were able to secure information that led directly to making the right deliveries at the right time. Raw material inventory turns (the number of times an inventory is turned into actual sales) for our customer went from 12 to 14 per year to as high as 200 to 250. Our need to build safety stocks also diminished. Building upon the new level of trust that this experiment engendered, we improved our information interfaces, thereby eliminating much of the former antagonism and wasted effort that existed. The result was a more streamlined system that saved money for both companies.

In this system, we were able to blend the forecast information we had historically received with actual usage data, information on store promotions, and on-line schedule changes. We no longer shipped raw materials for machines that were out of production for maintenance, or for planned usage that did not materialize. We did ship materials that were often taken from the truck to the machines that were finishing a new setup. We increased or decreased follow-up stock according to how successful the promotions were. Throughout the experiment, the need for safety inventories was reduced, and space in the customer's factory that had previously been used for storing materials was turned over to operations for use in manufacturing.

This experience suggested to us that similar efforts would work on the delivery end of a supply chain if the constituents would more closely align production and delivery with actual store sales. As we pursued this concept, we found many organizations already developing such interactions. We also discovered that progress was often delayed because of a lack of trust and open communication between the parties who were trying to capitalize on the kind of improvement features we knew could be made. When we first discussed such concepts as shared trucking and distribution facilities, we were greeted with skepticism. The potential to share data and work together on joint information technology projects was similarly derided in our initial contacts. When we recommended joint investments in capital projects that would dramatically enhance value and service, our audiences stared in disbelief.

As we persisted, we found a few organizations that were willing to set aside the old animosities and concerns and to start forging tomorrow's models. We were drawn to this group, to see if we could apply what we had learned on the upstream side to their progress on the downstream side, so that a total chain of improvement could be developed. We came to see partnering as the inevitable ingredient that could enable the parties to overcome resistance and to pool resources for their mutual benefit. It became extremely easy to find hidden resources that could be accessed for working out useful solutions. We also saw that it was possible to bridge the traditional chasm that separates the parties most in need of finding joint values, discovering that this bridge had to cross the most basic of all inhibitors to joint progress—the lack of trust between those who would form mutual-interest alliances.

The Fallacy of Trust

The constituents of the supply chain must share a strong bond of trust, or they will never share resources or reach anything close to optimization. As we pursued our investigation, we heard a lot of talk about this concept, but we found an abundance of mistrust and apprehension that slowed its implementation. The main barrier, we discovered, was the traditional attitude that any negotiation must produce a winner and a loser. In spite of strong protestations by buyers and sellers that the intent of negotiations was to develop win-win situations, our interviews confirmed strong desires on both sides of the negotiation process to come away as having "won" a concession from the other party. These concessions invariably benefited one party, not the business alliance or the supply chain system. What usually happened was that one constituent transferred costs to another, which was usually upstream, rather than helping to remove the costs from the total network. These results led to the perpetuation of an ongoing struggle for power and control in short-term positions, with the winner boldly claiming success and the loser seeking recourse to regain lost margins.

As we analyzed the data from our interviews, it became apparent that those who directed the people involved in the buying and selling negotiation process were placing too much emphasis on seeking the upper hand, rather than building strategic alliances for the future. Perhaps the pressure they felt to do this came from a need to dominate the negotiating process or simply to display some macho type of control over the process. In any event, the result we saw again and again was that the bosses for the buyers and sellers insisted on driving the negotiations so hard that any hope of building a trustful relationship became nearly impossible. Although a few of the negotiations we studied did result in win-win conditions, the majority benefited only the buying organization. Most frequently, the selling organization simply absorbed the cost transfers.

Few organizations managed to develop a win-win condition in the beginning, but the numbers are growing. The pioneers are trying to forge strategic relations built on the concept that trusted suppliers should have preferred positions; these suppliers can become valuable resources in finding new enhancements throughout the network of interactive relationships. But the pioneers are constantly challenged, often by people within their own organization who question why a more forceful, one-sided, and confrontational approach isn't employed. We have even been involved in situations where successful win-win relationships had been generated, only to be terminated by a new management that insisted on a more one-sided position. In short, the fallacy of trust is that even though it receives much oration, the favored approach is to wring concessions from a compliant supply base, with the misguided perception that the savings that are achieved from the interaction are permanent. However, nothing could be further from reality. If that perception were extended to its logical conclusion, every major buying organization would drive its entire supply base to the brink of bankruptcy. Those who favor the macho win-lose approach should take the time to consider how these poor, compliant suppliers are managing to make a profit. We find that it is because they become clever at passing back all the costs they seemingly acquiesced to through bargaining.

The Fate of a Dollar Saved

Once, when we wanted to test the concept we are promoting, we asked a retailer what would happen if we entered into a partnering arrangement and found one dollar of new savings. Our somewhat perplexed retailer needed elaboration. We replied that we wanted to know where a single dollar we might find from a value search in our interactive system would go? The quick reply was "On the shelf." When we asked why, the retailer replied that twenty-five cents of the dollar would be put into profits. The balance would enable the retail firm to discount the cost of the item. This would mean that more customers would come to the store to buy the lower-priced product. That action would draw more sales of the product through the system. In addition, the customer might buy other items in the store, and store revenues would be enhanced.

We agreed with the traditional logic of that argument but had to ask, "Then what are we to do with the other four dollars?" Our customer wanted to know about these "other dollars." We continued by explaining that we had actually discovered five dollars of savings in the system, but we had only offered one of them to see what its fate would be. We pointed out that once we found that the entire savings went to the retailer and consumer, essentially helping only the retailer, we had little incentive to bring the other four dollars to the table. Our customer quickly replied that if we helped to discount the product we made and offer that discount "at the shelf," we would move more product together and make additional profits on the extra volume.

Our retort was that if we gave the consumer fifty cents of the first dollar and kept twenty-five cents for each of us to build more efficiencies into both of our organizations, we would have created the incentive to find—and share—the other four dollars. The ultimate consumer would save money on the purchase, but the system would have retained a portion of the savings for other investments. Because the first dollar was shared with the supplier, retailer, and consumer, we would now have an incentive to dig out the other four dollars. The fate of that first dollar would have set a positive tone for working together on system improvement, rather than simply making cost concessions.

Partnering as the Solution

Optimization is a feasible objective for those who are willing to work together to develop the most effective supply chain. They will face many obstacles in that quest, most of which are grounded in the traditional competitive nature of business relations. We will elaborate on these problems in Chapter Five. To overcome those obstacles, however, the parties must have an ingredient to bind them in a mutual effort that leads to the kind of optimization we now know can be achieved. That ingredient is partnering, described in detail in Chapter Seven.

Our thesis is not based on speculation, but on the results we have seen organizations achieve. The alliances forged between Procter & Gamble and Wal-Mart, Rubbermaid and Kmart, Quaker Oats and Dominick's Finer Foods, General Motors Corporation and Ryder System, and many others tell us there is more than hope. They give us proof that significant improvements can be achieved. Each of these alliances contains a high level of partnering that is grounded in mutual trust and gain, the building of win-win relations, and the sharing of the fruits of the improvements.

As we have investigated these relationships, we have found that those involved have conducted extraordinary efforts to find leading-edge positions, considerable shared savings, and competitive advantages. They have also displayed a very high level of cooperation, expressed not only by the sharing of resources, time, and energy, but also by the benefits they have achieved. They exemplify true win-win alliances, in which it is inappropriate to use heavy-handed leveraging of supply position for cost concessions. Instead, an atmosphere has developed that consists of building mutual-interest projects and providing resources to work in cross-organizational teams to find all the improvement opportunities that may exist.

The constituents across the supply chain network must seek partnering as part of the solution; if not, they will never overcome the traditional obstacles. They must come together across the network in a mutual search for savings and efficiencies that benefit all participants.

Sharing All the Dollars

As each dollar is extracted from the supply chain system through reducing inventories, cutting costs and cycle times, eliminating redundancies, and so forth, advanced alliances will share each dollar saved. In this manner, the system becomes both customer-responsive and more effective by virtue of reinvesting some of the saved dollars in further enhancements.

It is through shared savings that the proof of win-win relations is demonstrated. A system that is dominated by the retail constituency will send the dollars down the ramp toward the consumer, increasing pulled throughput but seriously crippling the members upstream by not giving them any of the dollars necessary to sustain a leading-edge position. Quite simply, the constituents must share in the savings or they will find no long-term incentive to strengthen the network. Organizations that are hardy enough will survive the constant transfer of savings to the retailer, but poor returns on effort could eliminate or dramatically reduce the forward progress of strong technological innovators.

Information Technology as the Catalyst

If partnering is the missing ingredient, then information technology is the enabling and enhancing catalyst. As we developed example after example of how savings could be generated in supply chains, it quickly became apparent that success could not have happened without the level of data transfer and productive use of information being brought to the highest level of efficiency. This

means that the development of information technology supporting the data transfer had to be treated with the same importance
as finding inventory and cycle-time solutions.

The software and hardware that make interorganizational connections possible have to be brought to high levels of effectiveness.
Many organizations have concentrated on this development with
selected partners. The next necessary step is to disseminate these
improvements across the entire network that makes up a supply
chain. The shortest possible cycle times will remain unreach-
able until the interlinked systems have been made customer- and
network-friendly. The chances for value enhancements to inventory turns and just-in-time deliveries will depend on communication that is compatible and conversant. The use of clear, real-time
POS information instead of warehouse releases to trigger supply
replenishment, for example, will depend on having reliable recording devices, along with people who understand the value of efficient data collection. Information technology has become more
than the darling of organizational improvement; it has become a
necessity in supply chain optimization. It enables the system to
function at high levels of efficiency and enhances the financial
return to the participants by extracting unnecessary costs.

Action Study: The Universal Credit Corporation

*To satisfy a desire to own a house, a significant portion of the U.S. pop-
ulation resides in manufactured housing units, commonly referred to as
mobile homes. These units have provided affordable dwellings for millions
of Americans. To meet the demands of this segment of the housing market, many manufacturers construct individual units and move them to
market through the sales lots of hundreds of independent dealers. To
finance these units, the dealers use many funding agencies, from banks and
savings and loan institutions to such large financing sources as Universal
Credit Corporation (UCC). Our action study relates how UCC (a fictitious
name) decided to increase its share in this market by increasing the flexibility, speed, and ease of financing in the dealer transactions for mobile
homes.*

Figure 1.3 is a simplified model of the interactions between the suppliers, mobile home builder, dealer network, and consumers and the financial sources that support these constituencies. Our story begins when the general manager of the Manufactured Housing Finance Division of UCC, reacting to significant increases in competition from other funding organizations, called his senior management team together to develop a "blowout" strategy that would meet the competition and attain a market advantage through superior new features.

Following a review of current market trends, existing internal improvement projects, and issues associated with current competitive offerings, the division decided to build a business tool set that would offer network participants real-time access to valuable information that was not normally available in the supply network, with speeds that were available only through computer-based interactions. The first step in this new approach was to clearly identify the customer and the real customer needs. This led to a focus on the inventory financing being offered to the mobile home manufacturer. A secondary finding was that by meeting and exceeding the financial needs of the dealer network with pragmatic funding, the manufacturers would be able to enhance product movement. UCC could be the catalyst in this interaction and could gain a market advantage by satisfying two organizations' need for leads and with funding for their services.

FIGURE 1.3. Mobile Home Supply Chain Model.

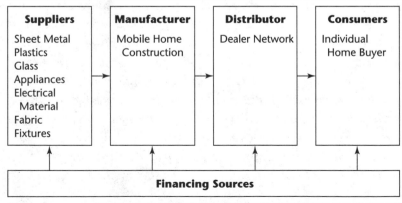

The vehicle that created the innovative feature was a printed listing giving the open-to-buy status for virtually all of the dealers in this market. Open-to-buy is a term used to indicate the line of credit established for dealers less the outstanding balances due. This yields the funds that are available for further financing. An analogous situation would be the difference between the line of credit and payments due to Visa or MasterCard. With this information, the manufacturers' telephone-based sales force could quickly identify which dealers had access to additional credit to purchase new units for their lots. Looking at next-day mail as another option for providing these data, UCC saw a way to obtain a competitive edge over the competition and provide dual financing—to manufacturers and dealers—that would be within the limits of outstanding credit.

As the idea gained acceptance, the UCC team went one step further. To cut the cycle time for data transmission on open-to-buy and the request for financing, a decision was made to offer personal computers to selected manufacturers and dealers to automate the interchange. Another new concept was introduced in the form of enabling software called Quick Access. Using personal computers, an existing data base, security-sensitive software, and the interlinked manufacturers and dealers, UCC was able to help its customers access the open-to-buy information on a real-time basis. The manufacturers used this new knowledge to spark a call to dealers with open credit and initialize a transaction. The system was eventually expanded to include suppliers of raw materials, completing the network interchange.

As a final enhancement, the Quick Access team elected to develop special classifications of dealers, from silver to platinum. Platinum performers would be those who used UCC for 100 percent of their inventory financing; gold, 75 percent; and silver, 50 percent. Platinum members would be given a free personal computer and the essential software, along with training and access to the data base. Other classifications would be given benefits based on their level of commitment. The purpose was to get the dealers to increase their level of business in order to reap the benefits of the Quick Access system. In the first full year of deployment, Quick Access achieved a $200 million increase in revenues.

This story is just one of many early attempts to use supply chain partnering and innovation to enhance network results. In this particular story, a service organization applied the type of improvement that is normally associated with a manufacturing network, and the manufacturer was the beneficiary of the work of the service organization.

Summary

Much activity is currently focused on eliminating supply chain inefficiency. This activity is driven by the consumer, who is becoming more particular and demanding of the retailer. As retailers seek the means of surviving, they turn their attention upstream in the supply chain and demand the benefits of improved efficiency. The resulting "power plays" leave a lot of money on the table as manufacturers, and their suppliers, carefully bring savings forward to the retailer. A general lack of trust inhibits this power playing. A superior format is possible, built around better communication, use of mutual resources, and efforts focused on finding values that can be shared across the supply network.

Chapter Two

The Pursuit of Supply Chain Optimization

• •

The typical supply chain network is undergoing major changes. In the past, when a heavy demand existed for brand names and national manufacturers developed new products, they usually allocated a portion of their output to the retail outlets of their choice. Stocking positions and displays were usually arranged to favor the most prestigious brands. As market shifts have occurred and retailers have gained more control, concern has arisen about effective use of total shelf and floor space and ways to bring products through the supply system that match consumer preferences. Now, instead of simply pushing products toward a friendly outlet, companies in the supply chain are finding that they must answer to the ultimate consumers, who determine what will be purchased and, therefore, what should be pulled through the supply chain and onto the display shelves.

These changes have increased pressure on all the members of a typical supply chain. Retailers, struggling to keep consumers, are focusing on cost reduction and want to move traditional expenses back through distribution to the manufacturers. Manufacturers, wanting to maintain margins, look for potential improvements that can be shared downstream with their customers and look upstream for concessions from their suppliers. Because the fruits of these efforts are continually passed to the ultimate consumer, supply chains and their constituents run the risk of becoming involved in a zero-sum game. Under these conditions, in which all savings go out of the system, margins fall for all members of the network. A better system looks for total system savings that are shared between chain members and the consumer. Much work will have to be accomplished to create this better world.

Firms that began the quest for improvement early made notable gains and are forging ahead of the competition with tangible enhancements and savings. A few of these pathfinders have even developed ways of saving part of the enhancement for themselves. A larger army of followers seems to be poised for action but unable to establish meaningful implementation. Our exposure to the many organizations seeking to change and improve their supply networks includes substantially more groups investigating the potential than actually reaping the benefits of action. In this chapter, we discuss the reasons for these mixed reactions by detailing the perspective that is driving the quest for change and outlining how a few leading firms are forging new paths.

The Supply Chain Vision

When Kmart convened its "Quick Response" meeting in March 1992, Joseph Antonini, then president and CEO, delivered the keynote address. He told the audience, "For centuries there's been a love/hate relationship between buyers and suppliers. And while the buyers were making suppliers jump through hoops, the consumer was left short-changed. If a product was out of stock, excuses . . . were handed out . . . to the shopper. Frequently, they left the store . . . filled with frustration, vowing never to return" (Rouland, 1992, p. 42). Under these conditions, it is not difficult to see how problems with a direct impact on earnings are introduced into a system designed to satisfy customers. To keep those customers happy and prevent them from going to other retail outlets for satisfaction, companies like Kmart felt the need to change the buyer-seller relationship and make sure that the consumer was not "short-changed." But several questions arise. Who pays for the retraining? Who pays for the redesign of systems to make certain that the desired product is available at the time of want? How do you calculate what is lost when these negative things happen? Buyers have historically received temporary accolades for forcing suppliers to make concessions, but the store, suppliers, and customers could be left with a less than desirable situation. Under these conditions, nobody wins.

Obviously, a better solution was needed. Antonini went on to detail some of the efforts being made by his organization to change the relationship between buyers and suppliers for the better. As he did, he presented a more effective method of reacting to supply chain demands, known as quick response (QR). Antonini said that Kmart had begun its investment in QR in 1987 (Rouland, 1992). The vision he outlined was "a closed-loop environment in which everybody wins—the store, the supplier and . . . the consumer" (p. 42). QR has become one of the areas in which supply chain members can turn the network into a more responsive and profitable system. It requires taking out all nonvalue-adding, cycle-time-extending activities. The result is quicker replenishment at lower cost.

Late in 1990, Kmart installed POS equipment in all its stores, with registers to pick up the data on all sales at the moment of purchase. The goal was to capture detailed information on "every sale at every Kmart store" (Rouland, 1992, p. 42). The initial objective driving this significant investment was the desire to introduce the ability to replenish products in concert with actual consumption, and thereby to reduce the typical three to four weeks that were required for an order-to-receipt cycle to five to seven days. When the company achieved that target, it quickly set a new goal at twenty-four hours. This pattern is typical in manufacture-to-retail chains today. Wal-Mart, in particular, is driving its supply base to a seventy-two-hour schedule, with some products on a twenty-four- or forty-eight-hour basis.

While a few leading retail firms were experimenting with this concept of rapid replenishment, many other companies were simply attempting to meet the changing needs of their consumer markets by placing more inventory into the system, or by moving it from place to place in an attempt to make adequate responses to sales without increasing inventory-carrying costs at the stores. These firms invested in high-technology registers and scanning equipment that provided valuable data on customers and their purchases, but they tended to not use this POS data to drive the replenishment cycle. Instead, most retailers quickly focused their attention on transferring inventories upstream in their chain of supply. Their initial motivation was to take as much stock as possible out of the supply areas behind the storefronts, to increase floor space for sales. Some firms transferred their goods to a local warehouse, others to an obliging distributor or manufacturer. As these warehouses grew in size and importance, they became distribution centers, satisfying the selling needs of a network of surrounding stores.

Today, the distribution centers are trying to find ways to lower the levels of stock they contain, which are there essentially to cover inefficiencies in the delivery system. With an emphasis on just-in-time deliveries, firms that do not have the manufacturing flexibility to meet short-cycle demands have no recourse but to place safety stocks in these centers so that shipments can be made on demand from the retail outlets. Because the network gains no real cost savings under this format, just a rearrangement of capital costs, the search continues for more effective methods. In the meantime, data bases are filling with register information that can give a better picture of what is actually being consumed and, therefore, what needs to be inventoried and replenished.

The current emphasis remains on reducing the amount of supply needed to meet store demands by creating systems that respond in shorter intervals and with more accurate replacement quantities that are linked to actual consumption. Under ideal conditions, the least amount of inventory necessary to meet the current demand will pass through the network. The consumer will find the exact article desired at the store of choice. No sales will be missed and inventories of unsold goods will not pile up in a holding area. No obsolescence will occur, and the cost of capital invested in inventory will be minimized for the total supply network. This ambition calls for methods, systems, and procedures that eliminate the inefficiencies that result in one or more parties in the supply chain building insurance or safety stocks.

For now, the Antonini dream of using POS information to trigger quick responses from minimal inventories is still in the development stage. Replenishing supply is still based primarily on releases from the distribution centers, where the data are considered more reliable and where assembling full loads for the stores can most easily be accommodated from the stored inventories. Development of superior methods of distribution and data interchange will require further exploration and significant dedication to pilot operations that prove the validity and resolve the problems of advanced supply chain initiatives. Before the process can become established, more companies have to explore the opportunities and get involved in implementation. This condition, which is well understood by those engaged in supply chain activities, creates a paradox in which firms wait for further substantiation of the emerging model and are reluctant to be participants in what they know is needed experimentation and implementation.

In subsequent chapters, we will cover some of the front-edge efforts in greater detail and show how success can be achieved. To better understand what keeps some supply chain players from trying more efficient methods, we need first to consider what is happening in the retail consumption arena now that makes it necessary for retailers to focus on quick response and more effective stock replenishment, and we have to consider why the traditional supply systems no longer meet the needs of today's consumers.

Matching Supply with Consumption Patterns

A major study of the grocery industry, a typical industry in search of a more effective supply chain system, revealed the presence of 104 days of overall inventory to support current levels of sales (Salmon, 1993). Most analysts agree that this level could be dramatically reduced, to 60 days or less. Some gains have already been made on a selected basis—that is, with a limited range of stock-keeping units, or sku's, usually in a particular family of high-turnover products. More often, the effort manifests itself in attempts by the retailers to move the inventories back to the manufacturer. This condition creates an atmosphere of gamesmanship, in which the carrying costs appear to be switched but are buried in the cost of supply. Fortunately, more fruitful efforts are being focused on the new patterns of consumption and on ways to meet demands with total network solutions that do not foist the costs of implementation on the suppliers.

A penetrating analysis of methods to effectively improve existing systems begins with the recognition that today's consumer operates under a fundamentally different set of objectives than his or her grandparents did. This consumer has adopted new buying habits that require suppliers, manufacturers, distributors, and retailers to work more closely together to bring extra value to the shopping experience, particularly in terms of selection, innovation, and service. Loyalty of any sort has become an elusive commodity with this consumer, so it takes considerably more than national advertising to ensure return visits. Arrangements between suppliers and buyers, manufacturers and distributors, and distributors and retailers in a network, which until now have been more adversarial than cooperative, must become mutually focused on the consumption habits that affect the total supply system and encourage the consumer to choose the network over that of any rival.

As these former adversaries engage in this new endeavor, they are reevaluating how their supply chains function and are taking a new look at procedures that for too long have been taken for granted. The purpose is to better establish their position as a member of the preferred network of selected markets, by having the best costs, selections, prices, and services. This means that the manufacturing system, in conjunction with the suppliers and distributors, has to become linked to meet and exceed the evolving demands of today's consumer. And, recognizing that very few networks satisfy customer needs all the time, an element of flexibility has to be included. The alliance also has to keep an eye on what competing networks are accomplishing in order to build the best practices into every part of the redesigned system. This is the only way to sustain a competitive advantage.

A loyal customer, if such a person can be developed today, will spend an average of five thousand dollars annually (in 1994 dollars) at a particular retail outlet. Emerging market strategies indicate that individual stores should develop unique merchandising techniques and systems to match their offerings to what these potentially loyal buyers are seeking. Although such techniques have many variations, depending on local conditions, certain generic supply conditions help to match what is offered with the evolving habits of consumption. Today, quality has to be built into the product or the consumer will return it and eliminate the store or department from her or his list of possible outlets. Service, suitability of the product, and convenience are new, additional factors that determine consumer loyalty. Consumers seek products, particularly foods, that are healthy; that are geared to smaller family sizes and singles; that recognize the needs of an aging population; that cater to those with limited discretionary income and limited savings; and that always give the perception of low pricing.

This list is followed by diversity of choice, broad product displays, and specialized options of a localized nature. We live in a time of "floor-ready" retailing, in which manufacturers have to transport products that are ready for purchase to the retail floor or shelf. In a service environment, this means that the person meeting the customer is prepared to conduct and, ideally, conclude the transaction without extra contacts. A service bureau that provides personnel, software, or computers to a financial institution is under as much pressure to have what look like custom-designed solutions ready for its customer at the best possible cost as a retailer is to satisfy the ultimate consumer.

Because of the increase in global marketing and the penchant of major manufacturers for seeking customers on that scale, product offerings have proliferated in recent years, flooding the supply chains with goods and services of similar characteristics. In virtually every type of retail environment, the number and variety of offerings are escalating. During 1994, over fifteen thousand new products were introduced to retail shelves, including some that were nearly clones of others. The notoriously high mortality rate of these innovations does nothing to slow what appears to be an unstoppable trend. This condition has exacerbated the difficulties suppliers, manufacturers, distributors, and retailers encounter as they fulfill supply chain commitments. In spite of good intentions and redesigned systems, these chains still have too many errors and flaws; opportunities to make sales are missed, too much inventory exists that does not get to market in time, excessive markdowns are required to move less desired merchandise, and insufficient stocks of wanted goods occur too often. And all of this now exists globally, usually in a nonautomated system!

Continuous product development and promotional activities thrive in a market with razor-thin margins that hardly cover the incremental costs of adding these ever-growing numbers of sku's. This problem challenges everyone in the business networks to try to stay one step ahead of the consumers' changing buying habits, often by guessing at the next wave of changes. Our experience counsels that matching supply with changing habits is far more an art than a science. Habits will change. That is the unstoppable phenomenon. Therefore, supply chain optimization will only become reachable (or approachable) when joint efforts by the supply chain constituents anticipate these needs and develop joint response systems that are flexible enough to react efficiently in the shortest possible time, with minimal inventories.

Early Attempts at Systems Improvement

One technique that has proved beneficial for encouraging multiple members of a supply chain to approach optimization together is to share the costs and risks associated with having the goods necessary to meet changing consumption habits. Lever Brothers Company and Distribution Centers, Inc. (DCI), built, staffed, and now operate a high-tech distribution warehouse for the toiletries manufacturer. Both organizations share the benefits and the risks. If usage within the warehouse falls below a certain point of effectiveness, Lever Brothers helps to cover the overhead costs. In return, DCI shares the productivity benefits when usage increases. This arrangement helps both organizations to have the necessary goods at the moment of need, while spreading the carrying costs, as they jointly try to anticipate what products the consumer most prefers.

The next step in such an arrangement is to work collectively to cut the need for stored goods. This stage requires development of a reengineered response system that better anticipates actual consumption and reduces the need for inventory to minimal levels. With such a system, the supply partners move products swiftly and effectively to the ultimate consumer through a network that benefits from the best practices across the entire chain. Examples of success in this phase of the effort are scarce, but there is an indication that major companies are pursuing such a full-system endeavor. A four-way alliance between E. I. Du Pont de Nemours (producing fibers), Milliken & Co. (converting fibers to fabric), Leslie Fay (producing women's garments from the fabric), and Dillard Department Stores (selling the garments) has attempted to remove all nonvalue-adding steps from its network and to shorten its cycle times while minimizing the need for inventories. This full-chain alliance is one example of total network supply improvement. Other examples are those of Rubbermaid and Kmart; Procter & Gamble and Wal-Mart; Whirlpool Corporation and Sears, Roebuck & Co.; and H-E-B Food Stores and the Coca-Cola Company, but they have been limited to a doublet connection between manufacturer and retailer. We see a great competitive opportunity to build more of the three- or four-way alliances while they are still relatively rare and before they become the accepted way to improve supply networks.

Even though the efforts cited have been recorded successes, most firms involved in supply chains remain poised for action but have not rushed toward replication. One industry in particular manifests this penchant for combining observation with inaction: the U.S. grocery industry. A look at this industry will help to illustrate why the subject of replenishment receives much attention but limited action. Challenged by a rash of new competitors, the grocery industry decided to take a hard look at such intrusions in their markets and to find ways to counter them. The industry faced the competition of mass merchandisers, club stores, deep discount chains, and other novel selling arrangements, all offering aggressive pricing practices. These actions put heavy pressure on grocers who were already operating on thin profit margins.

Aware that traditional responses would likely fail to offset the long-term impact of these threats, a core group decided to take a fresh look at the grocery supply chain and its practices. Their objective was to search out inefficiencies that could be eliminated, and thereby to generate new savings that would enhance grocery margins. In 1992, five sponsoring trade associations, listed in Figure 2.1, joined with fifteen select sponsors, listed in Figure 2.2, to form an efficient consumer response (ECR) working group. The consortium retained a consulting group, Kurt Salmon Associates (KSA), to conduct a supply chain analysis, because KSA previously had been instrumental in developing quick-response initiatives in the general merchandising industry. KSA was commissioned to look for potential improvements in grocery chains, from supplier through distribution to customer. The consortium hoped that grocers could use the information that was developed to respond to the threat posed by the encroaching group of nontraditional competitors. The KSA study found ample opportunities for improvement and recommended reengineering and redesigning the supply chain from manufacture to retail sale by changing the core processes in ways that would improve effectiveness. Issues it scrutinized included the following:

• Deciding what to carry, how much, where, and at what price
• Developing procurement and distribution techniques to provide in-stock availability
• Servicing customers in the stores
• Communicating product offerings to the customer
• Developing and introducing new categories
• Designing new stores

FIGURE 2.1.   Sponsoring Trade Associations.

Uniform Code Council, Inc.
Food Marketing Institute
Grocery Manufacturers of America
National Food Brokers Association
American Meat Institute

FIGURE 2.2. Efficient Consumer Response Working Group Members.

Campbell Sales Company
The Coca-Cola Company
Crown/BBK Incorporated
Kraft General Foods
The Kroger Company
Nabisco Foods Group
Oscar Mayer Foods Corporation
The Procter & Gamble Company
Ralston Purina Company
Safeway Incorporated
Sales Force Companies, Incorporated
Scrivner Incorporated
Shaw's Supermarkets Incorporated
Super Valu Stores, Incorporated
The Vons Companies Incorporated

The KSA study has been widely circulated in the grocery industry and has been read by many other interested parties from different industries. The impetus it gave to interest in ECR efforts cannot be minimized. It has had a major, positive impact on the thinking within many retail arenas. The study concluded that from the $300 billion retail grocery industry, 10 percent, or $30 billion, could be saved. The collective supply chains would gain these savings, it was suggested, by cutting out all waste resulting from unnecessary business practices. Inventories could be reduced by a possible 40 percent. Eliminating excess costs and inventories in the area of enhancing product promotions could save $12 billion. Better merchandise replenishment could save another $11 billion. Better store assortments would save $4 billion, and more effective introduction of new products would save $3 billion. In the general merchandise arena, the study presented an estimated total potential savings of $20 billion on $120 billion in revenues.

As a result of better supply chain management in the retail grocery industry by firms that implemented such changes, typical replenishment has gone from sixty-two days to fifteen for many products. Inventory turns (the number of times goods in inventory are sold in a year) have also been improved to twenty-four times from approximately six for some front-edge practitioners. Targeted as another area of potential improvement is the elimination of unnecessary deductions and reconciliations caused by inaccurate pricing. Many other errors could also be eliminated throughout the system. But as we investigated the range of improvement possibilities and became excited by the enormous potential, we discovered that although many companies were taking some advantage of the opportunities—virtually every organization we visited had established some form of improvement effort focused on the KSA recommendations—we did not find a single organization that was taking advantage of *all* of the identified opportunities. Moreover, we found a decided lack of integrated efforts to find total savings. A. T. Kearney, the Chicago-based consulting firm, reporting on interviews with twenty-nine companies, verified this discovery as they detailed finding "no common vision of the future supply chain integration" (Kearney, 1994).

All the manufacturers and retailers we interviewed, however, were determined to continue the search for ways to secure a share of the huge potential for their company. Many conversations took place on the study details, some of the success stories, and estimates of what the savings could be for individual companies. In the grocery industry in particular, the members we encountered were very anxious to get their part of the $30 billion savings after they watched the leaders make progress. Procter & Gamble, for example, was able to find a savings of twenty cents per case in distributing certain products to grocers from its facilities. Wal-Mart talked of increasing turnover on some items to over one hundred times per year. Throughout the channels of distribution we studied, large savings potentials were discussed. In consumer-packaged goods, senior officials talked of eighty-four days of average supply from the total of manufacturers', distributors', and retailers' inventories. Most agreed that a cut of 50 percent was feasible, with a dramatic effect on the cost of working capital and freshness of the products. The Kearney study reported examples of a 13 percent reduction in transportation expenses from improved interfacility planning, a 15 percent reduction in finished-goods inventory in one year from improved forecasting processes, and a $7 million reduction in one year as a result of replacing a "sales plan roll-up" (an informal system of having inventory goods ready to meet actual sales) with a formal forecasting and production-planning process.

We became convinced from these discussions that the most likely ultimate outcome of the search for potential savings would be the linking together of the various strategies and tactics we saw developing. The remaining opportunities are simply too great for firms in common supply networks not to pool resources. Call it what you will—QR, CRP, ECR, or some other two- or three-letter acronym—all of these strategies involve reaching beyond the normal relationships to form a collaborative network that optimizes the best resources across the total supply chain. Effectiveness does not come from isolation, but from working in concert with partners who are operating in an atmosphere of mutual trust. Our interviews served to convince us of the opportunity and the need to join resources from all constituents in the supply chain to gain the total potential suggested by the authors of the KSA study.

Although the enormous potential gains are obvious, getting beyond historical paradigms and engendering cooperation between buyers and sellers has thus far been extremely limited. Too many firms cling to the old ways of bargaining. If savings are going to be reaped, the parties involved must recognize their mutual interest in removing extraneous costs, not circulating them among constituents. They have to look together at reducing time and inventory from the point of supply and production to the point of sale, thereby eliminating all the unnecessary safety inventory and human actions that introduce redundant costs across the supply chain. When the nonvalue-adding activities are extracted from such systems, products will move from manufacture to retail space with the lowest cost.

As the large retailers take the lead in forcing these costs backward in their supply chains, the need for such an effort should become clear to their upstream constituents. The wise organization begins the quest for improvement in earnest. All of the basic elements are currently available. The necessary electronic data interchange (EDI) between parties has been tested and proved. Unfortunately, many firms are still waiting to make the necessary investments in people and systems. That is a fatal flaw. Major investments in capital improvements can be delayed, but the funds must be allocated now to form the joint alliances that will secure the future, and to develop the key human resources required for the redesign process. Additionally, information systems have to be designed now as the enablers and enhancers of the improvement process.

Efficient Consumer Response Becomes a Rallying Cry

We made especially interesting discoveries as we studied the most promising of the improvement initiatives, efficient consumer response. Most companies we interviewed have the ability to implement the elements of quick response and effective replenishment at substantially improved costs. The dilemma is that they have been slow to execute these initiatives. Extremely tentative action surrounds all the potential gains that could be made. ECR is steeped in high ideals and valid concepts, but these features elicit fear in some would-be participants. Independent retailers and wholesalers in the chain become worried about the investment in technical systems that is necessary. Some of the retailers we met expressed concern about sharing scanned data with wholesalers. And a few major manufacturers expressed concern that systems savings would be offset by lost revenues that would have come from pushing extra inventories toward the consumer.

We found that ECR has been presented as a means to eliminate most, if not all, of the inefficient practices in supply chains, with the additional benefit of creating shared savings opportunities. Unfortunately, the idea has found as many deaf ears as willing advocates. Richard Kochersberger, chairman of the Academy of Food Marketing of St. Joseph's University, elaborates: "While the concepts [of ECR] are simple, the execution is complex and sophisticated." With a somewhat irreverent view, he adds, "In most food wholesale and retail companies, distribution is still viewed as a necessary evil" (Kochersberger, 1993, p. 15). Glen Terbeek, international director for Andersen Consulting, calls attention to another important factor: "There's no question," he states, "that as far as ECR is concerned there's a lot of feeding frenzy. . . . I'm not really sure a lot of people understand what ECR really is. . . . Much of the ECR activities are attempts at optimizing the current way of doing business rather than creating new practices" (Mathews, 1993b, p. 5). The point is clear: it is hard to reengineer something that was never engineered correctly in the first place. ECR was meant to incite people to redesign bad systems. The reality may be that they never had any system to begin with, just a network of negotiators trying to best each other. The time to change that circumstance is now. The need for change is at the heart of ECR.

As we studied current practices, we found the additional problem that many firms throughout supply networks do not know their actual costs closely enough to establish the true value of their efforts. The executives told us that they knew the savings were there; they just weren't sure how much they could get in return for the effort that they sensed would be necessary. We understand that if you do not know what you are chasing it will be hard to mount an intense effort, but our response has consistently been that firms will never know how much real savings can be generated until pilot attempts are made. The potential is so great that we see little risk in mounting a limited effort and documenting the actual results as progress is made. As we pursued our discussions, we became far less concerned with the direction of this type of effort and more convinced of the need to get started. The pilot attempts that ensued from this conviction will be described in later chapters to illustrate how they can fill the gap as companies introduce the activity-based costing that will show exactly what the costs and opportunities are.

Partial Successes Incite the Hunt

Ryan Mathews, editor of *Grocery Marketing,* counsels using similar tact when he advises building a system with the ultimate customer in mind: "It is critical to remember that ECR is a single process within a larger process, and not an end in itself. It is . . . just one tactical step in a closed loop information system designed to facilitate the construction of an effective strategy for the deployment of industry resources toward the eventual aim of better satisfying the demands of a consumer driven marketing system" (Mathews, 1993b, p. 5).

When such a goal is visualized, we see why the efforts are so important. The developers of the Kurt Salmon study reported, "To validate the projected benefits of quick response, the Crafted With Pride in USA Council sponsored three pilot projects with leading retailers in three distribution channels—department stores (Dillard's), national chains (J. C. Penney) and mass-merchants (Wal-Mart). Each retailer selected a vendor partner for the pilot covering a range of product categories. The results exceeded expectations. . . . All three pilots showed sales increases of 20–25 percent and improvements in inventory turns of 30 percent. In-stock performance improved to over 95 percent from 70–75 percent" (Salmon, 1995).

As Kmart continued the search for improvement, some interesting results developed in the area of inventory turns. Beginning in 1990, they found turns with one large supplier (the cost of goods purchased divided by the average cost of inventory) was 5. Following collaborative effort, that figure went to 24 in 1991 and reached 40 to 50 in some departments by 1992. Robert Knorr and John Neuman of the Meritus Consulting Group (Knorr and Neuman, 1993) report that a few manufacturing leaders are breaking away and pulling ahead of their peers. They find that with this group, "quick response and supply chain partnerships are built on a new kind of trust-based relationship between the manufacturer and retailer and on redesigned business processes throughout the entire supply chain" (p. 61). They further report that some of these leaders have 90 to 95 percent of their sales volume operating in QR applications. Such QR techniques have enabled Palm Beach Company to go from having 80 percent of its business in large orders on long lead times with ninety-day windows to having 50 percent in small orders—one to two garments—delivered in hours.

A Current Perspective

The eventual optimum solution to ECR will be grounded not in these isolated successes, but in a concerted effort by consortia that are driving for full realization of the total potential. Their vision will soon coalesce into a timely, accurate, paperless network that has been redesigned to function with the smallest inventories and the best possible delivered cost. These networks will be characterized by trusting relationships through which valuable resources are shared to find the optimum solutions. However, before the collective thinking can move in that direction, we have to understand the current perspective on what is happening and where the trend is going. As we review the results to date, we notice that a significant gap is opening up between the "wannabes" and the networks that have forged ahead with implementation.

In optimized networks, costs are known and linked into electronic interchanges that are geared toward customer satisfaction and profitability. The real change in these networks is that where formerly they pushed masses of merchandise through a distribution channel to the retail shelves and floors, now actual consumption pulls the necessary replenishment to the POS by the most effective means possible. Leading practitioners are functioning under these conditions today. Reports like the following are becoming more common as a few organizations move inexorably forward: "At the end of each business day, sales data from Marks & Spenser's (UK) scanners is transmitted to a distribution facility where it is translated into a manufacturing or shipping order, which is received, filled and shipped in less than 24 hours" (Mathews, 1993a, p. 17).

The key issue that must be confronted and satisfied to produce greater participation is the need to see store performance dramatically improved, with replenishment of purchased goods at prices the buyer will accept as reasonably competitive. The apparel industry appears to be in the lead now, as its constituents chase quick response as the driving force. The food and grocery industry will stay with ECR as the process that offers the greatest opportunity. The general merchandise industries, suppliers of hard goods like appliances, tools, luggage, and furniture, and suppliers of soft items other than food and clothing will probably pass apparel and food and become the first to approach optimized supply chain conditions.

The ideas are available and the necessary tools and equipment are largely in place. No new technologies have to be invented or deployed to achieve the desired gains. Furthering of the initiatives will have to come from decisions to pool resources across full supply chains and to doggedly pursue a network-wide process map to find ways to remove all extraneous costs and activities. These actions will most likely start with some of the existing major players, but they can be equally fruitful for smaller niche firms who pool key talent with other organizations. In concert, this talent can dedicate time and effort in return for a piece of the enormous savings potential for their companies.

Small firms that believe that the gains from such efforts are only to be achieved by the major national-brand companies should take a second look. We worked with an industry that is marked by small- to medium-sized firms that move medical products through much larger distributors to a demanding customer base. For this group of manufacturers, we recommended working with some common suppliers, a cross-section of their members, one major distributor, and one or two customers. By arranging this consortium and working through the mapping process, we found over forty opportunity areas that could collectively be pursued for network-wide savings. The group went on to form action teams and successfully implemented the resulting improvement ideas in several of the highest-priority areas on that opportunity list.

Action Study: Plastics Corporation

Our action study for this chapter is representative of the early efforts at supply chain improvement. It does not represent a full-network solution, but it does explain how a manufacturer improved processes for selected retailers. It also illustrates how a simple beginning can lead to significant improvements and automation of manual processing.

The Plastics Corporation (a fictitious name) is a consumer products company that generated over $1 billion in revenues in 1995 through sales of household products, containers, and parts for consumer toys. These products were moved to market from twelve manufacturing plants through one private and eight public distribution centers. The public locations were warehouses that stored products for many companies. The private location was for use by Plastics alone. A typical supply chain for this organization would proceed from supply of materials through manufacture of packaged products, then through the distribution centers, to consumers such as Shaw Community Supermarket, Wal-Mart, the Kroger Co., Sears, Safeway stores, and other grocery and retail outlets.

Plastics had concentrated for years on making its supply chain as efficient as possible, but in 1992 the company decided to embark on what it termed supply-side reengineering. The firm's customer service sector, selected as the nucleus for this effort, had responsibility for forecasting and planning, distribution, transportation, and warehousing and operated a unit called the consumer information center. Its targeted objectives were to increase customer satisfaction and distribution efficiency, develop improved special packs, and create a leading-edge total category management system. Senior management's endorsement of this initiative was secured, with the directive to cross all functional areas and to use QR and ECR techniques as the enabling actions while increasing customer satisfaction.

The consumer information center immediately established a team that drew a process map of the current network for replenishing stocks, shown in condensed form in Figure 2.3. An early determination from this activity was the need to locate product activity data and purchase order acknowledgments in an automated electronic system. The teams used standard formats for this task, American Standards Institute standard 852, 855, 856, and 962 processes, respectively. With the system that was developed, products are shipped to customers, in response to store consumption, from one of the distribution centers, and the data are captured on the customer's computer system. The inventory movement data are used to create an 852 product activity transaction set, which is then transmitted to the company's electronic mailbox by way of a Value Added Network (VAN), a cooperative computer system used by multiple participants.

The 852 information is sent via e-mail to the firm's mainframe computer for translation into the correct nomenclature and for retransmission to the company's Distribution Replenishment Planning (DRP) system. The customer service account specialists use the DRP system to review the customer's inventory position with the demand forecast for each product at each distribution center. Replenishment orders are created as needed and an 855 purchase order acknowledgment is transmitted to the customer via the VAN. With this simplified and automated network, the correct flow of supply is enhanced and the need for inventory and paperwork is dramatically reduced.

As this version of ECR was developed, cross-functional teams were used, made up of personnel from the distribution centers and the customers. Their early steps included identifying key contact people who needed an accurate flow of data to carry out their functions. Plastics developed the necessary information flow for these individuals. The positions included account representatives, inventory planners, customer service personnel, and members of manufacturing, distribution, and information systems. The teams then selected an array of products for testing with the output of the improvement effort, set performance goals, and began to track the effort for discussion and further improvement at follow-up meetings. The basic requirements for making this system work included two years of warehouse movement, by week and by sku. The team added a list of standing purchase order numbers and set up their network on a computer-to-computer basis without clerical intervention. A decision was also made to build the capability to ship in a minimum of one layer or tier for each product. Transportation requirements were set for meeting standing appointments and for having EDI capability. The requirements for the warehouse were to transmit accurate information, have no errors or cuts, ship on time, and retain good carrier relations.

The immediate complication the teams encountered was the need to balance a system that was set up to manufacture goods to inventory or to order with a system that pulled these goods by the piece or by the truck. The decision was made that about a truckload of product per week per location made the most sense to Plastics and its customers, so the model was built around that concept. Operationally, the customer's stock status and inventory movement are used in conjunction with POS data and a sales forecast to initiate the DRP scheduling. This scheduling then triggers a

FIGURE 2.3. Network for Replenishing Stocks.

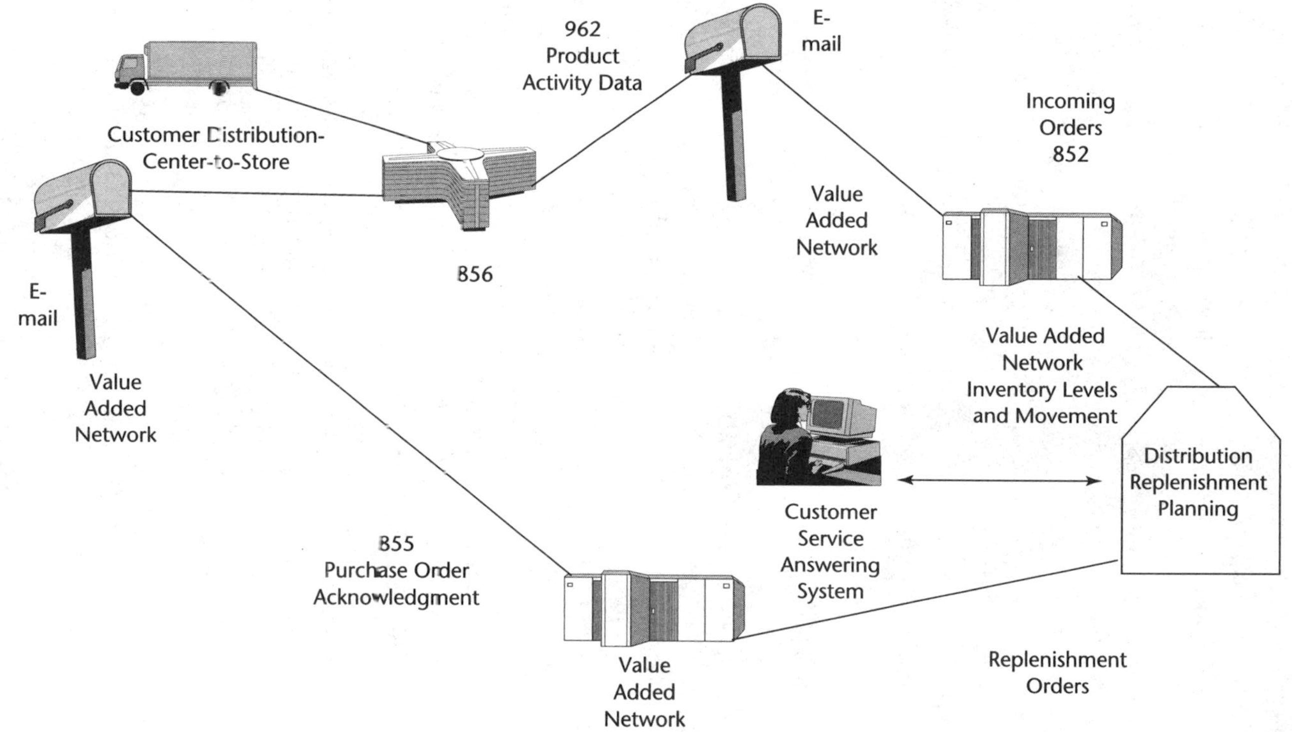

Incoming Orders 852

E-mail

Value Added Network

Value Added Network
Inventory Levels and Movement

Distribution Replenishment Planning

Customer Service Answering System

Replenishment Orders

962 Product Activity Data

856

Customer Distribution-Center-to-Store

Value Added Network

E-mail

Value Added Network

855 Purchase Order Acknowledgment

recommended order, based on pull-through consumption, that is used to develop the actual order processing. The keys to success are to have no delays in information, appointments, or unloading.

The benefits for the company include increased sales because of fewer stock-outs, reduced administrative costs, a smoother flow of orders, improved merchandising information, and reduced deductions. The retailer benefits from increased sales because of fewer stock-outs, higher inventory turns with lower stocks, improved receiving operations, and more accurate invoicing. The Plastics team tracked progress from beginning levels of 5 to 6 inventory turns and 92 percent in-stock levels to 30 to 39 turns with 95 percent in stock; inventory levels were reduced from 2.6 to 1.5 weeks' supply, a win-win situation for the firm and its customers.

Summary

If supply chain optimization is to become a reality, the existing mentality that pervades the typical supply network has to undergo a change in philosophy. The fundamental alteration is to move from a buyer-versus-seller concept to one in which the network attempts to forge a customer-focused virtual network that has the maximum effectiveness. Such a network will only be established when the constituents across the full chain are working to build a supply system that has a single organizational purpose. This condition is a long way from the "let's only worry about our company" thought processes driving much of supply chain management today.

The required solutions can become more focused as models are built for various industries that map the flow of inbound materials to the point of ultimate consumption. The timely sharing of data across these maps, along with information gleaned from documented practical applications, will provide the fuel for cooperative efforts. The result will include flexible, short-cycle schedules supported with the minimum inventories. Delivery of what is wanted will be made at the time of need. Traffic routing will be consolidated, allowing more complex routing without increased costs. Sophisticated information technology will be commonplace as the redesigned network operates in a concerted fashion on a comprehensive business strategy, rather than with local optimization at the expense of other members of the supply chain.

Supply chain optimization is not a figment of some wild imagination. Too many successes are being recorded for it not to happen. What still has to occur is the pooling of resources across logical supply networks—which make sense as a network for a particular market—with all members of the alliances contributing their part of the answer, so that a total solution can be fitted together like a huge jigsaw puzzle. If the leading-edge players can combine what they have learned with the advances being made by the interacting organizations upstream and downstream of them, they stand a much greater chance of moving toward that optimization than they would by doggedly pursuing the effort in isolation. In the next chapter, we will outline a model for developing such cooperation.

Chapter Three

The Interenterprise Solution

With an understanding of supply chain operations and an appreciation of the large potential gains that can be extracted from a typical system, we are now prepared to investigate a specific model aimed at realizing those gains. An abundance of execution models exist, many fostered by well-known organizations including major manufacturers, large retailers, and consulting firms. What separates our version from most of the others is its attention to a four-step process rather than the traditional three-step version. Three-step models normally focus on the supply chain from manufacturing through distribution to the retail outlets. In fact, most of the actual execution in these models has been accomplished in "doublets"—in an area between only two sectors of the supply chain. For example, some organizations have made notable strides by effecting improvements between manufacturing and their warehouse or distribution center system. In these cases, inventories were reduced or procedures developed to move large-volume items through the system with minimal handling. Paperwork improvements were made, and some special arrangements for sharing facilities were achieved, using cross-docking procedures or improved truck utilization.

Other firms have concentrated on making improvements between the distribution centers and the stores. Here the successes
have been measured by shorter cycle times and the holding of
fewer goods at the stores. Primarily, the stores have taken the lead
in these actions, because of their desire to better utilize floor space
by reallocating space from the back of the store to the front. The
removal of inventory from the back reduces the need to store
goods and allows the store manager to put more goods on display.
Several firms have also made strides by working to reduce forecasting errors using EDI and by eliminating paperwork, particularly purchase orders and billings. Service organizations such as
hotels and banks have usually made progress by working with
their supply base to improve costs and delivery and service features, again in a doublet arrangement.

These examples are noteworthy, but tremendous opportunities
still await the extension of these improved processes across a full
supply network. It is not enough to look just at the chain of supply downstream from manufacturing. We need to look at suppliers to manufacturing, too. This concept might not be new, but in
terms of actual practice, it is not being implemented. To maximize
cost reduction and ensure full analysis of the total chain, we prefer to look at the total supply chain as a four-step process.

The Four-Step Model

A three-step improvement model will bring attention to the potential enhancements that exist between a manufacturer, distributors, and stores or retail outlets, but it runs the risk of missing key
components of cost upstream of these constituents. A service
model will look at supply to the servicing institution and possibly into a customer base, but will overlook any connection to the
primary suppliers. A four-step version (see Figure 3.1) adds the dimension of the suppliers' relationship to the manufacturers or the
primary suppliers' relationship to a servicing supplier. Although
it might be argued that this concept could be extended to more
suppliers, creating an excessively long chain, this is unnecessary.

FIGURE 3.1. The Interenterprise Supply Chain Model.

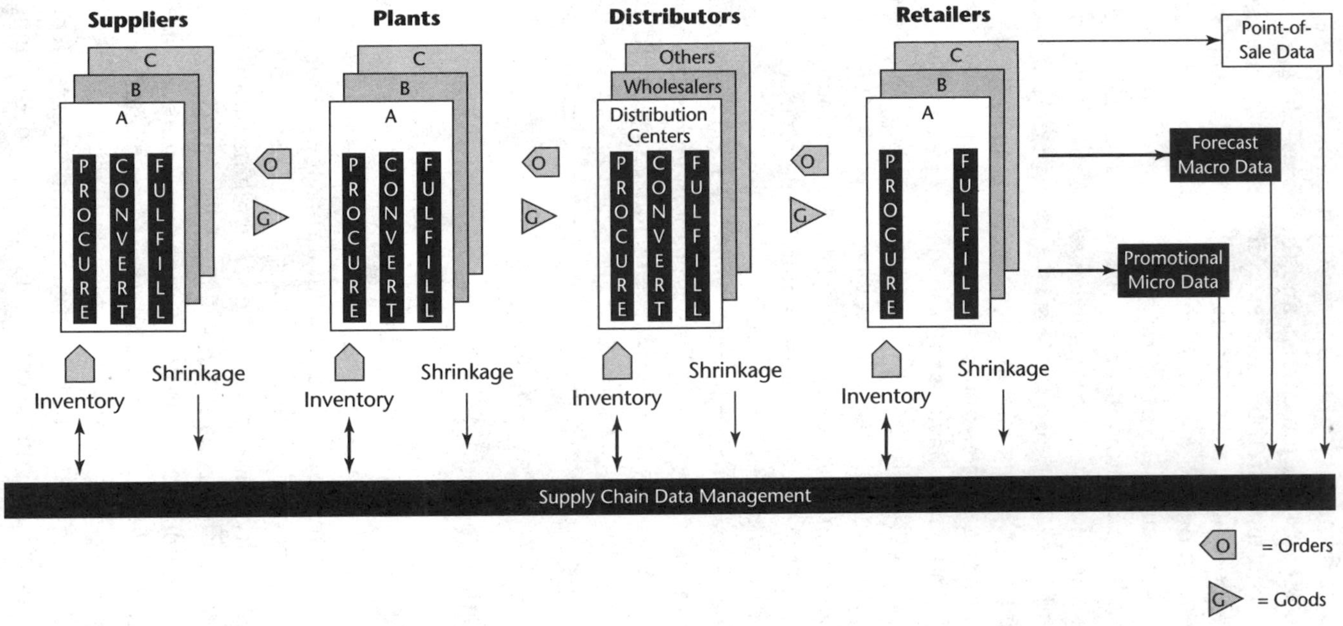

Virtually every business we studied was able to identify five to ten suppliers responsible for 75 to 80 percent of incoming costs. Our model begins with these strategic suppliers. Improving effectiveness with a manageable number of key suppliers yields the gains that are being sought; extension of the improvement ideas can be made to smaller vendors as resources and potential improvements allow.

As depicted in Figure 3.1, the model next progresses from these suppliers to the manufacturer, then into distribution, and finally into the retail outlets for consumption by the ultimate consumer. In a service environment, the primary suppliers would bring materials to the firms that provide forms, software, equipment, people, and technical instruments to the service organization, enabling creation of final services to the ultimate consumer. The model suggests that the key information that drives the system should be the POS information that comes from scanning actual purchases. These data are merged with the forecasts that are typically generated in any supply system. We refer to these data as the *macro data trends;* they derive from historical information and are used to trigger purchase orders for the current period. In the service model, this information would come in a similar manner from the forecasts and historical data on sales that are used to make purchases based on anticipated future service levels.

The *micro trends* in the model come from the promotions and special sales events and their results, which often raise or lower the amount of goods currently needed. Capturing these micro trends is extremely valuable in any system designed to trigger actual replenishment needs and to plan manufacturing schedules. The service world also has many instances of special promotions, such as hotel and resort packages. Typically, this promotional information is not shared with constituents upstream in time for them to do adequate preplanning and coordinate supply with the results of the promotion. In the limited cases where we were able to extract this information early and share it ahead of the distribution function, significant gains were seen: constituents were able to respond with fewer fluctuations in the manufacturing schedules and with less supporting inventory.

These three pieces of data are merged in the model and then

deposited in a proactive data base, which we refer to as supply chain data management. This data warehouse is absolutely critical to the success of the interenterprise network system being depicted. It must contain the three sources of information mentioned above and must be accessible to the parties upstream of the retail outlets, in a compatible format: that is, any necessary translations must be made in terms of products, sku's, or item-specific information so that each party understands clearly what the items are as well as the replenishment needs. In the data base, each item is preset with reorder or "trigger" levels that initiate the ultimate pull needed across the entire supply chain to meet consumption demands. With this information, the members of the network can initiate activities for replenishment while keeping inventory supply at minimum levels and still satisfying the end-user demands.

The interenterprise model will be used extensively in this chapter as we describe how a total network system can be built and optimized with the proper relationships and cooperative ingredients. The crux of this model is that its execution requires a change, from thinking of the system as one that is driven by the management to thinking of it as functioning in response to the ultimate consumer. Thus the emphasis shifts from pushing product toward consumers to pulling product through, as needed, to replenish what has been consumed.

Changing a Push System into a Pull System

Historically, manufacturers held the upper hand in supply chain systems, particularly if brand loyalty had been achieved. These manufacturers could demand and receive special treatment such as preferred shelf space and store locations. The supply system that was created in this environment pushed products to the retailer for sale to a predisposed consumer. An interim period existed when retailers were able to literally sell slotting allowances—shelf space—to new manufacturers or for new items. Today, the retailer is more interested in having what the customer currently wants rather than what used to be heavily demanded and therefore is in a position to make demands on the manufacturers concerning which items and how many of them will be brought through the system. Ultimately, we see control passing to the final consumer, who will have an enormous range of buying options via tomorrow's electronic systems. For now, we will concentrate on what is happening and what can be improved within the retail-dominated supply chains.

The subtle change in the character of who controls supply systems has moved the emphasis from making ample supplies of products and pushing those products toward the stores to a system where the actual consumption of products triggers release information and goods are sent toward the store shelves to meet current customer demands. In the latter case, the opportunity is created to reduce the costs that are traditionally associated with carrying the extra inventories and slow-moving products.

Many firms have not adjusted their thinking or their supply systems to meet this change in product flow. Instead, we witnessed many systems still built to accommodate long-run economies in the manufacturing sector, regardless of actual pull-through demands in the network. The firms still utilizing these systems were content to rely on the use of warehouses to store the extra product rather than working on the flexible systems that would adapt them to the current supply chain demands. Weeks of excess inventories were encountered throughout our visits to organizations in all four sectors of the model.

That is a critical mistake. Today's supply system has to be geared to near-total flexibility. This means that the manufacturer concentrates on achieving the shortest possible changeover times, responding quickly to the need to make a product in demand instead of the one running on the machines, and develops a distribution system that gets this product to the point of consumption in the shortest possible time. The ultimate outcome of the current trend is for retailers to demand smaller and smaller quantities that match actual consumption at the stores, ultimately one unit at a time. Responding to these local demands by drawing from a convenient inventory satisfies the need for product availability, but it introduces extra costs that must ultimately be borne by the consumer or pushed back upstream for absorption by manufacturers and suppliers.

The need for flexible change does not end with the manufacturer. It progresses further upstream, placing demands on the manufacturer's suppliers to be equally flexible and to respond without building inventories. Done properly, the more flexible network of supply, manufacture, and distribution becomes an optimized system that creates an advantage over slower and more costly competing networks. It becomes capable of responding to changing consumption patterns and localized retail needs without eliminating the chance of making a profit in the process.

As the model implies, the four-step system begins to trigger production after the product has been consumed. When the stores record a sale, the POS information becomes the key ingredient in initiating replenishment. Current sales are transmitted to the interactive data base using standard EDI formats. These data are then merged with information that has been preloaded from the forecast as expected sales, to develop an understanding of the differences and to make responses more in tune with actual pull-through. The adjusted forecast is then balanced against any current needs of a special nature, or in response to special sales events or promotional efforts. The total of these three ingredients will create the actual consumption data that will bring the system into balance in response to real throughput. The parties upstream of the stores will then receive standard EDI-formatted data that have the necessary information for response and replenishment of actual needs. The traditional push system is thus converted into a pull system based on actual demand.

The model is a representation of what can be developed and what we have been able to create on a pilot basis. Currently, most supply chain systems make far greater use of forecasts, with all the inherent weaknesses in that mode, and rely much more on distribution center releases than is implied in the model. Efforts to improve the accuracy of forecasts have proved to be very beneficial in triggering supply response, when that medium is the relied-upon source of information. An array of programs and advisers is available to demonstrate how a historical data base can be used in conjunction with current sales activity to generate higher reliability in forecasted volumes. IRI Logistics, based in Chicago, has made significant strides in reducing forecast errors and validating forecast information for use in distribution planning systems. Efficient Marketing Systems, headquartered in Deerfield, Illinois, has made similar strides in developing interactive data bases from POS information that can be used effectively to improve replenishment systems. We recommend these kinds of services to improve forecasts. We counsel, however, that to achieve true efficiency in chain replenishment, actual POS information should be the primary source for determining the need for replacement of goods purchased, augmented by the sales forecast and promotional and special sales activity data.

The caveat we would add is that the reliability of the POS information is an issue that has to be fully resolved before most organizations will embrace it as a source for triggering responses. Additionally, retailers have to take ownership of the use of POS as the key ingredient in response systems. Only when they see its value for their stores and are willing to use it extensively will this tool reach its full potential. The number of possible users is large, but the number of actual implementers remains small because of concerns about the "cleanliness" of this form of data, which we will discuss shortly, and misunderstandings about who will benefit from this direct link to consumption. But progress continues among those who are dedicated to using this front-line information source, and it is the most-favored trigger point in the application of the interenterprise model. If replenishment is to be accomplished with the least variability in the manufacturing schedule and minimal inventories, then releases have to be tied to actual consumption as tightly as possible. This condition requires a move toward POS and away from preliminary forecasts.

Pulling from Consumption Instead of Forecast

Most of the supply systems we studied required improvement because of slow execution times, the need to discount goods to have them consumed, overdependence on inventory to obtain supplies, excesses in supporting paperwork, or a multiplicity of redundant costs. Those who were charged with the improvement effort professed an earnest desire to make the conversion to the use of POS in order to help alleviate some or all of these conditions. Many of these same individuals, however, provided myriad excuses for their reluctance to migrate to a POS-driven pull system. The basic complication in their plans was their inability to pull replenishment directly from consumption. Most organizations were so locked into the traditional forecasting system that change was virtually impossible to achieve.

The typical system is driven by information created at the retail end of the chain, based on historical actions, and balanced with marketing data provided by large manufacturers, consultants, and trade publications. In essence, these forecasts are seasonally smoothed guesses, following a model based on a one- to five-year history of previous sales data. The more sophisticated the organization, the more complex the program for generating the forecast information. Supposedly, more reliability is attached to the figures with larger data bases. In 100 percent of the cases studied, however, we could find no group that consistently relied on the forecasted data beyond the first few days of each new period. Adjustments abounded, particularly in periods of unexpected promotional activity.

A few organizations that have worked hard at refining their forecasts, particularly those that have done so to use them as input to distribution resource planning systems, were able to demonstrate notable improvements. A larger group suffered through and accepted the limitations inherent in their forecasting. One major organization shared with us information that showed forecasting errors to consistently be in a range of 30 to 70 percent. They had become adept at living with this problem, but they knew that large embedded costs resulted from this magnitude of inaccuracy. By working with professionals and doggedly pursuing improvement, they were successful in pulling these error rates down to 8 to 18 percent. This level was still high enough to require additional supplies and techniques for responding to the implications of the error rate, but it is indicative of the magnitude of improvement that can be made.

Most firms relied on the forecast to begin each of the twelve segments into which the sales projections were divided and to develop the necessary financial planning information. This meant

that each new period had an expected outcome and a set of specified materials, manufacturing ingredients, and system outputs
that would be needed in the supply chain to meet the projected demand. Regardless of actual performance, most companies started
each new period with the forecasted figures. Certainly, the anticipated financial results continued to be tied to these projections.

By the third or fourth day into a new month or quarter, however, the expediting, changes, add-on orders, special shipments,
and so forth started in earnest. We watched as some of the most
sophisticated organizations generated bills of material and data
for their materials resource planning systems (MRP and MRP II)
and DRP systems, based on the projected demand information,
only to be overridden by experienced schedulers and planners
adjusting to actual conditions. We saw carefully constructed distribution planning schemes being adjusted with manual interven-
tions to accommodate the slightest variations in customer demand. We also watched as these same firms relied heavily on daily
production meetings to keep customer satisfaction at the pre-
ordained high-level targeted results.

After careful study, we concluded that a forecast is still essential to the supply system, if for no other reason than to drive the
financial planning. It is also the best starting point to determine
what capacity has to be available to meet the estimated demands
for the current year and to give the buyers a chance to know how
much of the incoming supplies will be needed for the current
period. Planning and scheduling also have to be based on some
sort of projection that has a semblance of validity. Beyond these
features, the forecast diminishes in value for practical, day-to-day
purposes. With the appropriate plant, equipment, supplies, personnel, and other resources to meet the projected demand, what
the system desperately needs to know is how much product will
be consumed tomorrow. Now the focus shifts to the POS data.

Combining the Forecast with POS and Promotional Data

With continuing information on the previous day's consumption
or that of a day in the near future, the forecast can be adjusted to

reality. Then the possibility becomes real of constructing replenishment plans that are synchronized with consumption. The necessity, of course, is for a high degree of accuracy in the POS information. Early attempts at using this valuable resource were stunted by inherent flaws. In scanning products, it is a natural reaction to simply add a number of similar items for a single entry at the checkout register. In many cases, however, the items are dissimilar. For example, six rolls of paper towels might be recorded together, because the price per roll is the same. In terms of supply replenishment, however, the entry data are flawed if the six rolls have different printed patterns and, consequently, six different sku numbers. Several retailers have opted to code the POS device so that it forces each item to be handled individually, whether it is scanned or keyed. It is essential to train the cashier to understand the need for clean data if this source of information is to be used for replenishment. This training will be demanded when store managers begin to realize the value of this information in computer-aided ordering and the ways it can keep their own costs down as replenishment moves to a system with less safety stock and shorter cycles.

Once the machinery has been installed to pick up the correct product identification, what remains for better implementation is a system for ensuring that no human intervention or flaws are introduced into the reading of that information. As accuracy reaches necessary levels, the usefulness of the replenishment plan also increases. With highly accurate purchase data, the members of the supply chain can prepare for actual replenishment instead of relying on hoped-for levels or warehouse releases to set replacement needs.

Completing the loop by accessing promotional or special sale information provides a total picture of current pull-through demand. Promotions are not going away in the supply-to-consumption chain. They are an embedded part of merchandising and have to be handled in any system that purports to optimize response. Forecasts, or historically based information, can be merged with yesterday's actual sales to get a picture of what is changing in the plan and why. This combination has to be merged with any promotional overrides to develop a real-time look at the system.

Every promotion we watched followed a pattern. The item was identified and the plan was set in motion for the promotion. Orders were placed for the necessary stocks, as much by guesswork as by accurate calculation. As the promotion progressed, available stocks were exceeded and extra orders were sent back to the suppliers. These orders were delivered, but then the promotion began to slow down and extra stocks were left over. With the use of the combined data described above, necessary replenishment could be signaled upstream to the suppliers in closer congruence with the actual progress of the promotion. Then a logical flow of new stock could be sent toward the stores, without an excess of safety inventory.

Building a Proactive, User-Friendly Data Base

Once the decision is made to use forecasts in combination with POS information and promotional data, the requirement shifts to creating the data base in which this information will reside so that it can be accessed by the upstream constituents. This effort requires not only a few years' history of product movement; it also demands that the information be accessed in terms compatible with each user's internal information system. Sku's at the point of purchase from a grocery store, a department store, or a mass merchant outlet cannot be assumed to be the same. Nor should it be assumed that all manufacturers will use the same code or identification. The data base has to start with what was purchased, but the data need to be made understandable to the upstream suppliers to be of any value.

Triggering Product Flow When Needed

The practicality of this type of data interchange comes from the ability to trigger the replenishment activities based on what is being consumed rather than what was expected to be consumed. This condition is tantamount to setting up product flow on an as-needed basis. Safety stocks can be carried for special needs or for slow-turnover items, but the ultimate result of such a system is shipment of the correct amount of product to bring the stores back to their predetermined stocking levels for any regular, seasonal, or promotional circumstance. In an ideal situation, a single item could be replenished within a single day. Although that condition is very futuristic, consider the more mundane improvement of having the correct amount of goods flow through the system during such seasonal peaks as those associated with major holidays. A world-class system will do just that; it will accommodate the largest swings, traditionally connected with major holidays, and will have the right amount of the most-demanded goods available at the time of need.

Even though such a condition is not completely practical today and could prove to be economically difficult for some items and stores, the direction is what is important. Product replenishment, to be effective, should be triggered by current consumption. As the system moves in this direction, the flow of supply will rely less on projections and more on what was truly absorbed from the supply chain. All of the inventories, handling, paperwork, and expediting will move toward optimization of resources as the network becomes more and more tuned in to having product available to meet the true demands.

Inventory Minimization

The need for less inventory is not only a factor between distribution and the stores. If the data base has the pertinent information and can trigger a pull scenario on a real-time basis, each constituent will come to realize that less stock is needed as the reliability of the data is improved and stock is delivered in a more timely fashion. This condition makes production scheduling considerably easier. In this scenario, with more reliable information, the manufacturers and suppliers to the retailers can plan with shorter cycles. In essence, the upstream facilities shift their emphasis from manufacturing for stock to producing for replenishment.

This situation creates an environment in which the manufacturer stops making lot sizes to fulfill a composite of customer orders and instead sets aside machine time to fulfill individual orders. Products are scheduled and produced to match specific needs rather than in quantities that may or may not match consumption. Determining what lot size to produce also becomes a local decision in which the economies of production are balanced against local carrying costs to determine the optimal size. Decisions to make lot sizes that correlate to consumer demands are now affected by the knowledge that the responding system is going to meet the demand in any case, without having to create excess inventories.

In this type of flexible system, it becomes equally imperative for cycle times to become shorter throughout the supply chain. The idea is to build a network that can respond more swiftly than any competitor. Suppliers to the manufacturers have to work on shorter cycles and quicker response times as much as the distributor to the stores does. This improvement adds another dimension of flexibility to the manufacturing process. With needed supplies arriving in a "kanban" (the Japanese term for only enough material to meet the needs of the manufacturing system) or just-in-time basis, with just the amount of need, the manufacturer has more freedom in planning and scheduling. Now a simple calculation can be produced that reflects what size order is best to run, or run and hold, based on the timing of actual orders and delivery.

In the interenterprise model, the flow of products goes across at least four constituencies before reaching the ultimate consumer. Our experience with mapping the flow of these products and the associated fulfillment process has revealed a significant opportunity to radically reduce cycle times. In one instance, when we plotted the flow of ingredients and packaging to a major manufacturer, we discovered two weeks of waiting time in what was thought to be a short cycle. Lead times were unnecessarily extended, with resulting excess inventory and safety stock throughout the network. When we went further and investigated the flow from the manufacturer to the distributors, we found another week and a half of pure waiting time. Throughout the entire process, we identified a month's worth of unnecessary delays. The resulting reengineering of that process removed these inventory excesses and shortened the cycle time by 50 percent.

In another case, we were asked to look at a larger cycle time, that of creating a new product and bringing it to commercial realization. Although this project went beyond the supply chain factors being considered here, the findings have a parallel application. The process map of the product development cycle demonstrated that a twenty-four-month cycle was involved, which was considered too great for current market demands and competitive capabilities. The first focus on the process map was on the amount of nonvalue-adding time built into the current system. As we do in supply chain applications, we isolated the largest ingredients of nonvalue-adding effort. In this case it was the time spent waiting—for approvals, for samples, for releases, for shipments, and so forth. Through re-design, the product development cycle was reduced to one fourth of the beginning conditions, primarily by extracting the causes of the unnecessary delays. These measures not only led to cutting the cycle time; they also enhanced employee satisfaction by stream-lining what was perceived to be bureaucratic waste.

Plotting the processes involved in supply chain replenishment will quickly reveal avoidable delays that lengthen the cycle time for forecasting, planning, scheduling, manufacturing, and deliv-ery. Cycle-time improvement is one of the more obvious tangible values of pursuing supply chain optimization.

Eliminating Redundancies

The next area of concentration should be the elimination of any redundancies that exist across the supply system. The model in Figure 3.1 can be used to show overlapping stores of inventory be-tween each link in the chain. Just keeping track of these inven-tories creates a potential for duplicated efforts. Transferring in-ventories to meet needs creates a second area of improvement opportunity. We have watched as people prepared certain goods for transfer to the next organization in the supply chain and have carefully noted their activities, especially the actions of those clos-est to the final operation, such as delivery or shipment. We have then followed the path of the goods, watching and recording as the first person at the receiving site inspected the incoming goods, recorded what was received, and entered the data regarding the shipment into the firm's data base.

When we compared the data on the activities of the delivery and receiving personnel with representatives from both organizations, we found a significant overlap. Most of this overlap was grounded in a lack of trust between the two parties. Each side had established an extensive "auditing" process to oversee the product exchange activities. By adopting partnering techniques that placed the responsibility for delivery of exact-count, quality goods at the sourcing site, we witnessed a substantial reduction of personal effort on both sides, providing resources that could be reallocated to value-adding activities. And when we documented the savings from these changes, the trust level increased surprisingly in other areas of interaction.

Redundancy resides throughout most supply chains. It can be found within the order entry process, in which two people at two different locations and work stations print and transmit purchase orders and receive and transmit acknowledgments. Both functions are easily automated but, more important, only the effort of one person should be required for this type of transaction. A simple analysis of the actual duties assigned to people in communication at the connecting links in the supply chain will reveal many other redundancies that should be targets for elimination as the network moves toward optimization.

Moving the Information Electronically

Systems are currently available and functioning in daily business activities that automate nearly all the paperwork transactions in supply chain networking. The action study in Chapter Two is an indication of what can be accomplished. Other firms have advanced the use of EDI to remove the need for verbal expediting via phone or fax, as well as to reduce billing to an error-free, electronic funds transfer and to set up restocking programs that rely on electronic information rather than direct person-to-person correspondence.

EDI has received far too much discussion and little actual

implementation. Its purpose is to enable an organization to complete business transactions faster, with less expense, and virtually without errors. Other benefits can be derived from increased control over work processes and efficiency in handling. Common benefits include lower inventories, improved customer service, lower human resource requirements, and considerably better information access at the time of need. Unfortunately, our investigations reveal that most organizations, other than the leading-edge practitioners, stop with order entry and billing. They are reluctant to bring more functions into EDI systems until they observe more documented successes. Their caution impedes a logical extension of cooperative supply chain interactions.

Some of the major retailers, sensing the value of the potential savings, have insisted that their suppliers become EDI-capable or risk being taken off their supply list. This threat has caused a commotion, but we see limited evidence of a strong movement toward becoming EDI-capable. Only with a consistent supply chain electronic transfer system will we see the kind of effective optimization we are espousing. EDI becomes the enabling tool to speed cycles, eliminate errors, make obsolete the need for paperwork, and bring replenishment systems to world-class standards. Using this tool wisely across the supply chain requires progressing through several steps:

- A process improvement plan, based on a reengineered system that meets customer needs under optimum conditions, has to be formulated and clearly understood.
- A detailed tactical plan must be created for developing the software and hardware requirements.
- Breakthrough strategies have to be included that will dramatically cut the existing system resource requirements and costs.
- Defect and delay points have to be succinctly delineated during the reengineering effort so that error elimination is completed and the new process becomes totally reliable.

The logical way to accomplish this progression is by mapping the total process and conducting a full-scale reengineering effort, with all members of the supply network participating.

Recognizing the System Limitations

Making changes in supply replenishment has limitations. Keeping replenishment at short intervals with a high degree of accuracy, for example, requires state-of-the-art information technology. This is a functional issue. Another requirement is to have a large enough volume in the items being replenished to keep the trucks moving the goods to the outlets as close to full as possible. This is a magnitude issue. Although the less than full truckload has to be a factor in supply systems, the improvement effort should be geared toward keeping trucks as close to full as possible to optimize delivery costs.

Some items will not lend themselves to an optimized system. Items such as baker's yeast, special seasonings, and low-turnover garment and tool items have to be stocked in stores, but a pallet load or one bin could be a year's supply. To maintain freshness of perishable items and keep supplies at needed levels, such items must be inventoried. Other limitations will have to be recognized and addressed, but not allowed to interfere with the overall concept. The improvement model should be fashioned for high-turnover items and expanded to include the lower-turnover sku's as development proceeds. The potential to combine items and use cross-docking techniques in the distribution centers to fill out truckloads has to be investigated by members of the total supply chain to get the critical mass of product necessary to keep truck utilization at practical levels. More cooperative arrangements have to be worked out so that whole industries can move toward supply chain improvement. This is the only way that full optimization can be approached.

Some Early Examples

An early endeavor to prove the validity of using a supply model to improve effectiveness occurred when Rubbermaid and Kmart decided to partner in an effort to enhance their replenishment network. Figure 3.2 shows the three-step model used, with the

FIGURE 3.2. Rubbermaid and Kmart Replenishment Network.

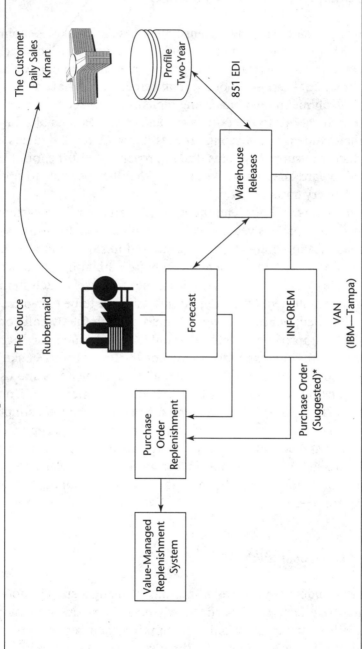

Note: Two years' data for start-up.

*Suggested point of sale: Maintain service at agreed stocking levels.

warehouse releases representing the model's distribution sector. Beginning with daily sales transactions gathered from the Kmart stores, information was accumulated until a two-year data base was created to help verify what Rubbermaid items were actually consumed. This information is currently being used to establish a profile of expected consumption and improve the forecasted pull-through. Using a standard 851 EDI program, the current actual scanned sales at the point of purchase in the stores are accumulated and compared against this profile, then adjusted by the warehouse releases (for purposes of ensuring accuracy) and compared against the forecasted sales.

Warehouse releases are also sent to a value-added network (VAN), where suggested replenishment purchase orders are generated to coincide with the actual pull-through that is occurring. The data coming from the forecast analysis part of the system are then compared with the suggested purchase order to establish a specific replenishment release. Next, this information is put through a "value-managed replenishment" program to trigger an actual release to Rubbermaid manufacturing. The release pulls product from manufacturing rather than having it sent to inventory beforehand in anticipation of consumption. Inventories at the warehouse (Rubbermaid's distribution centers) are only kept at the low levels required for store delivery. Throughout the transactions, service is maintained at previously agreed-upon levels.

This effort is progressing to the fourth step recommended by the interenterprise model by including suppliers. With growing information on actual consumption and the quicker connection through EDI, the possibility becomes real of connecting supplies of resins, tools, packaging, and labels to pull-through consumption, rather than accumulating these stocks based solely on forecasts.

In an effort to create an advantage in one of the most competitive of all modern industries, consumer electronics, Philips NV embarked on a quick-response system that would pull product reliably through its entire chain of supply. The idea was to replenish retail shelf stock without stock-outs and at the lowest cost to the "partners" in their chain, including suppliers, manufacturers, and retailers. Figure 3.3 depicts their vision, which has become a reality for the firm.

FIGURE 3.3. Philips NV Quick-Response Vision.

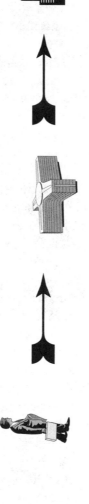

Consumer purchased product at retail store.

Purchase data enters POS system at cash register.

POS information is transmitted to both the distribution center and supplier.

Distribution center maintains minimum inventory, serves as tranship location.

From POS information, distribution center fills orders from stock or transmits order to supplier.

Supplier receives order to ship to distribution center or store.

Order is pulled from (minimum) inventory or produced to meet schedule fulfillment date.

POS information is used to forecast demand.

Pull-through in this system begins when a consumer buys a Philips product, such as a television set, at a retail store. This action triggers a POS data transmission back to the distribution center and the supplier, in this case the Philips manufacturer. The distribution center has been transformed from a holder of inventory to a service location that responds to the pull-through with minimum stocks. Using the POS data, it sends supplies to replenish the current orders, if available. The same information is received at the manufacturing location, where an order can be created or product taken from the line to match the pull-through needs. In this three-step system, the customer's purchase is used to pull the replenishment product. An extension to the manufacturing center's suppliers would complete the four-step model being recommended. Similar efforts are being conducted by Dillard Department Stores; J. C. Penney Company; Levi Strauss and Company; V. F. Corporation; Sears, Roebuck & Co.; and the recognized leaders, Procter & Gamble and Wal-Mart. Procter & Gamble's story will be detailed in the action study.

Action Study: Procter & Gamble's Continuous Replenishment Program
·····

Working with a number of customers, notably Wal-Mart, Procter & Gamble developed the most widely recognized three-step supply chain improvement system. Its technique, termed continuous replenishment program (CRP), became the company's vision of how to respond to the growing need for quicker, more accurate customer service and stock replenishment. From the Procter & Gamble viewpoint, CRP changed the traditional customer-supplier relationship. Under CRP, the reorder process was simplified and streamlined for greater efficiency and effectiveness. Using process reengineering techniques, the order response system was redesigned to eliminate nonvalue-adding costs and cut cycle times as much as possible.

The CRP system that resulted is outlined in Figure 3.4. This process starts with orders that are received from stores at the customer distribution centers via EDI, along with Procter & Gamble's on-hand inventory and receipts. These orders are aggregated and sent, in the form of an electronic pull-through demand that has been compared with on-hand inventory, to the

FIGURE 3.4. Continuous Replenishment Process.

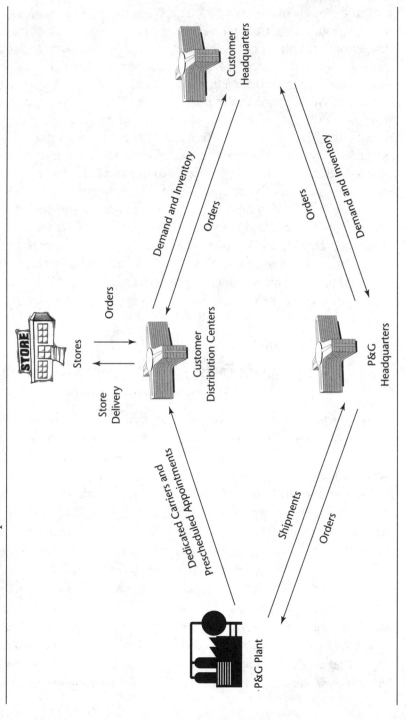

customer headquarters site to enable Procter & Gamble to establish optimum reorder quantities. After making overview analyses and adjustments for promotions and special activities, the headquarters group routes the actual orders back to the distribution centers and to Procter & Gamble headquarters.

Plant-specific orders are then sent from Procter & Gamble to the individual manufacturing sites for production. After the needed stocks have been manufactured, dedicated carriers with prescheduled appointments are designated to move the replenishment goods to the customer distribution centers. The replenishment goods and the on-hand inventory are then sent to specific customer stores. In this system, inventories are minimized by keeping the stocks in the distribution centers at very low levels and relying on the flexible manufacturing systems at the Procter & Gamble plants to meet most of the store needs.

Although the actual process is more detailed than we have outlined, all the functions that make the system work are included. The effect is a system in which the customer and Procter & Gamble benefit from a lower-cost, speedier process, and the ultimate consumer gets better selection at lower prices. Documented customer benefits include:

- *Customer warehouse inventory that was reduced from nineteen days to six*
- *Inventory turns that increased from nineteen to sixty, with a one-time cash flow increase of up to $200,000 resulting from the lower amount of working capital tied up in warehouse inventory*
- *Better utilization of distribution center space, through the reduction of customer-owned inventories*
- *Reduced administration costs, through the use of electronic interchanges and elimination of paperwork*
- *Improved store service levels, from 96.4 to 99.2 percent on specific products, by having the right amount and variety of replacement stock available*

Procter & Gamble recorded these benefits for the company:

- *Improved customer service and satisfaction*
- *Increased order volumes of up to 30 percent*
- *An increased market share of more than four points*
- *Reduced distribution costs*

- *An improvement of 4 to 12 percent in vehicle utilization*
- *A 60 percent lower rate of returns and refusals*
- *A 20 to 40 percent reduction in goods damage*

Through the use of this program, Procter & Gamble now knows, from the incoming data on POS transactions, what to ship even before an actual order is generated by the customer. Planning and scheduling are greatly enhanced by this capability. For example, products like disposable diapers used to suffer from wide fluctuations in scheduling needs depending on the particular type of diaper being consumed: regular, super-absorbent, or special grade. Under CRP, manufacturing fluctuations have been substantially reduced, because the plant knows which types are being pulled out of the system. Together, Procter & Gamble and its customers involved in the CRP process can offer the customer lower shelf prices resulting from system savings, reduced out-of-stock situations, improved product freshness, and decreased package damage.

The Procter & Gamble system, recently purchased by IBM, is one of the leading-edge practices that will help to bring supply chain optimization to reality. As this type of system is developed by others and is expanded on the upstream side to include the suppliers of the materials needed to make the replenishment products, the opportunity for system optimization starts to be real. The requirement is to recognize that the types of enhancements that can be worked out by cooperative efforts between a retailer, a distribution system, and a manufacturer can also be developed upstream with similar efforts. The same methods of working out better interactions can be used between suppliers and manufacturers as are used between manufacturers and stores. Improving a four-step process simply expands a supply chain's documented three-step successes in a logical fashion to build a truly responsive supply network.

Procter & Gamble is now hard at work introducing the next version of its supply chain improvements—termed "streamlined logistics"—and developing tomorrow's solutions for today's problems.

Summary

A plethora of execution models are available for those who want to go in search of supply chain improvement. The model outlined and described in this chapter was developed to address the short-comings we found in these models, especially the absence of a step that included the primary manufacturers' suppliers. In building an optimized solution, it is imperative for the four vital links in the supply system to progress through a reengineered version of supply replenishment; if they do not, the network runs the risk of having a weak link in the process. This is why we foster a model that includes the key primary suppliers and focuses on sharing with those suppliers accurate and timely POS data, combined with forecasts and promotional and special activity information. The examples we illustrated are progressions toward improvement. They need to be expanded to complete their contribution.

The interenterprise solution includes the entities and the transactions that have to be scrutinized before optimization can occur. Many organizations are chasing improvement in their own manner. Our experiences reveal, however, that only a few are looking at the full supply network. Those seeking help should not overlook the importance of partnering with all the constituencies that affect the intended end result: an error-free, low-cost, low-inventory system that is electronically linked as completely as possible and that totally satisfies the ultimate consumer. Such a network will benefit all the constituencies that come together and share in the effort and reward, while providing the best satisfaction and service to the end users through a network that has an advantage over other competing groups.

Chapter Four

A New Look at Business Partnering

Up to this point, we have developed the case that a supply chain can be optimized. We have illustrated a typical chain and presented a four-step model for bringing that chain to levels of improvement that will approach optimization. The potential savings have been discussed, as have the likely pitfalls. Most of the examples cited have been successful with a two- or three-step model. The task now is to introduce a concept that has to be woven into the fabric of the supply network to induce firms to work across a full chain and mutually seek optimization. That concept is *business partnering.*

In this chapter we will revisit that concept, which has become an overworked, misunderstood, and often-abused idea. It has to be fully appreciated and accepted if the kind of supply chain cooperation being advocated is going to be a reality. With all of the work currently being conducted by individual firms to bring improvement to existing supply networks, we have found only a handful that truly appreciate the importance of this crucial ingredient.

The Concept Defined

A supply chain must have an ingredient that binds the members together or the network will have little substance. In a scenario that is typical, but that offers little chance for optimization, this ingredient is the leveraging of position. The more powerful members—the ones with the large volume orders—simply exert their influence over the weaker participants—those firms seeking the volume—and extract unwarranted concessions to ensure continuing to be a supplier, particularly during times when market conditions make some suppliers especially interested in increasing volume positions. These circumstances only weaken the network.

The weakness in these situations derives from the fact that leveraging only serves to create a loose-knit association of member organizations that attempt to make as much profit as they can from each other, rather than working for the mutual benefit of the network. The parties will appear to be developing close relationships that often span many decades of working together. Closer analysis often reveals, however, that one party has traditionally dominated the relationship. It only takes a period of short supply to reveal how superficial that relationship has actually been. When the opportunity arises to gain an upper hand that has been denied for years, even docile suppliers have been known to make unprecedented demands on customers that have overpowered them in the past.

The superior network builds on the fundamental element of trust—in the partnering concept and in each other—and uses the concept of business partnering as an ingredient that benefits all members of the supply system. Because this ingredient is often mentioned but rarely understood, we propose a definition and working arrangement that will make it the catalyst for supply chain optimization. At its core, partnering is an association of parties acting for their mutual benefit. The operative word is, of course, *mutual.* Most alleged partnering arrangements we have observed were that in name only. Invariably, what we encountered were very good customer service stories that had been passed off as examples of partnering. For example, the use of such special-delivery devices as helicopters and chartered airplanes provides wonderful stories of how a supplier went the extra mile to service a customer. It does not speak to partnering, because it lacks mutual benefit. Stories of ways in which a supplier's employees worked long and unusual hours to make certain that a needed delivery was at the required point at the required time are also great examples of servicing and pleasing a customer. They are not illustrations of partnering.

Beyond the feature of special customer service is the element of shared resources and benefits that accrue to both parties. When a supplier has mobilized special resources and made unusual shipments in a time of desperate need, the reward is typically a special order or an increase in position. This kind of reward should be given to a good source, but it does not approach the kind of leading-edge arrangement that can come from extra effort by both parties to find a competitive advantage. We prefer to work on alliances that are focused on business partnering, which we define as a process through which the involved parties establish and sustain a competitive advantage over similar entities, through pooling resources in a trusting atmosphere focused on continuous, mutual improvement.

Under the circumstances established by this definition, the partnering firms have to be prepared to give up a part of their traditional independence or their power position in the pursuit of greater opportunities. In short, the parties have to share, on an equitable basis, in both the investment and the benefits. Suppliers, for example, must shift their thinking from satisfying any and all demands to taking a proactive role in increasing their customers' competitiveness through mutual-action projects. Buyers have to look beyond their ability to leverage volume for lower costs and find ways to seek out the ideas and participation of suppliers in actions that have greater benefits for both parties. Both organizations have to work with other members of the supply chain with the objective of investing resources in the future of the networking relationship.

Because the focus of this book is on optimizing the supply chain network, we should position that concept in a framework based on business partnering. Optimization means that the parties to the relationship have found the maximum value from participating in the supply chain rather than following the traditional approach of concentrating on what happens at only a few links in the chain. As optimization is pursued, it may be discovered that a few links have to be suboptimized for the good of the network. In that case, the increased cost should be shared, and not borne solely by one party.

As an example, inventories require special attention as the chain seeks high-order fill rates and high levels of service and customer satisfaction. Partnering requires the parties in the network to analyze how to keep these high levels of satisfaction without introducing the competitive disadvantage of carrying high levels of inventory. If total costs can be reduced by pooling supplies in strategic locations, those costs should be shared across the network. This allows the network to become more competitive while reaching high service levels.

In the 1980s, manufacturers and retailers worked in their separate areas without deference to the upstream side of the supply chain. Now they are realizing the flaws in neglecting the total system. The traditional mode bred a win-lose environment, in which there was ample reason not to develop high levels of trust. Each party looked for opportunities to raise margins without regard for the total cost to the system. Such actions had short-term benefits for one link in the chain but could jeopardize the strength of the supply system as it competed with other, more effective networks.

To elaborate on this point, any cost that was pushed away from the retailer usually stayed in the system and was borne temporarily by an upstream chain member, only to be passed backward later. Every supplier has a profit-and-loss statement that records the health of the firm. Absorbing costs only detracts from that statement and invites the supplier to look for opportunities to pass the costs back to the customer. Some firms are more clever than others at this type of action, but we saw ample cases where suppliers accepted cost pass-backs only to see them go forward at a later time. That is not the way a partnering system is meant to function.

Early Abuses in Implementation

In many of the early cases we studied, organizations professing to have entered into partnering arrangements attempted to regale us with stories of how they had partnered with another company. As we sifted through these stories, we found very few that truly fulfilled the partnering definition. Nearly every case was an example of how one firm, typically a supplier, had gone out of the way to provide an extraordinary service for a valued customer. Seldom did we see examples of customers going out of their way to help a supplier. In most cases, the concept of mutual benefit was not met.

As we probed more deeply, we found many abuses scattered among these pretenses we were hearing. A typical story would begin with the storyteller describing a superficial understanding of partnering, with an emphasis on being seen as practicing a hot business technique. Then the story would move to a recitation of how one party had made very special efforts in exchange for a larger-volume position. When we continued the investigation of these stories by querying the suppliers, we found many of the abuses to which we have alluded.

In one particular case, a major company with many operating divisions had started the partnering process by forming a buying council intent on obtaining greater value from suppliers. In this case, supplier partnering was the espoused ingredient and the reward was to be participation by a smaller supply base in the consolidated purchases of the total group. The council initially indicated that it had already made a reduction in the number of suppliers, based on past performance in terms of quality and price. The reduced base was then given a portfolio of expected conditions required to attain a position of continuing supply, and asked to prepare long-term proposals, with partnering features focused on value enhancements rather than price as the key ingredients that would determine the eventual reward of business.

Taking the council at its word, most suppliers prepared proposals containing features that could generate cost savings significantly beyond those normally existing with the member companies. Competitive pricing was submitted by all bidders, with
discounts based on expected actual savings from economies of
scale caused by expected volume increases. More important, special value enhancements that contained opportunities for significant, shared savings were generally presented. Following the presentations, from which final decisions were to have been rendered,
a strange set of circumstances emerged.

Incumbent suppliers that were not supposed to be among the
finalists in the process found copies of the competing proposals.
Individual members of the council countered the submitted, final
proposals with demands for extra concessions for only their business unit, often also indicating that one of the incumbent suppliers had offered further reduced pricing. Pricing, in fact, became
the dominant issue. Guaranteed savings became the vehicle to ensure that any value enhancements accrued solely to the buyer. In
short, the council members saw and seized an opportunity to
leverage their combined position over the less innovative incum-
bents to gain cost transfer. As the days stretched into weeks, the
leveraging continued until a core group of suppliers refused to go
any further with concessions. The contracts were finally awarded
with little semblance of anything that looked like a partnering
arrangement. The language heavily favored the buyer and left little
or no room for the suppliers to share in any enhancements that
would be developed.

The reality of this situation was that, for a time, the council did
succeed in dramatically reducing internal costs. It also succeeded
in temporarily weakening the profitability of its alleged partners.
Most suppliers were simply left with an out-of-pocket loss for
being a preferred partner. As a postscript to this case, when market conditions allowed the suppliers to recoup lost margins, they
did so with delight. The council members now look back on the
deteriorating quality and service levels the organization also experienced and have concluded that their partnering effort was not
a success.

Our portfolio of stories contains many such examples, most not worthy of repetition. However, we did develop an understanding of how abuses can occur in spite of well-intentioned efforts. This list of pitfalls helped us to understand what it takes to make supply chain partnering work. The foremost complicating item on this list is an incompatibility in the business philosophies of the intended partners. In today's fiercely competitive environment, most companies approach their supply base as a necessary evil from which any and all cost concessions should be extracted. The number of firms believing that suppliers have as much right to a profit as they do is much smaller than might be expected from conversations in this area. More often, we find buyers espousing the philosophy that huge savings can be wrung out of suppliers.

We saw a large number of organizations with wide cultural differences trying to come together to find huge savings, without any intention of sharing those savings. Firms that were being hammered by their customers for unwarranted cost reductions became just as unmerciful to their supply base. Companies that generated significant improvement ideas for their customers became focused solely on how to hold position rather than on developing a format for sharing those ideas. With the understanding that the buyer was going to continue leveraging the volume position for future savings, the suppliers typically went into a defensive mode. In that position, only minor savings were generated, never those of a breakthrough nature. Trust became a lost element as prices were raised to former levels at every opportunity and quality and service were relegated to lower levels of importance.

In spite of all protestations to the contrary, we witnessed most partnering examples deteriorate into one-sided bargaining situations in which early efforts to find enhancements quickly evaporated. The emphasis went from finding hidden values to getting back what had been given up in the negotiations. With little joint commitment of resources, the suppliers often withdrew early offerings as they found the need to apply those resources to internal projects.

As we interviewed parties from both sides of the negotiating table, we found each group convinced that it had done the best in the negotiations, but when we later reviewed earnings, which should have been enhanced from these superior bargaining skills, we rarely found any evidence of such superiority. Business seemed to continue as before, with the negotiators waiting for market conditions that would allow temporary price increases, and earnings remaining in single-digit percentages in the interim.

In summation, we found that most management groups saw partnering as an opportunity to improve their position at the expense of suppliers. Their expectation was that suppliers would contribute substantial ideas and savings whose total benefit would accrue to their profit-and-loss statement. Suppliers were expected to do most, if not all, of the work. The reward was to have a continuing or enlarged position of supply. These circumstances spell the death knell for partnering. At the first tight market opportunity, these seemingly compliant suppliers will reverse roles with relish.

Successful Applications

Although many of the early attempts at serious partnering arrangements did not prove to be fruitful exercises, a growing number of applications have proved the validity of the concept. In general, the leading stories are coming from the retail industry, particularly in hard and soft goods. Driven, perhaps, by an urgent need to improve precariously thin margins at a time when buying alternatives are increasing, members of these industries have been hard at work to find ways to build strategic relationships that will bring benefits, usually cost savings, to all of the parties to the alliance. Enlightened suppliers, looking for more fruitful partnering experiences, are stepping forward to help in the mutual effort.

Several basic tools have become central features of these emerging successes. Leading-edge electronic interchanges are always involved. The use of highly accurate bar coding with the Universal Product Code fills the implicit need to track the flow of goods with high accuracy. As product is transferred across multiple locations, errors are hunted for and eliminated. Electronic scanning determines how goods are transferred from supply through point of purchase, with the information digitally shared throughout the supply system. Warehousing, distribution, and transportation use highly reliable information to find the most effective systems. Metrics for measuring success are oriented around customer service levels first, followed by efficiency. EDI has been raised to a competitive tool by most of these emerging alliances.

Benetton, the colorful clothing retailer, has been among the leaders, with a system that now provides a benchmark in terms of replenishment to individual stores. Product flows from Italy to stores in American malls, based on information on actual consumption that has been electronically tracked and returned to the manufacturing locations on a daily basis. At these sites, suppliers provide the materials and services necessary to create the quickest of responses—for example, by dyeing plain garments to the specific colors of the incoming replenishment information and getting the shipments to the precise locations in a one- to two-day cycle. The Gap and The Limited stores also receive high marks for the accuracy, efficiency, and responsiveness of their systems. At its Atlanta distribution center, Avon Products has worked out a system with suppliers and logistics support in which its automated procedures are state of the art. Bar coding is used to sort, route, and pick all replenishment orders, with an incredible degree of accuracy by current standards.

These successes are grounded in partnering principles. Joint strategies have been worked out at the most senior levels, with buy-in at all intermediate levels. In this system, interactive, cross-organizational groups meet and define their mutual objectives, always in terms of customer satisfaction followed by earnings improvement. From these basics, plans are developed that focus on the use of mutual resources to attain a competitive advantage through the application of technology and more efficient use of human resources. Typically, the early interchanges focus on the more obvious flaws in the current network systems, but they proceed rapidly to the development of innovative solutions that provide a competitive advantage.

Dana Corporation, an automotive-parts supplier, and Ford Motor Company, two leaders in the development of supply chain activities, have created a model system for the shipment of automotive parts (Alter, 1993). As often as four or five times in a day, Dana employees access a menu that lists the parts they regularly supply to Ford assembly and parts locations. They check for parts needs, shortages, on-hand supplies, parts being used that day, and how activities compare with historical usage, documented in their interactive data base. Decisions are made on the replenishment of drive shafts, tie-rod assemblies, and other critical parts. Because of the electronic communication capabilities built into the system, particular searches are finished in as few as five or ten minutes. Where necessary, the parts are quickly shipped, usually the same day, to the specific manufacturing site needing supply.

In this system, a new dimension in electronic interchange has been reached. The paperwork has been eliminated. There are no purchase orders, acknowledgments, or invoices. Moreover, people within the Ford system are not aware of the transactions. No computer, no individual, has placed orders from that part of the network. Ford has literally opened a portion of its data base to Dana employees, who have been empowered to use their new knowledge of actual usage to make decisions on replenishment. Ford's just-in-time manufacturing process has to maintain its integrity, but Dana helps that process by putting needed parts into the system at the exact point and time of need, without requiring even an electronic notice of transfer of shipment.

Joseph R. Phelan, Ford's manager of supplier communication, explains that Ford "started out in the transportation and the material end of the business, then expanded EDI to support our JIT programs" (Alter, 1993, p. 64). The firm uses conventional electronic data transmissions to send suppliers a weekly "material release" for its requirements in the coming months. Selected suppliers, like Dana, send advance shipping notices covering material that is on the way. They also make decisions that will keep the manufacturing system supplied, regardless of short-term changes. "If the supplier does the job right," says Phelan, "we don't have to go through an elaborate receiving process. We just get the trailer number, pull the electronic shipping records, book the shipment, and send the materials to the assembly line. We don't have to count and inspect" (Alter, 1993, p. 64). In the process, the supplier takes the responsibility for ensuring that Ford has the needed parts when it needs them. Savings have accrued to both parties, because the system functions at higher levels of efficiency.

The alliance between Procter & Gamble and Wal-Mart has

already been mentioned. The driver in this situation was Wal-Mart's desire to restock certain shelf items more effectively than any competitor. The advantage would be a lower on-the-shelf cost for Wal-Mart's stores. Procter & Gamble wanted to secure a nearly exclusive position on selected items from its portfolio of goods. The mutually developed replenishment system allows both parties to meet their objectives. The system keys off information generated from warehouse withdrawals, as opposed to POS data, to trigger automatic replacement of stock to predetermined levels. The process also requires a substantial number of customized, data-intensive interactions.

Procter & Gamble is now attempting to broaden the program to other key customers. One discovery driving this interest was the realization that a need existed for a certain critical mass of volume to make the economic returns desired in a crucial part of the process. As lower-turnover items are included in the system of re-plenishment, the ability to sustain full truckloads becomes an issue. However, as more firms embrace the process, it becomes possible to fill trucks with items from other suppliers.

General Electric's major appliance group offers another example of successful partnering, in this instance within its medium- to small-sized dealer network. Using this system, GE offers selected dealers the best pricing, access to inventory data to check on product availability, and the opportunity to order via an electronic catalog. The dealers gain an advantage over larger competitors; in exchange, they commit a major floor allocation to GE products, provide direct access to financial systems to allow GE to collect receivables on a monthly basis, and give GE access to customer sales data for marketing purposes. The result has been enhanced sales for the dealers and improved product, data, and cash flows for GE.

Finding Hidden Values Within a Network

As we scrutinized the growing number of successes appearing in the supply chain arena, we were quickly struck by the amount of extra value that could be extracted from supply networks. Often, the ability to extract savings was inhibited only by the reluctance of one or more parties to dig deeply enough across traditional boundaries to find new areas of mutual savings. Other parties were unable to achieve savings because they lacked enough trust in members within the network to adopt the new methods and procedures that removed traditional costs from the supply system.

In one case, we worked with a consortium of manufacturers who moved a large part of their product through distributors to the ultimate consumer. This practice worked well because most of the manufacturers in this network were small and produced many customized items; these were handled better by large distributors who could pool other items to make sensibly sized unit loads. The group asked for help in finding opportunities for cost, time, and service improvements across their typical supply chains. Upon mapping the flow of orders through a few systems, we quickly discovered a cache of hidden inventories that were not communicated between members of the supply network. Manufacturers worked from incoming orders and usually shipped from machines (by making product to order and shipping directly from the shop floor), with a small safety stock kept on their premises. The distributors, however, were found to have three to five times the predetermined stocking levels agreed to in the negotiation process, because they feared that the manufacturers would not meet surge demands.

Although this condition generated extra orders for the manufacturers, it also created an obsolescence risk and excess inventory carrying costs in the system. As the ultimate consumers, the firms that were drawing stocks from the distributors, started demanding lower delivered costs, attention was turned to ways to pass these demands back to the manufacturers. In between was a treasure load of potential savings. When information on the time the hidden inventories had been kept in stock was secured and analyzed, it quickly became apparent how much extra cost existed in the network. The consortium moved in an expeditious manner to reduce what was truly an excess network cost.

The first step was to map the flow of data necessary to fill orders across the network. Next, manufacturers and distributors worked with a few representative customers to determine how electronic feedback of actual consumption data would reduce the need for safety stocks to ensure reliable order fulfillment. Working in reverse, with information on what was actually being consumed, they redesigned the flowchart with new processes that cut the need for stored goods and improved the timing and flow of replenishment. All parties to the exercise contributed people, especially from their information systems group, to work out the improved processes. The result was the elimination of three weeks' inventory from the system and dramatic reductions in paperwork. An electronic funds transfer feature was a special enhancement, speeding payments across the network.

As supply chain members focus on real consumption, they often find major opportunities to make improvements in areas that are hidden from normal view. Inventory is the most obvious of these opportunities, but possibilities exist to remove paperwork, eliminate redundant functions, bypass unnecessary process steps, and eliminate a host of extraneous communication and expediting steps. What is required is a reengineered process that is focused on satisfying the consumer at each connection in the total process.

Starting Internally

To create a system founded on the concepts of business partnering, a business organization has to start on the inside, forging the first alliances between entities that typically do not cooperate. In many companies, imaginary silos are formed around areas of expertise in such a way that employees care very little about sharing information or resources across departmental boundaries. These silos are born of people wanting to guard their special areas, rather than seeking better opportunities for the firm. Turf issues are a result of this phenomenon and become real impediments to progress and must be treated as crucial elements to be defeated if partnering is to succeed.

Today's global environment will never have sufficient resources to deal with all of the issues and possibilities that exist for further improvement. Downsizing has become such a natural element in the lexicon of management control that hardly a firm has avoided being restructured. In the same period of time in which hundreds and often thousands of jobs have been eliminated, a drive has arisen for increased earnings. The net result is that a typical firm is seeking more profit with fewer internal resources. In the face of this dilemma, it becomes critical to apply internal resources to reach the most beneficial objectives, rather than to implement narrowly defined projects prescribed by departmental managers who seek only to protect their area of control.

Partnering starts with a prioritized list of objectives that creates the strategies and actions needed to accomplish these objectives. From this beginning, the resources of the organization should be applied to reaching the objectives in the highest-quality, most effective way possible. Cross-departmental sharing has to become the action mode. Team problem solving must extend to every available employee in a way that effectively pulls the best-quality results from the total human resource pool, creating a new level of cooperation with the focus placed on continuous improvement for the overall organization. Only when the people inside an organization are working together in an effective manner, on objectives crucial to survival and sustenance of a competitive advantage, will optimization become a reality.

A good way to begin this type of internal cooperation is to map the internal processes that exist to produce and fill orders. Building an as-is situation for the order fulfillment process typically quickly exposes opportunities for internal improvement. Moving to a better system requires parties from each of the sectors within the process flow to determine how the available resources can be best applied. A simple technique that helps in this exercise is to have each group identify its internal suppliers and customers. The group then sends communications to the internal groups and asks for an evaluation of performance in terms of the current working arrangements. Our experience has shown that up to 40 percent of the existing processes become candidates for change, usually because the internal customers do not find that these processes have sufficient value-adding need.

This exercise will take considerable patience and could require over a year to achieve benefits, but the final results will have a positive impact on the network's understanding of cultural limitations and of what is needed to build a higher-quality internal effort.

Beginning with What Has Worked

As the internal exercise proceeds, the next step is to develop an understanding of the strengths of the current organization that should be retained. The list should include the capabilities that are necessary for securing further gains and advantages through redesign or reengineering efforts. With this information, the participants prepare a list of resources needed to achieve success. For example, if a sector that is identified as critical to future success lacks a strength it needs, resources have to be provided in that area. With budget constraints, this could require transferring personnel from less value-adding functions into the more critical area.

The tendency of many organizations is to quickly try to jump into some type of redesign or reengineered process that will affect quantum improvements. The people involved do so more out of a desire for a quick fix than from an understanding of what the firm truly needs to enhance performance. One reason such actions result in failure is that they may force the organization to cast off parts of the existing processes that could be very effective in securing future competitive advantages. We prefer to assess the existing systems to determine what should be retained and what should be changed.

A technique that has been successful for us has been to develop an opportunity to find "quick-hit" savings that validate the partnering concept and provide funds for further initiatives. The technique begins with the identification of an internal site that is in need of improvement. This could be a plant that is losing money or that is substantially under budget, or it could be a department with a weak performance record. We have evaluated manufacturing facilities, technical centers, and customer service departments and have found significant opportunities for improvement. At such sites, we normally focus a group effort to map the process and identify areas that can be improved. The idea is to pinpoint improvement opportunities that can generate immediate savings. Such quick hits have included reductions in setup and delay times, waste, and errors; cycle-time improvements; and organizational changes. A portion of these savings can be then be set aside and applied to other internal initiatives; in this way, the larger redesign effort takes on a self-funding aspect and does not drain current cash flows.

Expanding to Suppliers

When internal partnering has reached levels that successfully break down the traditional turf barriers and lead to high levels of cooperative actions focused on necessary objectives, the organization can then turn to the use of outside resources. Suppliers offer an excellent vehicle for gaining the resources needed to solve problems and build on opportunities. Most suppliers are far more willing to help on focused projects than might be presumed. The caveat is that they want to be treated fairly, listened to when they make suggestions, and given a chance to share in the benefits of the actions taken.

It is not necessary to bring all the suppliers in to help. Such an action would probably create chaos. It is far more appropriate to select, from among the key strategic suppliers, a small group that can offer valuable suggestions and cooperate on joint teams focusing on projects having a significant impact. One firm approached this situation by segregating its 3,000-company supply base into three tiers: traditional sources, those that had gone through a certification process and achieved preferred status, and the top 100 sources with which it wanted to partner.

To this list of 100 sources, the firm sent a simple letter inviting the CEOs to attend a briefing at the company's headquarters. At this session, the firm shared some important information on its future strategic plans and described how the suppliers could help the company achieve success. The firm then asked the sources to submit improvement ideas that could help it to accomplish its objectives and indicated that it was willing to listen to any suggestions, in what was really an idea generation program. Further, the company would form joint teams with the suppliers to work on the suggestions and would set up a program by which the savings could be shared on an equitable basis. The result of this exercise was an avalanche of improvement suggestions, with a value in eight figures for the first year alone.

This firm and another with which we worked not only benefited in terms of savings enhancements by finding some low-hanging fruit; they went on to develop special supply partnering arrangements with strategic suppliers that have generated substantial extra earnings for both sides of the partnership.

Using Logistics as the Catalyst from Distribution to Consumer

Once key suppliers have been brought into the network and are contributing to improvements, firms seeking supply chain optimization should begin to use logistics as a primary source for finding many of the valuable savings that exist in the network from supply to consumption. This subject will be given greater attention in Chapter Eight, but we touch on it here because of its critical importance to the partnering relationship we are espousing.

Toyota Motor Manufacturing Corporation, at its Georgetown, Kentucky, assembly factory, applied this approach with the cooperation of Ryder Dedicated Logistics. At this location, Ryder was actually brought on-site and given office space within the large assembly building, where its employees function much as they would if they were employed by Toyota. Coordination is at nearly optimum levels at all times. At this location, Toyota has essentially outsourced the logistics function to a qualified expert in order to concentrate on the core competency of automobile assembly. We watched with fascination, during our visit to this site, as truck after truck containing necessary assembly materials arrived at the receiving dock without specific instructions from the manufacturer. They had been dispatched electronically from the supply locations in response to the needs of current orders and a specific sequence of new car assembly. Incoming inspection was not necessary because the truck driver had inspected the load before accepting it for delivery.

In a typical case, we observed a trailer load of car seats being automatically unloaded and scanned by robots. The individual seats went immediately to a waiting queue to be placed in the steady stream of cars being fabricated on that particular day. As we saw green following blue, then red, then gray, in a variety of models, the seats arrived precisely when they were needed in the exact color necessary for proper coordination, matched to the customers' orders. When we asked the assembly workers when the last mistake in the sequence had occurred, the response was that no mistakes had been made since they had started to work at the factory. When we asked the Ryder representative assigned to the site if he knew of any problems, his reply was that there could not be any. Problems would damage the relationship, because it was built on trust that there would be no flaws. Ryder, Toyota, and their key suppliers have worked out a new distribution system that moves currently needed supplies directly to assembly in a sequence built on current manufacturing needs. Orders from consumers in this system are the triggers that move the supply chain.

Sears, Roebuck & Co. also used logistics effectively as it went in search of savings. Working closely with a core group of strategic suppliers to fashion a model for more universal application, Sears analyzed the process map from store needs back to replenishment of a range of products that are high-turnover items at all stores. Such improvements as eliminating purchase orders and making payments directly from advance shipping notices enabled this retailer to dramatically reduce inventory needs and shorten delivery cycle times. In this pilot exercise, strategic sources are tied directly to store needs and respond by replenishing to predetermined stocking levels. No paper orders are generated, just an electronic accounting of product consumption, collected through barcoding processes. The advance shipping notice alerts Sears and the stores to what is on the way. The same system triggers a transfer of funds based on the goods indicated on the shipping notice, speeding the payment cycle to the suppliers.

Considering the Total Enterprise

The objective of business partnering should be focused on optimization. In this mode, the growing network of cooperation moves from internal to external partnering by taking a serious look at the total network as a field of opportunity. Success stories include the following types of improvements as typical outcomes from serious partnering efforts across supply networks:

- Inventory reductions of 40 to 60 percent, resulting from working out communication systems and just-in-time deliveries that reduce the need for safety stocks
- Inventory turns of five to seven that rise to twenty-five to thirty because of more pull-through of demanded product with lower inventories and fewer stock-outs
- Cycle-time improvements of 50 to 60 percent as a result of collectively mapping and analyzing flowcharts, from the creation of new ideas to commercial realization, with the largest factor being elimination of nonvalue-adding steps
- Increased sales and market share up by 35 to 55 percent, as a result of jointly creating the most responsive system and inducing the final consumer to shop the network
- Profit improvement of 15 to 30 percent, through waste elimination and cost reductions that result from improved process design
- Improved customer relations of 20 to 40 percent, through seeking and responding to customers as they identify true supply needs and ways to satisfy the ultimate consumer

As partnering continues to develop among the leading-edge practitioners, companies are discovering an ever-increasing number of areas that offer improvement potential. Those in the lead are now extending that lead over competitors mired in the traditional negotiating process, who never seem to get deeply into the type of process improvement that a true environment of hard work and trust will foster. Total business cooperation becomes the core philosophy for the front-runners; they are moving inexorably toward leads that will be nearly impossible to overcome.

Determining the Necessary Alliances

Once a network of effectiveness has been created internally and extended to key suppliers to develop front-edge capabilities, attention shifts to the most important factor, satisfying the external customer. Effective process redesign in any true partnering alliance must turn on the list of customer needs, and the selection of customers who can help to identify these needs is crucial to success. Most firms simply have too many customers to analyze a complete listing. In a similar fashion to the one used to segregate suppliers, the manufacturer or service firm looks at the key customer accounts with which the future must be tied to achieve success. An effort should be made to segregate existing and potential customers into a hierarchy so that the scarce analytic resources can be applied in the most effective manner.

Starting again with a key group, alliances should be forged that have the same type of application as is described for strategic suppliers. The purpose is to develop what the system should be trying to achieve to become the most effective network and secure the loyalty of the ultimate consumer. An evaluation should also be made of the true partnering possibilities, so that any model that is created will have value and application across the full spectrum of customers. Many manufacturing firms are applying this concept on a strategic basis to gain long-term relationships with and commitments to retailers that have been designated as crucial to future viability.

The strongest advice we can offer is to take the senior decision makers in the organization off-site for a day or two and discuss the industry, the strategic customer list, future trends, the firm's strategic intent, and who should be on the partnering short list. The preceding factors will all spawn a list of possible candidates. The process should proceed slowly as the lists are merged into a final form (or whatever small number starts to make sense). From this list, consideration goes to:

- Who will be the future survivors in the selected industry?
- Who will achieve or maintain market dominance?
- Whose revenues will grow at a rate that demands consideration?
- Whose concepts, ideas, and strategies are most compatible with ours?
- Who has the type of management philosophy that favors a partnering arrangement?

- Who will show sincere interest in sharing resources to find mutual benefits?
- Who will accept sharing of the rewards?

The first list of four finalists should be challenged and amended until there is consensus on the grouping. Role playing helps by having individuals play the part of known senior executives at the selected customers. Discussions that come very close to the real circumstances often develop and reveal key people who could obstruct the alliance.

The balance of the session revolves around prioritizing that list and deciding how to arrange a pilot project, the purpose of which is to test the ability to work together in a meaningful manner. The first firm selected is naturally a crucial decision, so great care should be expended on making the final choice.

The task and the challenge when working with customers is to apply resources to working with the organizations that offer a real chance of securing a mutually beneficial long-term relationship. Not all customers are equally important to the future. The partnering process demands that resources be applied in the most important areas; if not, a drain will be created that dissipates the effectiveness of key people. Therefore, scarce internal resources must be applied to building leading-edge alliances that result in better efficiencies, which are subsequently applied across the total business network in which the firm operates.

Action Study: Baxter Healthcare Corporation

Baxter Healthcare Corporation, the large medical technology firm, operates a distribution organization called United States Distribution (USD). This unit receives manufactured goods from suppliers and also converts incoming materials into its own manufactured products. USD serves health care customers ranging from physicians' offices to acute care hospitals and including the ever-increasing number of consolidating health-providing organizations. Our action study (based on a presentation by Edward J. Ram, Jr., Supply Chain Manager, Baxter, Inc.) follows this division as it

decided to study a supply chain that moves from suppliers to manufacturers to USD, which acts as the distributor, and finally to the range of
customers mentioned. The objective was to create an "Effective Business
Partnering and Supply Chain Strategy" that would provide the highest
customer service, while maximizing the efficiency and effectiveness of resources in the total supply chain.

The key functions of USD were marketing, purchasing, and inventory;
orders were filled from supplier stocks and Baxter-manufactured products
in the USD system. The primary functions of the supply base were sales
and marketing, customer service, and manufacturing operations. The concept was to link these functions together through a structured interface (the
supply chain management model) that would open channels of communication both inside and outside of each organization and result in the redesign of processes to optimize the model. Better data on what the groups
agreed were the key drivers for the total system resulted in joint efforts focused on improving these drivers, even if this created suboptimal conditions for one segment of the network. The first effect of the effort was a
change in focus from functional objectives to organizational goals for both
sectors of the network.

To lay the groundwork for an effective alliance, investments were made
in resources and technology that would provide tools needed by the business partners. Emphasis was placed on end-user information access, viable business models, and EDI capabilities. A second wave of investments
was made in the processes identified by the joint teams as needing enhancement to provide greater flexibility for the system (a factor deemed to
have great importance because of the changing customer base and customer demands). Suppliers and manufacturers concentrated on short cycles and quick changeovers. USD looked at ways to handle stocks so that
it would be easy to switch into various finished goods, depending on variations in customer requirements. USD wanted to enhance the system's
ability to meet the "pull" needs of customers with quick, accurate responses. Third, a scoreboard was created to measure the supply chain and
the performance of its constituents.

The primary measures were days of inventory on hand (DIOH), lead
times to get the product in the system, and customer service levels.
Secondary scores included fill times from order to delivery, excess stock, return on managed capital, and EDI usage.

At the start, many meetings took place between the distributor, manufacturers, and selected key suppliers. The focus was on developing the working arrangement and the scoreboard and working out improved processes. The central objective was to improve the supply chain and create higher levels of customer satisfaction. Attendees included representatives from distribution marketing, supplier sales and marketing, and supply chain personnel from both entities. Representatives from other constituents in the supply chain, including key customers, were invited to participate at appropriate times in the process. The effort went through three "cases" as they jointly developed their supply chain solutions.

In the first case, titled "Early Technology," the distributor inventory group initiated discussions with the supplier operations group. Representatives from many functional groups participated, because the effort focused on the predetermined key drivers. EDI was assumed to not be available, and the scoreboard concentrated on DIOH, lead times, and service levels. To keep the project simple initially, the groups worked on the highest-sale items. Forty percent of all sales were in three hundred items, from which a dozen were selected. The manufacturing cycle was tracked at five to six weeks, not very flexible by partnering standards. Inventories were measured at fifty days for the suppliers and forty days for USD.

Following review and critique by the joint team, changes to the existing supply system were implemented. (See Figure 4.1.) USD and the suppliers agreed at the outset to equal sharing of the net benefits. This was a crucial element in the partnering effort. Among the changed features, suppliers were allowed to ship bulk products directly to the distributor's manufacturing site. The distributor's distribution planning system was then used to allocate products (supplied goods and goods manufactured by Baxter) to the distribution centers operated by USD. Safety stock was no longer required by the suppliers. Variability from the suppliers dropped from 50 percent per week to 5 percent per month. Total system inventory dropped from ninety to fifty-five days. A complex financial model was built to track costs and benefits. In a way that was the opposite of most supply chain efforts, the major part of the benefits flowed to the suppliers, with incremental savings coming to the distributor.

In the second case, titled "Mid-Technology," the joint team moved on to assuming that EDI transactions were available. The scope of this technology included sku's, prioritized as A, B, and C items in terms of annual

FIGURE 4.1. Supply Chain Partner.ng, Case 1: Process Flow.

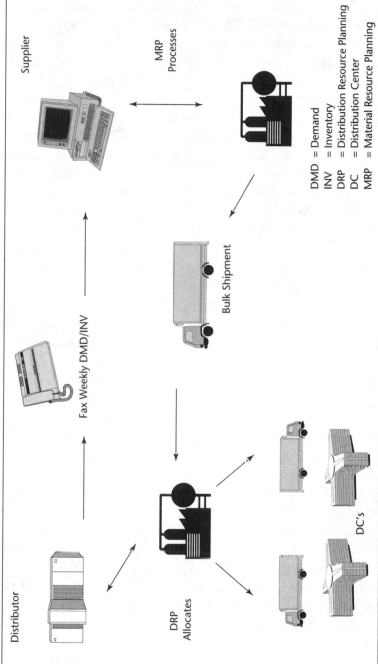

Distributor

Supplier

Fax Weekly DMD/INV

MRP
Processes

Bulk Shipment

DRP
Allocates

DC's

DMD = Demand
INV = Inventory
DRP = Distribution Resource Planning
DC = Distribution Center
MRP = Material Resource Planning

volume. A pilot was established that included nine items from each category of sales. Pallet-level bar coding was introduced and advance shipping notices were utilized. The details of the interactions are not described here, because they involve complex networking arrangements, but the result of the effort was that the suppliers took responsibility for a vendor-managed inventory system. Daily transactions were sent to the suppliers, then fed into the Baxter materials and distribution planning systems. Product was then allocated to the distributors' centers. The shipping notice created the receiving transaction, with the pallet bar code being scanned for matching verification.

The second case led to further savings. The complex joint financial model was no longer required and purchase orders were eliminated. The suppliers now performed the allocation and shipped directly to the distributor's distribution centers. Inventory decreased for both the supplier (50 percent) and the distributor (20 percent). Lead times went down by 50 percent and the suppliers' fill rate became 100 percent. Service levels for the distributor were close to 100 percent. Total working capital was reduced as a result of the lower inventory levels.

The third case was titled "High Technology." It was instigated by one of the suppliers in the new system who wanted to achieve special recognition. The assumption was made that a much broader EDI capability was to be used. The scoreboard was enlarged to cover all agreed-upon drivers, and joint investments were made in the enabling technology. An agreement created a fully vendor-managed inventory with a consignment process.

The essence of the third-case achievement was the combination of all the leading-edge capabilities the team could identify. Baxter has five cross-docking centers that were being underutilized. The team worked out how to make maximum use of these facilities. Optimized pickup schedules and freight lanes were set up. Under the consignment process, in a test made at the time of this writing, the distributor sells product to the health care provider. The distributor also sends daily trace sales electronically to the suppliers and internal manufacturer. The suppliers write an accounts receivable transaction and the distributor writes an accounts payable transaction from the daily trace sales report, all automatically. The distributor pays the suppliers using electronic funds transfer, based on payable terms.

Under this full-automation scenario, all of the previous benefits have accrued and the customers are rating the system as extremely effective. Expenses to accounts payable and accounts receivable are reduced. Both the suppliers and the distributor have tangible savings to pay for the effort. Invoices have been eliminated and working capital has been reduced even further. The groups continue to meet on an ad hoc basis, working to improve their business partnering alliance and their supply chain model.

Summary

As we developed material for this book, we found that virtually every firm of any size that we interviewed indicated that it had an improvement initiative under way that would enhance the effectiveness of the firm's supply chain. However, on closer inspection, we witnessed such a wide variation in results that we became convinced that a better way to go in search of supply chain optimization was to enlarge the scope of the efforts and to include resources from more constituencies.

The firms that could document progress in their efforts, usually using a three-step process, had found elements of partnering that built greater strength in their supply relationships than those that lacked these vital ingredients. But all of them fell short of utilizing a full supply network in their improvement efforts. Throughout our search, we were hard-pressed to find examples of true trusting relationships, although we did find savings, for a time, often in significant early reported numbers.

Where we found sustained savings and signs of market leadership, we also found that the parties upstream and downstream in the supply chain had put aside traditional relationships and had forged new alliances. These alliances were grounded in the idea that the supply chain offers a tremendous opportunity for enhancement and mutual savings, but only when the parties approach it by partnering. The effort has to proceed on the assumption that opportunities and reasons exist for all parties to benefit and for the consumer to see real shelf savings. The effort becomes optimized when all key resources are focused on total network improvement. Competitive advantage over competing networks is gained as one particular group keeps working through its alliances to find all possible improvement opportunities.

Chapter Five

Overcoming Obstacles to Success

••••••••••••••••••••••••••

Virtually every business firm of any appreciable size has pursued some form of improvement to its supply chain network. Our interviews with a representative sample of these organizations have confirmed a wide disparity in both techniques and results. The organizations at the top of the list can point to impressive gains in several vital areas. Typically they can document savings in paperwork and error elimination, improvement in levels of inventory and annual turnover of inventory, specific product cost savings, shorter cycle times in a variety of areas, and lower warehousing and shipping costs. Most of these same firms have developed measurement systems that verify the profit enhancement, although many have a way of letting these profits drift toward the ultimate consumer and away from building their infrastructure.

The firms that head our roster of successful implementers have also found a way to share savings across their full supply network. They do this by carefully measuring the real savings and typically dividing the amount equally. In that way, customers will have the benefit of competitive prices and suppliers will have enhanced earnings as an incentive to find more areas of potential improvement. Although most of the current successes have been with two- or three-step efforts, the best networks in our study portfolio are those that have used a model similar to the four-step interenterprise solution to take extraneous steps and costs out of each link in the system. These leaders also look for methods through which benefits can accrue to all the parties that helped in the implementation effort.

The companies at the other end of our spectrum can show documented savings, but of a lesser degree and without a focus on improvements across the full supply chain. Typically, these firms have worked, often as diligently as the leaders, to find the enhancements they know exist in their networks. Unfortunately, they lack the willingness to avoid traditional adversarial conditions, thereby failing to develop the scale of improvement of the more effective leaders. As we searched for the reasons behind this gap in results, we quickly discovered a pattern of interference in the less successful organizations. We will consider this pattern of barriers to success in this chapter.

Perceptions That Inhibit Success

We observed consistently that the firms with the highest degree of success had a cultural perspective that was strongly oriented around customer satisfaction, shared resources, and an understanding of the need for all members of the network to make a reasonable profit. We found that the organizations with the lowest records of success failed to embrace similar philosophies, remaining trapped in traditional perceptions that became barriers to improvement.

At the senior levels, every firm we interviewed indicated a strong ethic of satisfying or, if possible, delighting the customer. However, as we persisted to lower levels, we found widely varying interpretations. The successful firms carried the idea throughout the organization, whereas the others lost the idea as we went down the organization. In one multibillion-dollar company that produces consumer packaging, it was discovered that in spite of senior advocacy for a strong orientation to customer satisfaction at the expense of short-term profits, this credo was not implemented beyond the chief executive's suite. Even though the CEO forcefully advocated the philosophy in public, the measurements by which compensation was awarded favored an orientation toward short-term cost improvements at the expense of satisfying customers. Any special efforts that were focused on a particular customer were rudely criticized by everyone except the members of the sales department.

In this firm, the customer was important only during visiting days and when large orders were received. At other times, the measures that mattered were shipping the product in a way that suited the efficiencies of the manufacturing schedule and perpetuating the low-cost metrics being used to calculate success. This attitude meant that the orientation on the shop floor was to ship both good and bad products and let the customer sort out the difference. Shipments were not made with an eye for delivery schedules, but for optimizing the use of capital and machinery in the plant. This also meant that investment funds were appropriated to generate projects with a productivity orientation or a quick financial payback, as opposed to those that created innovative products or increased customer satisfaction levels. These latter projects were typically scoffed at during review sessions as being nonproductive.

In the less successful firms, as the customer-oriented facade was removed, we found an underlying belief throughout the organization that the customer was an entity that could be taken for granted until a complaint was received. At that moment, people in these companies typically split into two camps. In the first camp were those who wanted to resolve the issue quickly with apologies and replacements. The second camp consisted of those who wished to blame the problem on the customer or on another internal function. In these organizations, it was virtually impossible to create a true customer perspective consistent with today's market demands. Those in the first camp simply wanted to talk the customer into using the problem goods or accepting a minimal charge for partial replacement. Those in the latter camp wanted to replace the goods and use the incident as an example to those involved in the poor processing. In this environment, customer problems are not perceived as opportunities to establish an improvement procedure. Each incident becomes a problem that widens the rift between the internal camps. In the service organizations we studied, a similar pattern was found. The managers insisted on recruiting and training people with a customer orientation. But lower in the firm we found a disparity in attitudes toward carrying out that orientation, particularly with difficult customers.

We watched with some amazement as one senior manufacturing officer, disturbed by a situation being described, tried to enforce his will on the organization. He demanded a true customer orientation as the secret of future success. With impassioned and forceful rhetoric, he laid down new laws for the organization. Unfortunately, closer inspection revealed that those who were not in the customers' camp simply avowed that "this too shall pass." No real changes were made to such customer measures as quality, returns, complaints, on-time shipments, or fill rates. Nor were any alterations made in the way that compensation or promotion was determined. Special letters were sent to all departments from the officer explaining the need for the stronger customer orientation. Promotional materials were generated to support the new orientation. And it all lasted six months.

Some improvements were recorded in the desired metrics, but the numbers were found to be bogus when they were compared with actual customer data. What had happened was that those who were responsible for showing the requisite improvements simply allowed better numbers to be recorded by relaxing the rules regarding what was documented as a customer failure. A later customer survey revealed that the customers were recording returns, fill rates, and on-time shipments at levels considerably worse than those shown by the supplying firm. We concluded that it took considerably more than momentary, impassioned exhortation from the boss to generate the correct customer perception. Instead, measurements and rewards were required that focused directly on customer satisfaction.

The perception necessary for optimal success has to start with an understanding that there is no future unless the customers' needs are filled beyond simple satisfaction. With so many options available for consumers in current markets, the idea has to be ingrained throughout the organization that the customer will move to another source at the slightest provocation. In this environment, satisfaction gives way to delight, or to a totally rewarding experience, for companies that want to be on the front edge of success. All senior executives would lead their discussions with guidance on satisfying the customer and establishing metrics that focus not only on the financial strength of the firm, but on the increasing loyalty of the customer base, gained through unparalleled satisfaction. They also would involve themselves in operations regularly to test the perceptions of those who directly engage the customer.

A perception of satisfaction is attained by talking to key customers, particularly those with a reputation for being the most difficult to serve. Management must take the time and be able to verify that the metrics being used to determine results are showing compatible numbers. Unfortunately, when we conduct interviews with key customers, we find that they do not report satisfaction measures nearly as high as those being posted by the suppliers.

A simple example is on-time delivery. Working with one organization that avowed an intense desire to have such a metric in the high ninetieth percentile, we found a large disparity in the customers' and suppliers' figures. The firm was showing that 94 to 95 percent of all deliveries were made on-time. When we talked to key customers, we found that the real number was closer to 80 percent. The difference was in a liberal interpretation by the supplier versus a very strict definition by the customer. The supplier booked all orders on a schedule that listed delivery in a three-day window. The more particular customers issued orders with delivery on a docking schedule that was specific to hours in a single day. If the supplier's truck appeared late and was made to stay overnight before being unloaded, the customer recorded a late delivery. The supplying firm recorded an on-time delivery because the truck was unloaded within the three-day window. No effort was made to record the additional cost of the overnight delay or extra driver time. The supplier was fooling no one outside of the organization and was on a disastrous road in terms of keeping its key customers satisfied. In the final analysis, when decisions are made about which suppliers will be preferred, customer satisfaction becomes the ultimate determiner, measured in terms of what the customer rates as good service.

We find another disparity in perception regarding the issue of shared resources. For those at the upper end of the success spectrum, the issue is clear. Those organizations that can help a manufacturer or retailer to further success are solicited. At the other end of the spectrum, the organizations also look diligently for potential improvements, but they expect the firms upstream of their operation to supply most or all of the resources. This is a formula for mediocre performance. Even when the supplier offers to provide useful resources, the level of improvement can be expected to be less than when everyone shares talent and the funds needed to implement the actions. Management's support is also much higher when both firms put up some cash to cover the cost of the mutual effort.

In one unfortunate experience, we watched as a supplier, wanting to help a major customer, fielded a talented group to help the customer find savings in their mutual supply system. The initial reaction was positive as the supplier's team mapped the process to find areas of potential improvement. Interviews were conducted with managers, help was solicited from plant floor personnel, and other vendors were contacted for useful advice, all in an effort to find savings for the customer. The initial results led to documented savings opportunities through fewer changeovers, higher line efficiencies, less scrap, and less delay time. As the effort proceeded, however, the enthusiasm declined significantly. In a very short time, the supply team saw themselves becoming a target for criticism by some of the customer's people, particularly those who were responsible for the areas where improvement potential was being found.

As savings in the seven-figure range were exposed, the exercise deteriorated into squabbling. Those who could have gained the most from the improvement ideas became extremely defensive and spent the better part of their time arguing over how to measure the improvement and suggesting that the team look at other departmental areas. Moreover, as new ideas were introduced in review sessions, excessive time was wasted in deciding who should get credit for the originality of the change concepts versus how to secure the savings. Gradually, the members of the supply team asked to be relieved as it became apparent that any implementation would be characterized by the customer's more reticent people as "something we knew all along."

The more fruitful exercises always include members from both organizations and, typically, a few third-party participants to stimulate innovative thinking. This means that the improvement exercise is conducted by internal as well as external personnel. In this situation, the perception becomes one of a joint effort, with mutual rewards.

Procter & Gamble Paper Products Co. offers an example of the positive side of the partnering relationship. In August 1990, the tissue and towel plants in this division of Procter & Gamble were carrying $7.7 million worth of raw material inventory (wood pulp) on their plant sites and en route from the supplier in Grande Prairie, Alberta, Canada. The supplier had another $6.5 million invested in pulp stock targeted for Procter & Gamble. Procter & Gamble was also incurring the cost for storage, handling, and freight, as well as any demurrage on this store of pulp. According to Doug Warner, "This costly procedure and large inventory protected against a perception that Procter & Gamble had a unreliable supplier and inconsistent rail service" (Warner, 1993, p. 75).

An alternative was formed that included Procter & Gamble's tissue and towel mills, the Grande Prairie supplier, and the railroad carrier. Working together to better manage the inventory led to the application of a continuous-replenishment process. By June 1992, Procter & Gamble and Grande Prairie were carrying $10.6 million of pulp for a 26 percent inventory reduction, while increasing pulp usage by 15 percent. Cash that was no longer tied up in inventory was $3.6 million. With the elimination of carrying costs, the annual savings were projected at $775,000. This experience has now been extended to most of Procter & Gamble's domestic paper plants (Warner, 1993).

Every firm has a greater need for improvement resources than are currently available. External members of the supply chain offer an important supply of potentially value-adding resources, which are usually easier to access than expected. If a manufac-

turer wishes to improve transportation costs, for example, suppliers and customers can provide logistics personnel to work together
on ways to cut warehousing, distribution, and shipping costs.
Railroads and trucking firms can provide valuable help, as shown
in the Procter & Gamble example. The participants pool ideas
they have independently developed for their organizations, or by
the shared use of equipment, into something that makes sense
across the network. The sole requirement is to make equal demands on the internal organization and the external resources, resulting in a mutuality of effort. This condition creates a joint team
with the right perception—that both sides will be involved and
credit for successes will be shared by all parties.

The final obstacle to success is the perception that all members
of the supply network are entitled to a fair profit. As simplistic as
this concept may appear, we have documented comments from
major organizations indicating that buyers from less successful
firms have a different preference. Countless interviews have un-
derscored the perception of buyers that they have always received
the lowest possible prices. We are left uncertain as to where the
few organizations are that must be paying the higher prices. The
retail buyers have a nearly universal belief that no competitor
could receive lower prices than those they have negotiated. This
situation is at odds not only with the fact that prices are established by market conditions, but with the fact that organizations
on both sides of the bargain are still making a profit. Our experience with supply networks is that, through partnering, savings improvements can be ten or more times greater than those garnered
from negotiating.

The perceptions that drive the leading firms in the supply chain
are oriented around the customer, mutual resources, and mutual
benefit. Most firms accept these concepts, but many become clever
at hiding their true beliefs, thus reducing any opportunity for optimization. One of the ways to test the level of positive perceptions is to study a firm's willingness to accept outside counsel.
Firms that do well in this aspect tend to find more valuable resources than those that have perceptual blinders regarding the
value of outside thinking—that is, those that cater to the "If it
wasn't invented here, it can't be any good" syndrome.

Failure to Accept Outside Advice

In a typical situation, when we visit a firm interested in value enhancement, we encounter people at high levels who make this statement: "We will accept all the good advice we can get, especially if it shows us how to increase earnings or satisfy customers." Although most of these people are well intentioned as they tell us how they welcome outside counsel, a difficulty in this process becomes an obstacle to success. If the outside advice leads to significant savings, the internal people may be criticized for not having found the solutions themselves. This condition is unfortunate because it makes the internal people reluctant to look for or accept counsel that could lead to supply chain improvement. Let us take you through a stock situation to illustrate our point.

A multibillion-dollar organization, which manufactures a recognizable consumer product that is sold through grocery and retail outlets, asked us to visit, based on our success at a similar but noncompeting firm. In the first meeting, at a senior level, we discussed the interenterprise solution and related some documented stories of how mutual savings had been generated. At the conclusion of the presentation, there was general agreement to move forward, but with the reservation that the investment had to remain small because of short-term cash needs. Our response was to look for a specific location within the supply chain where we might find some quick savings. Not only would that verify the value of the effort, but it would create the funding required to carry out larger-scale improvement efforts. The notion of self-funding appealed to our audience and a commitment to go forward was obtained.

When we mentioned the caveat regarding some firms' reactions to outside advice, we received the typical remark quoted above. Our experience has taught us to be cautiously skeptical, however, and we persisted in explaining that some of their people could actually be offended if large savings were found at the test site. We were repeatedly assured that nothing would make this customer happier than to find significant savings.

A particular site was selected and a preliminary visit was made to form a joint team that would look for potential areas of improvement. This site was a manufacturing plant that produced a very popular food item. It was currently under intense pressure to achieve cost reduction and higher throughput, because the product was currently in high demand. Once the joint team was organized, it visited the site and started to look for areas of bottleneck, low efficiency, and waste improvement. The team asked questions regarding current complications and looked for opportunities to shorten changeover times, reduce delays, and increase running speeds.

The team included industrial engineers trained in line efficiency, quality experts, material-handling specialists, logistics and transportation professionals, and others. Representatives from both internal and external resources were used. They probed to find where simple changes to procedures, systems, and methods could augment the existing improvement process. They watched low-efficiency machines make changeovers across several crews and run product that was currently in such demand that large back orders had been generated. They followed the flow of product from incoming materials to finished goods sent to storage or loaded on trucks. In a very short time, a significant number of potential improvement areas were identified.

The team generated over seventy bona fide improvement suggestions. The savings attached to these ideas by the joint team would total over a million dollars annually—for a single site. In spite of the assurances by senior management that the firm would be delighted with significant savings, two complications arose. First, the president of the firm publicly chastised the head of operations for having a site under his command in which an outside team could find so many savings in such a short-term study. Second, the head of operations immediately sent word to the site, telling the employees to criticize the findings. The fact that a joint team had recommended the improvements became lost in the resulting fray, and most of the suggestions were denigrated. Considerable follow-up and patience brought the results very close to the original forecast, but enormous wasted effort was expended because the senior executives had not lived up to their commitment to accept counsel without criticizing their internal personnel.

Firms tend to have a definite cultural imperative where this issue is concerned. There is also no clear correlation between how a firm perceives the value of outside help and results. Firms that insist that there are no good ideas except those that are generated internally limit themselves to the strength of their recruiting and promotion. Their idea generation is only equal to the skills they hire. As these organizations reach a crisis point, their only solution is to downsize the organization, cutting back on their resources and further limiting their capability. They can continue to succeed, but as their remaining resources become focused more on survival than on the effectiveness of the organization, idea generation declines further.

A good example of a more desirable condition has been that of the automobile industry. These firms were typically dominated by groups that exemplified the need to perceive that only the manufacturer can generate good advice. Domestic firms have been particularly criticized by the press for their lack of innovative thinking and the shackles placed on them by their own bureaucracies. Recently, however, this industry has moved strongly into the area of accepting outside counsel and it shows great progress in this shift in attitude. Joint engineering projects with suppliers and the outsourcing of engineering and development of components to more qualified sources have led to dramatic improvements in costs and to reductions in the cycle time for introducing new models. Other industries are starting to look at the experiences in the automotive sector to find valuable resources external to the traditional departments that were supposed to be the fonts of all knowledge. Too much expertise is residing in too many different arenas for a firm to be tied to the obsolete concept that if there is a way to find outside counsel of value, then it has hired the wrong internal resources. No one firm can have such a corner on talent in today's globally competitive environment.

The Value of Synergistic Analysis

Our experience has frequently shown the value of collaborative effort. It is important to stress this point, because objections to this type of effort create a large obstacle to success. To progress in our argument, let us introduce the concept of synergistic analysis. The simplest definition of synergy is combined action. Synergism becomes the ability to draw together multiple thinking to exceed the value of individual thinking done in isolation. This can be simplified by saying that two heads are better than one. Synergistic analysis goes one step further and says that there is great value in combining talented people from different disciplines to take action together; in the business sense, this is done by focusing on specific problems or opportunities. By working collectively on situations that have a major impact on the viability of an organization, we have witnessed truly amazing results from such cross-disciplinary efforts. Synergistic analysis is nothing more than organizing smart and energetic people, from any sector of an organization that can help, to look for answers that can improve a business. In the search for supply chain optimization such actions are critical to success.

Bringing together experts from different areas to focus on a necessary solution to a defined problem can generate almost magical results. The time allotted to these experts gives the internal employees the opportunity to demonstrate the value of their experience and to have a direct impact on an identified high-priority problem. They feel good about the exposure and the results that come from listening to their counsel. They become stimulated by the discussions, the critique, and the acceptance of their ideas by knowledgeable people. A reverse benefit occurs as the experts have an opportunity to be exposed to people who would normally be beyond their point of contact. They get closer to the actual conditions in which their ideas can be implemented. In fact, they get to learn even more through these experiences and are injected with additional learning that can be beneficial for their efforts in their normal area of responsibility. The situation takes on an aura of shared commitment and extra effort, with impressive results.

The largest obstacle to success is that most firms believe that all good ideas have to be generated internally. As a result, they wait until the internal mechanisms are complete and then introduce their ideas into the market. If they were correct in their perception that all good ideas are internal, success rates should approach 100 percent. In reality, the percentage is far lower. Drawing on the resources available across a total supply chain provides significantly more opportunities to increase the chances of success. Failure to consider the value of cooperative ventures, or synergistic analysis, with suppliers and customers loses an inexpensive opportunity to enhance the improvement effort. By working with others, the smart firm also gets a laboratory in which new ideas can be tested and critiqued before facing actual market conditions. Utilizing these resources will increase the opportunity to add extra value before introduction in the market and increase the chances of market acceptance.

Another important concept that has to be adopted for supply chain optimization to succeed is that potentially cooperative organizations must develop compatible business philosophies as they build their supply networks. Buyers and sellers have to be synchronized in their concepts as they develop the purchasing and supply strategies of the future. Any element of waste or inefficiency becomes a target for group review to determine how it can be eliminated, minimized, or borne by the appropriate party for the benefit of the network. This is the paradigm that has to be accepted, the concept that will lead partnering firms to their future advantage.

The Search for Total Value

Many organizations stress the need to avoid establishing relationships within the supply chain that focus only on short-term advantages. Virtually every firm we interviewed expressed the desire to look at the total costs to the system as opposed to the lowest price on a single item or commodity as a means of promoting that concept. But a review of the actual track records of these firms differs a great deal from their advocacy. Too much pressure is applied to improving current earnings in most business firms for this pressure not to be an obstacle to partnering success.

Chapter Eight will be devoted to logistics as a force behind supply chain optimization, but a brief look now can help make our point. We can draw out the specific area of transportation, a part of the logistics function, to illustrate the obstacles that are encountered. No matter where a product is created, a means of getting it to market must exist. The efficiency of this process is a source of great opportunity for improvement for most organizations. In traditional relationships, the manufacturer looks to the suppliers to absorb as much of this cost as possible, asking for delivered prices that include shipment. Retailers similarly look to manufacturers to absorb the responsibility for transportation. Some firms are convinced that they achieve the best possible transportation system and costs by using their own fleet of trucks to ship products. These companies bury the cost of shipment in the delivered price of their products, losing the opportunity to work with other firms in the supply chain to find further enhancements.

Regardless of where the burden of responsibility falls, transportation is typically handled on an individual, local basis. Centralized groups may exist to negotiate contracts and to work out the best routes, but usually a large portion of the shipments use local discretion and can bypass the centrally prescribed methodology. The reality is that transportation is a system that cries out for mutual effort. Too many trailers pass each other on our highways with less than full loads that could carry more product if only the logistics and arrangements were worked out between interrelated companies.

Some well-meaning people have worked hard to make improvements in this area, but we always find more opportunities for enhancement. Trailer utilization is a universal opportunity. A local effort will focus on improving that factor at a single site or for a small group of plants but will fail to consider the total network system. Often, suppliers will be asked to submit opinions on how trucks can be pooled or how back-haul arrangements can be worked out to make some use of returning empty trailers. Third-party handlers will be investigated to see if improvements can be generated by pooling an individual firm's shipments with a larger grouping. The more forward-thinking firms will look at the total supply chain to seek opportunities to dramatically cut transportation costs, not by foisting them upstream, but by attempting to eliminate anything less than full loads on the way to the ultimate consumer and reducing or eliminating the cost of any redundant capabilities. Although this condition may not be practical in all instances, it is the driver for these front-edge organizations.

As total cost to the system becomes the overall initiative, the leading organizations begin to evaluate the supply network from initial raw materials to final consumption. In between, every aspect of shipping interchange is investigated for potential improvements. Investments are made, but in projects and equipment that create a mutual benefit. The typical barriers of trust and traditional negotiating roles give way in these instances to a focus on how the network can satisfy customers at the lowest cost, but with a transportation system that has been optimized from the supplying system to receipt of product at the stores. Pooled resources are used, joint investments in equipment and warehousing are made, and information technology becomes focused on ways to enhance the entire effort so that there are no mistakes, cycle times are at the briefest possible intervals, and supporting inventories are minimized. Our action study illustrates one example of how this dream can be accomplished.

Action Study: The Goodyear Alliance

Take a look, when you are next driving on an interstate highway, at the number of large tractors that are pulling trailer loads of goods across this country to waiting consumers. One of the largest manufacturers of the heavy-duty machines that pull eighteen-wheelers formed an alliance with a major supplier of tires, the Goodyear Tire & Rubber Company, providing an excellent example of how to make a real partnering effort work. It is a true story that has a successful ending for both parties.

After being spun off from a parent company, the truck manufacturer decided to look at the partnering concept to determine if it offered any special potential when evaluated against results from their traditional supplier relationships. Their first step was to take a very serious internal look at existing procedures and supplier relationships. They found the following:

- *They had a neutral to adversarial relationship with 100 percent of their suppliers.*
- *Price buying was the dominant purchasing strategy.*
- *They had a fragmented procurement base.*
- *Limited opportunities existed for enhanced profits for both buyer and seller.*
- *Consideration of the needs of customers was a neglected factor.*

Rather quickly, it was decided that three areas should be investigated for specific opportunities to change these traditional circumstances and find significant improvements. The areas selected were engines, drivetrains, and tires. A multifunctional team was selected to initiate the process, which included members from finance, truck marketing, parts marketing, advance manufacturing, production and quality, planning, engineering, and purchasing. The Dana Corporation was selected as a partnering candidate for the first joint team, which was formed to investigate drivetrains. Tires became the second area of focus and presents us with the grist for this study.

At the time of the original effort, the area of tires had the following characteristics:

- *It was the third largest item in cost of sales.*
- *It had a fragmented supply base, with Goodyear as its largest supplier.*
- *It used centrally controlled purchasing.*
- *It had a high pull-through percentage, with little return of product.*
- *It had an existing standard position on how to conduct relations.*

The initial objective established was to develop a partnering arrangement, while making certain that additional profits for the truck firm would be part of the results. As the story unfolds, it will become clear that they quickly moved toward utilization of mutual resources for mutual benefit to achieve that seemingly personal goal. The team objectives became: to better understand the tire market, to identify potential business opportunities, to motivate suppliers to offer their best and most comprehensive proposals, and to have a significant positive impact on profits.

The team began by visiting tire companies and making presentations regarding their purpose and expectations. Interviews were also conducted with customers, dealers, and key truck firm managers to make certain that they were covering all important constituencies. When valuable resources that could help in the effort were identified, the team acquired them. These visits took the team to ten plants, a just-in-time facility, four training facilities, three test tracks, a half-dozen trucking firms, four research and development centers, seven headquarters locations, and the truck firm's Midwest assembly operation.

During this part of the process, the field of suppliers was narrowed to four: Goodyear, Bridgestone, Michelin, and General. A formalized evaluation procedure was developed and used to rate these contenders. The evaluation included such factors as their willingness and ability to be a partner and their commitment to the "trust business." Considerable amounts of prepresentation data went into the solicitation for proposals. Using an elaborate but very focused matrix of deciding factors, with appropriate weightings, the truck firm developed a scoring system that led to selection of the finalist. Goodyear received the highest score and was selected as the partner.

Paul Schlimm, Goodyear's director of original equipment sales, and the truck firm's manager of supplier relationships, were deeply involved in this phase of the process. They reported that several factors were key in building the original partnering relations. An early consideration was whether or not the organizations were compatible regarding decision-making processes. The ability to gather necessary information was another crucial consideration, as was the possibility of building a trusting relationship. The truck firm wanted to make sure that it would be moving in the right direction, and that both parties would be comfortable with the new alliance they planned to form, particularly because it would be used as a model for other alliances.

The partnering proposal that was eventually used fulfilled all of the truck firm's "must have" items and most of the "wants" as defined by its decision-making process. From the partner's perspective, the proposal also outlined basic Goodyear expectations in terms of attaining a growing share of the firm's business on a mutually beneficial basis. The agreement stated that the partnership would be open-ended and could be mutually terminated. Basic staffing and office commitments were outlined to provide for a core implementation group and a full-time partnering team that would oversee how the alliances developed.

During the initial tire group joint team meeting, a mission statement and driving goals were established. The mission statement set the tone for a real partnering situation. It begins, "A working partnership is a joint business alliance wherein two companies agree to favor each other's business activities," and adds, "Each partner dedicates resources in people, capital, and facilities to support future business and profit growth. . . . Progress is measured by the success of joint programs identified, prioritized, developed, and implemented through the cooperative efforts of the operating disciplines of both companies." The statement was endorsed and signed by both firms.

Within a short time, hundreds of improvement projects were suggested without restraint or comment from team members. These projects were grouped by their relationship to either a particular goal or a functional work group. They were then assigned to full-time business teams for evaluation and prioritization, using a simple point system based on potential benefits, timing, resources required, and risk. Of interest was the fact that projects that benefited either party to the alliance could be and were submitted.

Dave Larsen, of Goodyear, is an account executive assigned to the truck firm account. He reported that when the business management team was formed for the joint activities described above, care was taken to get a true cross-section of disciplines. The idea was to give attention to the need to avoid compromising one area within the company for the benefit of another. The original team included full-time participation from these disciplines:

Truck firm	*Goodyear*
Partnership management	*Truck tire marketing*
Tire and wheel purchases	*General product sales*
General product purchases	*Replacement tire sales*
Truck marketing	*Engineering*
Parts marketing	

The roles established for this team were: to manage all aspects of the team process, to develop and implement partnering business plans, to provide leadership and support to working groups, to provide a forum to address strategic issues, and to communicate results and promote the value of the alliance. Again, it is interesting to note the significant degree of empowerment that was given to the team. Senior endorsement was very high from both companies, but the actual development of the projects was carried out at the team level.

Working groups were also set up with a combination of full- and part-time members. These teams were responsible for developing action plans, forming specific task groups, acquiring needed resources, monitoring progress, reporting results, creating innovative solutions, and being the key source of idea generation.

One working team generated results that typify the kind of success that can be generated from a true partnering relationship. The Assemblies On Time (AOT) team was established with the purpose of designing a better system to mount final tire assemblies, an identified high-priority opportunity area. The AOT team developed one of the more innovative operating solutions in the trucking industry.

The focus began with an analysis of current tire procurement and assembly systems and procedures. Typically, tires and rims were ordered by the truck firm and stored with modest inventories. The rims would then be painted or treated and sent to an area for mounting. Factory floor space was dedicated to this function. Unfortunately, the team discovered that when the tires were mounted, the units were not always foolproof. Some were improperly mounted, underinflated, or incorrectly balanced. Although the percentage was small, the team saw opportunities in floor space savings, error elimination, and increased throughput in the assembly area.

The solution was a model of partnering principles. Before the partnering arrangement, the truck firm received all tires and rims and did the painting and mounting, producing the final assemblies. Because of the small but significant percentage of the final assemblies rejected due to poor quality, ten days' inventory of tires and rims were maintained as safety stock. Under the new conditions, the truck firm wanted Goodyear to assume responsibility for the tires and rims, including the painting, mounting, and final balancing. Accuride Corporation, the truck firm's major wheel supplier, was contacted and expressed interest in being part of the arrangement. This firm had the wheel and painting expertise, so a further alliance was quickly initiated. Goodyear formed a second partnering arrangement with Accuride, establishing that firm as the manufacturer of choice for the rims. A corporation was created—AOT International, Inc.

A new facility was built using property near the truck firm's plant. In *this plant, tires and wheels are sequentially ordered for assembly. Now, robotic arms flawlessly apply paint to the wheels. Another robot lubricates the tires and a technician orients the wheel for proper mounting. A computer-controlled program automatically inflates the tires to particular vehicle specifications.*

A fully computerized balancing station is next in the sequence. A technician applies the appropriate weights to the designated areas and the balancing is complete. This method assures customers of perfectly balanced tire and wheel assemblies. When the assembly is complete, the tires on wheels are stacked sequentially for installation on designated trucks. The final assemblies are automatically loaded into trailers by a computerized conveyor. These trailers are continuously ferried across the street to the assembly plant throughout the day, where they are off-loaded and put on a moving conveyor belt that goes to the assembly line. Technicians at the truck firm plant remove the finished units at the point of need and mount them on trucks.

In the process of implementing this activity, the team combines the strengths of Goodyear and Accuride into a high-quality tire and wheel assembly process, with a decided competitive advantage. The truck firm benefits from improved finished tire and wheel assemblies and saves valuable shop floor space that had been reserved for holding inventories. AOT has expanded its base and now ships units to the Canadian assembly plant on a just-in-time basis. The ten days' supply of finished units has been reduced to a supply of hours, a savings for all three parties. Detailed business plans are produced by the joint team, and mutual savings have been generated. One interesting side benefit has been that funds from the partnering savings have been used to buy a test truck for experimenting with other new products that are interesting to all the parties.

Reporting on the benefits, Paul Schlimm remarked, "Trust was demonstrated by the open communications that developed when the partnership was put together. [The truck firm] subsequently offered to co-locate Goodyear personnel to facilitate the necessary interchanges. Joint training of team members was introduced, and improved communications between all levels of the two firms was noticed to have improved." This was obviously a win-win situation for both companies that knew how to apply partnering the way it was meant to be applied.

Summary

Many obstacles stand in the way of making partnering work across a full supply chain. However, a growing number of examples are proving that the savings from true partnering greatly exceed what can be achieved by wringing usually unwarranted concessions from an acquiescing supply base. We see the latter approach as the obvious choice of those who are unwilling to put greater and more fruitful effort into finding the hidden savings that typically exist in most supply chains.

The obstacles usually start with flawed perceptions of the value of good relationships between parties in the supply chain. These perceptions are grounded in a lack of the trust that is necessary to make any alliance work. The needed perception is one that says that partnering will work, but that it must contain the application of mutual resources for mutual benefit. Anything less will doom the effort to short-term maneuvering by buyers and sellers, with no real improvement in the competitive advantage of the supply network.

Chapter Six

Reengineering the Supply Chain

• •

Having committed to an improvement effort based on an interenterprise model and taken the time to anticipate and allow for the obstacles that can interfere with the effort, an organization is ready to consider how to reengineer a supply chain network. This consideration begins with an understanding of exactly what the idea of reengineering, or more correctly process redesign, means in general terms and what potential impact using such a process can have on the organization. It then progresses to applying the technique at the appropriate locations in the supply system and continues as further opportunities to make dramatic and advantageous changes are identified. The ultimate intention is to never stop improving the process, but always move toward optimization.

The Concept of Reengineering

At the end of the nineteenth century, an American engineer, Frederick Taylor, gained widespread notice when he revolutionized the modern industrial world with a new concept. Taylor envisioned the mechanization of the workplace, using techniques developed from adapting industrial engineering practices. He focused on the structure of labor, task decomposition, and measurement of the work force. Taylor's basic belief was that management could increase worker productivity by applying engineering principles to existing factory conditions. The best-known facet of his work is the time and motion study, in which an "efficiency expert" breaks down a specific job into its basic elements and then times each step in the job. These time elements are then manipulated to find better ways to perform the functions. The structure of labor was to provide the ability to organize the industries that would be created to meet the demands of the growing worldwide consumer and military markets. These concepts became the heart of "Taylorism."

From Taylor's time until 1990, perhaps no single concept stirred the imagination and incited arguments to the same degree as Taylorism. Then an article that appeared in the July–August issue of the *Harvard Business Review* caught the attention and imagination of business managers. Michael Hammer, a former Massachusetts Institute of Technology professor of computer science turned consultant, published an article with the strange-sounding title, "Reengineering Work: Don't Automate, Obliterate" (Hammer, 1990). With this introduction, Hammer gave birth to one of the most misunderstood, misapplied, effective, and powerful tools developed for business in the twentieth century—the concept of business process reengineering (BPR).

From the original article, we have what Hammer wrote as the definition for BPR. It is the "fundamental rethinking and radical redesign of business processes to achieve dramatic improvements in critical measures of performance" (Hammer, 1990, p. 104). The emphasis was placed on the radical redesign element as the necessary feature that would obliterate the unnecessary, replacing it with totally new processes that would be dramatically more effective.

Soon after its introduction, BPR became a business improvement fad. Interest was shown everywhere and Hammer's explanatory seminars and definitive book became instant hits. The ideas discussed at those seminars fired the imagination of many of the attendees and inspired them to go back and apply the teachings as quickly as possible. The majority of these would-be disciples must not have been listening when the new guru announced that the technique had a failure rate of 60 percent or more. Undaunted, they tried to apply BPR indiscriminately across their organizations. A few of the early successes became the material for articles and stories supporting the technique, but the larger number of misfires were left essentially unrecorded.

Upon reflection, we now see that these disciples had much greater enthusiasm than understanding. The problem became how to use the concept in an appropriate setting or for an appropriate application, as opposed to indiscriminately applying it to every business practice. In an example of the latter case, an operations vice president for a division of a Fortune 50 firm classified a plant closing as an example of reengineering. An information systems executive at a two-billion-dollar corporation talked about BPR being the migration of computer programs from midrange computers to a personal computer client server environment. Both instances showed an obvious misunderstanding of the purpose of BPR. Advocates continued to foster BPR's potential, however, viewing reengineering as the next business panacea. John Sculley, at the time CEO of Apple Computer, was quoted in 1993 by the *Wall Street Journal* as saying that reengineering would provide the engine that forces a "reorganization of work that could prove as massive and wrenching as the Industrial Revolution."

So what is BPR, where is it headed, what can it do for an organization in search of improvement, and how does it apply to supply chain optimization? These are the kinds of questions that have to be answered before any organization attempts to apply such a forceful technique, especially in an area as complex as supply chain improvement. With so much activity already being devoted to enhancements in this vital link between suppliers and consumers, rushing foolishly into using BPR could actually cause more confusion and complications than favorable results. Those who have been hard at work trying to find the often-cited savings potential in serious change efforts could view BPR as an intrusion that might interfere with the reasonably good progress they are making.

BPR has been called by many different names since its introduction. *Process innovation, core process redesign, work process analysis,* and *process improvement* are among the favorites. Over the past three years, reengineering has become synonymous with restructuring, reorganizing, delayering, the next version of Total Quality Management (TQM), flattening the organization, downsizing and rightsizing, business improvement, and business enhancement. In reality, those who use the idea of BPR to mask methods that would strip away people and systems rather than build for the future have corrupted the intention and misapplied the tool.

Hammer advised that when we explore the key elements of reengineering and how these ideas relate to business practices, we must look systematically, and with a critical eye, at the processes that drive the business. It is imperative to understand the definitions of the jobs and tasks being performed and to reveal the structure of the organization—not just the structure on the official organizational charts, but the unpublished, true structure as well. Embarking on a course of reengineering will literally shake the foundations of the management and measurement systems, breaking long-standing paradigms in the process and often smashing into little bits the inhibiting portions of the culture that once drove the organization. Most changes are minor shifts in direction that usually perpetuate the culture, beliefs, and values that are in place. For those who wish to keep these past formats intact, BPR is not the tool of preference. Those who choose to apply it to supply chain activities must develop an understanding of value and challenge.

Promises and Limitations

Figure 6.1 shows some of the barrier categories that will be encountered as an organization progresses toward a real BPR effort. Some of these walls of confrontation and resistance are steeped in tradition; some are a recent phenomenon. Typically, we have found that almost all the firms with which we work are engaged in some form of improvement effort. The names of the efforts vary greatly, but not the intentions. The universal purposes are to cut costs as quickly as possible and to develop innovative ways of

FIGURE 6.1. Evolution of Business Techniques.

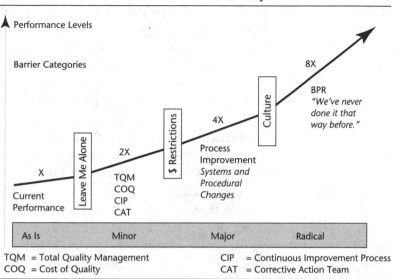

| As Is | Minor | Major | Radical |

TQM = Total Quality Management   CIP = Continuous Improvement Process
COQ = Cost of Quality   CAT = Corrective Action Team

doing things that result in higher customer satisfaction. An average firm works to improve current performance by a magnitude of 2 to 5 percent annually. A steady stream of improvement projects is presented, typically favoring midrange capital investments as a means of making process enhancements.

When pressure is applied to such an organization, the first wall of resistance appears, in which the participants essentially ask to be left alone. They resist outside analysis and hope for the small, incremental improvement levels that have been achieved in the past to be accepted as sufficient to enhance performance. To vault over that wall, most firms use new techniques, like those embodied in TQM, Cost of Quality, Continuous Improvement Process, and Corrective Action Teams. With these efforts, many companies have gone beyond the as-is condition of small annual improvements to what have proved to be larger, but still minor, levels of enhancement. As the figure illustrates, a doubling of results is not unusual for firms progressing into this area.

Now the restricting wall becomes a cry for larger investment dollars, usually in new, untested capital. The answer seems to be to install the latest technological advances, regardless of organizational preparedness. Billions are spent during this time, often in a vain attempt to find higher savings simply by buying new equipment and systems. For those who resist such a singular strategy and insist on fixing much of the equipment and systems in place, while adding new capital in judicious increments, the jump over the wall comes with the design of significant process improvements.

In this phase, the emphasis is on analyzing the key processes that drive customer satisfaction and profit enhancement. New systems and procedural changes are augmented as firms try to make major improvements without sacrificing all the gains made from past efforts. Organizations now wish to change a total process, such as order fulfillment or logistics and transportation, using totally new procedures and methods. Successful firms are able to find up to four times the traditional level of enhancement before running into the next inhibiting wall.

In this position, the culture of the organization becomes a particularly difficult element. People in all parts of the firm can be expected to complain that enough is enough. Certainly, improvements have been achieved, often of a significant nature. But the bar is always moved higher, particularly as ownership changes become the order of the day. New management always wants higher levels of performance as the measure it exacts for claiming the new ownership position. A typical first step is a dramatic downsizing of the work force. With fewer people left in place to face higher targets, improvement needs the radical changes typically contained in a BPR effort.

The first response in this stage is typically that larger-scale improvements have to include major investments. To climb over this most difficult wall, Hammer advocated rethinking and making new evaluations of the way the processes that drive the firm are carried out. Typical levels of improvement should be set aside as core groups look for totally new ways to accomplish what has to be done. Now the improvement team challenges the idea that culturally we have never done things in such a different manner. The team members attempt to focus on radical redesign to show some breakthrough examples of what could result. In the areas where

BPR does apply, orders of magnitude in improvement that were never dreamed of previously can be accomplished.

One of the best known examples of BPR, accomplished by Ford Motor Company, was described by Hammer in his article and seminar (Hammer, 1990, p. 105):

> In the early 1980s, when the American automotive industry was in a depression, Ford's top management put accounts payable—along with many other departments—under the microscope in search of ways to cut costs. Accounts payable in North America alone employed more than 500 people. Management thought that by rationalizing processes and installing new computer systems, it could reduce the head count by some 20 percent.
>
> Ford was enthusiastic about its plan to tighten accounts payable—until it looked at Mazda. While Ford was aspiring to a 400-person department, Mazda's accounts payable organization consisted of a total of five people. The difference in absolute numbers was astounding, and even after adjusting for Mazda's smaller size, Ford figured that its accounts payable organization was five times the size it should be. The Ford team knew better than to attribute the discrepancy to calisthenics, company songs, or low interest rates.

In fact, Ford found that complex, cumbersome, and unnecessary procedures, or non-value added activities, accounted for much of the discrepancy in relative size and cost of their accounts payable function. The solution, or quantum leap, required elimination of non-value work and reduced head count to 75 staff.

As with most management concepts, reengineering is not a magic pill. It is a powerful tool, and its use is fraught with pitfalls and bumps in the road. Many of those who have embarked on this path have done so at great peril, because of the uncertainties of the potential consequences. Among the companies interviewed in the research for this book, we were able to find many firms that entered into reengineering expecting the organization to quickly embrace the concept and, with equal alacrity, find substantial improvements. The final results often belied these early expectations. Savings and improvements did occur, but little correlation was found to the early expectations.

Most often we found that certain particularly good departments, which probably would have succeeded with any improvement effort, were able to find innovative ways of effectively redesigning their processes to cut costs and cycle times. What we did not find was a consistent pattern of applying the defined course of action for the reengineering tool across anything approaching the full organization. Underneath the discussions of the early successes we also heard of the failed and discontinued efforts. The result was a mixed bag of success and failure.

Overall, there is general consensus that a failure rate of 60 percent exists for firms that participate in BPR initiatives. These figures should raise concern over why companies continue to embark on a journey filled with such a high failure rate. Why do the people responsible for results in these organizations take such a risky path? Quite simply, we found that the organizational and personal rewards for a successful trip are so high that the risk is generally put aside in favor of an attempt at achieving great results. Consider the possibility of being able to reduce 80 percent or more of the process steps in a department or area of responsibility. Consider further that such an improvement could lead to double-digit savings in areas of constantly increasing costs. The real issue is whether the rewards are worth such a high risk. Most managers we interviewed expressed a willingness to take the chance, particularly as BPR remains a hot business topic.

Common Pitfalls

Given this undaunted attitude, we have advised caution before helping managers to proceed down the reengineering path. Like any management concept, BPR has many potential complications. From those who failed in their first attempts to reengineer, we discovered several consistent missteps that could have been avoided.

Not Recognizing Natural Resistance

Reengineering will threaten the livelihood of many of those doing the work. Most of these people have spent a good part of their life

building a career that could be terminated if the new design eliminates the organization's need for their services. The redesign
could also change the size and scope of the responsibilities assigned to them. Because of one of these reasons or just suspicion
of the unknown, the reengineering process will be perceived by
many within the organization as the beginning of an unknown future that most likely could have bad personal consequences. This
condition quickly leads to fear and a natural resistance.

Anticipating this condition is essential for success. Care has to
be exercised in handling the introduction and soliciting help in the
early, assessment stages. It is imperative to keep communication
about progress open and to document the improvements in terms
of measurements that have meaning to the stakeholders.

A helpful stratagem and influencing technique is benchmarking the key customer satisfaction measures to determine any hidden crises that would mobilize support for the effort. One client,
a manufacturer of industrial packaging materials, accepted this
premise; before initiating a BPR effort in the order-to-delivery
cycle, the organization took the time to benchmark a few key factors like sales per employee, days of inventory, lead times, on-time
deliveries, and fill rates. The firm also studied receivables and
payables and took a hard look at customer satisfaction ratings.
The purpose was to redesign the process to be more effective in
use of people, efficiency of filling orders, and ability to get good
products to the customer on time. The firm's interest turned to
shock when it found itself in the bottom third of most of these categories. After the typical period of denial and rebuttal subsided,
the senior management group was able to use the benchmarking
data to mobilize a strong supportive effort for what quickly became a survival initiative.

Assuming Acceptance of the New Methodology

It is a fatal flaw to conclude that the power of the BPR effort will
result in the design of new processes that will convince people of
the mistakes of their past practices and enlist their willing support
to implement the changed processes. At one company, we
watched as a project team designed new processes that could dramatically reduce cycle times for delivery, save thirty-five million

dollars in inventory, support larger revenues, and put eighteen million dollars a year into new profits. The team had designed these
processes to be more responsive in all phases of customer needs—
from new product design through delivery and follow-up customer service. The problem with this potential success story was
that many of the people who should have been at the forefront of
the effort supporting the redesign became reluctant to do so, because they were unwilling to accept the responsibility for such a
large process change. Their perception was that their immediate
area of responsibility would come under scrutiny for bad past
practices; this was sufficient reason to stall their involvement in
the improvement process.

A better approach than charging forth with BPR, expecting en-
thusiastic support, is to bring all relevant departments into the
process from the start. People become excited about participating when they help to construct the change process of which they
will be a part. They also see more clearly how their effort will affect the future of the organization. The existing culture must be
studied as closely as the change process to determine where non-
compliance will occur. A helpful procedure is to pilot-test the new
process. By setting up a model that includes the processes to be redesigned or reengineered, a sixty- to ninety-day pilot can be en-
acted that gives the mentors the time and actual experience to
determine the probability of lasting success, with the option of returning to the existing systems if the redesign does not create real
improvement. One firm with which we worked decided to undertake a major overhaul of its order-to-cash process. Because the
planned changes would have such a major impact on the business,
the decision was made to establish a six- to nine-month trial with
the revised process. During that time, several very critical modifi-
cations were made in order to improve the practicality of the redesign and to bring on much-needed support from several key
players.

Defining Too Narrow a Scope

In an attempt to find an early success, some firms embark on BPR
in a narrowly limited area. Although these efforts might achieve

some local successes, they do not provide the scale of benefits associated with reengineering efforts. One medical supply company looking for such a success attempted to apply BPR to its order entry function. It overlooked the broader issues associated with the entire order fulfillment process. Although one department involved in the total process had some documented successes, the net effect was that barriers to improving other, more significant, parts of the process sprang up and led to a failure to reap large-scale savings. The change group actually became pariahs in the company and slid back into the old and more familiar ways of performing the function. The firm eventually declared the effort a failure.

Defining Too Broad a Scope

As the scope can be too narrow, so it can be too wide if care is not exercised. A diagnostic phase is very critical in identifying the scope and value of the process under study before embarking on a BPR project. In the excitement of beginning a corporate initiative of the magnitude normally encompassed by these efforts, those at the helm often elect to try to do all things at once; this is sometimes referred to as trying to eat an elephant in one bite. The general rule in reengineering is that no organization can effectively undertake more than two or three BPR initiatives simultaneously. Furthermore, each of these initiatives should cover a fairly complete process, such as order fulfillment, order-to-cash, logistics and transportation, distribution management, or forecasting and planning.

Pursuit of more than three such efforts typically leads to great frustration and limits the potential for success. Understanding the corporation's own processes and how they affect customers' needs will provide a basis for deciding which opportunities should be placed highest on the priority list of initiatives. For BPR to create radically improved processes, changes must be made to the existing culture. Such changes will be resisted unless they are clearly seen as being beneficial. To make such a determination, the question we most strongly advise asking is: Will this initiative and the resultant changes provide our company with a distinct competitive advantage? Unless the answer is in the affirmative, the BPR effort could be a major drain on resources that will result in only a cosmetic enhancement.

A financial services company attempted to reengineer all its basic functions without adhering to the fundamental rules mentioned above. With great fanfare, the senior management team announced the initiation of a BPR effort that would totally remake the company, garnishing significant gains in performance and earnings. They quickly announced the team formations and the members of a leadership council. In total, twenty-one separate BPR teams were to be formed, which were given the challenge of making the effort a raging success and a precursor of the future. As much of the organization as possible was to be involved in the change effort. Shortly after the teams began their work, the efforts began to falter as the reality of trying to do too much became a recognized fact. Dissatisfaction over the lack of progress and the failure to achieve any significant accomplishments soon led to a breakdown in the reengineering process. To execute one of the twenty-one efforts in a specific area, each team leader was cast in the unexpected position of waging a constant political campaign for the use of critical resources.

Within less than six months, no active signs remained of any of the initiatives, and the firm concluded that BPR was an inappropriate tool for its type of business. This firm overlooked the necessary preparation steps. It should have defined the necessary objectives and the steps needed for accomplishment, established benchmarks that would show where competitors had advanced, and considered the cultural changes required before embarking on twenty-one initiatives. Remember the definition of BPR. Radical change has to be handled with care in a few focused areas to start with, not across a spectrum so large that there is no way to adequately provide the necessary human resources.

Providing Insufficient Resources

If an organization suffers from a lack of available resources or has a constraint on key talent, management should avoid too large a BPR initiative or too many of them. They should also look cautiously at reengineering in general unless they have access to additional talent. Insufficient allocation of resources leads to frustration, short-circuiting of required analysis, recommendations based on insufficient data, and premature implementation. We can cite many cases in which the organization was more prone to supply money than the required human resources to do an effective process redesign and implementation. That is a formula for failure. A common rule applies in this instance: those who are assigned to the effort associated with a reengineering effort need to be those who are the least available due to their importance to the business. By making the mandatory up-front sacrifice, firms maximize the emphasis on the effort and the strength of the implementation team. Consequently, when the organization needs additional resources to implement the team findings and recommendations, the proper allocation is made. With necessary resources applied to the task, the results typically outweigh any up-front loss caused by reassigning critical personnel.

Failing to Have a CEO Mandate

A guarantee of failure is the absence of a clear mandate by a firm's senior officer. In most U.S.-based corporations, the power held by the office of the chief executive cannot be overstated. When making such radical changes as those called for in a BPR effort, using the strength of that office to drive the change becomes imperative. This support becomes such a critical point of concern that if an organization attempts to undertake a BPR effort without the CEO being driven toward making the recommended changes, then it would be better to withdraw and attempt less radical or less substantive changes.

Xerox Corporation provides some valuable insights into how to go about readying an organization for major change. That firm's supply chain initiative illustrates how to combine thorough preliminary analysis with process and performance benchmarking to gather valuable input before launching a redesign. Xerox took time and care as it developed its Integrated Supply Chain

· · · · ·

effort (ISC) to effectively prepare for a major change process while avoiding the pitfalls.

The ISC effort was developed to support the corporate goals of cutting supply chain costs, increasing levels of customer service, and generating better asset utilization. To do this, it determined that streamlined processes would be required that increased the velocity of supply activities, through reduced cycle times, and yielded superior business results in the goal areas. From these central objectives a change effort was initiated to redesign the supply chain processes. Results to date have included three points' improvement in return on assets and $600 million savings in supply chain costs.

The fundamental that drove the changes was characterized as the need to move from segmentation to integration. That meant changing paradigms from building inventory stocks to configuring and shipping to order; from emergency orders being a normal practice to rapid deployment of selective customer needs; from redundant stock echelons to single, logical echelons; and from local to global stock visibility. These terms are specific to the Xerox transition, but it can be seen that the traditional means of delivering products and services had to undergo a major transformation, a difficult task for any organization. Most organizations would have thrown these nebulous objectives at a core team and told them to reengineer the process. Such actions contribute to the high failure rate for BPR. Xerox chose to take the time to find out what the gap was that had to be overcome and where others had made successful changes in similar areas.

Under the direction of Steve Tierney, vice president of ISC, a core, internal transition team was formed that included materials management, manufacturing, logistics, operations control, quality, and representatives from nine business divisions. This internal team developed a long list of "keys to unlocking supply chain excellence." They focused on issues as wide as delivery-to-request date, obsolescence and scrap, order fill lead time, value-added productivity, faultless invoices, ship-to-invoice cycle, forecast accuracy, warranty costs, materials lead time, and asset turns.

All of these categories were determined to be relevant measures of the effectiveness of the supply chain process. To provide the team with useful information that would establish the performance gap and the magnitude of possible change, a special benchmarking process was set in motion before the redesign was started. Partnering arrangements were made with external sources, including leading universities that could help provide data on successful efforts by other firms. An especially beneficial source came from the formation of an ISC roundtable that included 3M, Du Pont, Procter & Gamble, the Black & Decker Corporation, Digital Equipment Corporation (DEC), and Siemens. These companies provided resources to develop benchmarking data in the categories of interest. Key measures were identified and, with the help of the partners, data were generated on all of the specified measures. A base of 119 companies involved in similar activities was used to access this information and to make determinations of the best practices. Performance measures that showed the need for improvement included delivery timeliness, net inventory as a percentage of marketing revenue, total supply chain costs as a percentage of marketing revenue, cash-to-cash cycle time, total supply chain response time, asset utilization, performance of meeting request-and-commit dates, and total supply chain costs.

With this information as a guide to the best in class, ISC set out to build a customized, redesigned process that would capture the features of these higher benchmarks. The factor that became the driving force and secured dedicated effort was the desire to become the best in supply chain activities. A concurrent effort was instigated to look at financial and inventory performance benchmarking. That effort augmented the overall improvement process by establishing the need for focus in these areas and the need for supporting information technology (I/T).

From the benchmarking exercise, the team developed a road map for execution and proceeded to redesign the key processes that were determined to be important for the future (twelve ISC business processes resulted from this redesign exercise). Work continues on the effort, but the key was the care taken in the beginning to establish the need for the change process and the level of potential improvement, documented by actual benchmark information.

Applying the Tool for Supply Chain Improvements

Increased competition from all sectors of the business environment is bringing new pressure on organizations involved in supply chains to find innovative, useful approaches and radical changes that will enhance customer satisfaction. In the process, the concept of standing alone and forging the necessary changes in isolation no longer makes sense. With new ideas and technological advances arriving at an ever-increasing rate, to rely totally on internal strengths means bypassing new techniques unknown to those intent on pursuing a culturally correct approach.

Developing this type of new relationship takes great patience and steadfast determination. Even with strong senior endorsement, full organizational commitment comes slowly. In sessions we hold in which members of a supply chain come together to execute a pilot with the interenterprise solution, we spend whatever time is necessary to drive home the understanding that new paradigms are required and that garnishing short-term gains at the expense of a supplier or customer only results in more of the same game playing and ultimately in losing net income for all of the involved parties. To move toward a real optimization opportunity, the members of the chain must look at any improvement tool as a chance to find totally new ways to create a competitive advantage. When the tool is as powerful as BPR, then putting aside selfish interests and working together in a spirit of shared opportunity becomes the paramount tenet. BPR involves such radical redesign that only when the involved parties clearly see large mutual advantages will the requisite key resources be made available.

On the positive side, we discovered in this powerful tool an outstanding opportunity to apply reengineering techniques to the many and varied levels of interfaces among supply chain organizations. As we traced the movement of products and services from supplies of raw materials, through the factories and service groups, across the modes of distribution (internally and externally), and eventually into the marketplace for consumption by the ultimate consumer, we found myriad chances to conduct BPR analyses and quite often radical redesigns. Most firms insisted on applying the tool exclusively to internal functions and processes, turning to outside sources only with an insistence on receiving concessions. Slowly, we were able to move a few groups into the new paradigm of trying partnering techniques, in combination with redesign and reengineering, to reap far greater results. A few examples will illustrate the types of opportunity we encountered.

From Push to Pull

In most supply chains, products tend to move forward in a "push" manner. In this system, suppliers build inventories of their products and enlist sales organizations to push these stocks toward the manufacturers for consumption in the ultimate market. We have consistently been able to show how these stocks and the working capital needed to support them can be reduced through a closer linkage with data on true end-use consumption. Great opportunities exist to dramatically reduce inventories and cycle times when the chain of activities between supply and consumption is clearly mapped and redesigned.

The typical redesign includes radical, innovative changes to the information flow from actual consumption information to procurement of the materials and services necessary to replenish that consumption. Only by applying a technique as forceful as BPR will the members of the supply network make the real changes necessary to define a "pull" system that brings stock to the point of consumption at the time of need for replenishment. This type of redesign requires mapping the current flow of information across many companies and designing a system that utilizes the swiftest methodology and the correct application of technology.

Forecasting Demand

Anyone who has been associated with a plant's manufacturing activities has experienced the problem that comes with trying to establish reliable production schedules. The usual first difficulty involves the forecasts of demand that come through traditional interactive systems. Sales representatives are sent out to develop these forecasts in an annual foray to find the material for next year's business plan. Following many arbitrary changes and overrides by management, these preliminary forecasts are turned into strategic plans and monthly operating plans. A close examination of the substance behind those plans quickly reveals the nebulous nature of the forecasts, not on an annual basis, for which they are reasonably accurate, but in the embedded inaccuracies of the monthly, weekly, and daily forecasts.

In spite of the complications, we find that the validity and usefulness of the planning and scheduling that must derive from these forecasts can be greatly improved, as new and better forecasting processes are designed. As teams have traced current processes, they have discovered in virtually every case in our experience that better consumption data can be introduced into the information flow, along with the crucial element in today's supply chain networks—the information associated with promotional efforts. It is this latter information that causes the variations in otherwise effective manufacturing schedules and introduces the nonbudgeted costs.

What is required is a larger-scale cooperative effort in which teams document the current system and its inherent flaws and proceed to design, in concert, a new system that enhances the flow of information based on actual need and on-line consumption. As the joint teams focus on the current system, they will find areas where the changes can range from a simple sharing of previously proprietary data to the application of complex algorithms that have been designed to enhance the accuracy and timeliness of the forecasting process.

Improving Customer Satisfaction

Redesign of a process like order fulfillment can raise the level of customer satisfaction dramatically and also eliminate the resources required in the labor-intensive areas. By reengineering processes and eliminating wasted effort and nonvalue-adding

steps, companies have discovered that they have a great opportunity to leave behind old methods that slow their customer response time and to provide the right tools to do an improved job.
Many redesigns result in more freedom by personnel to serve customers. Once people are relieved of mindless tasks that were designed in another era and that add little or no customer value,
they use that freedom to make the right decisions to satisfy the
customer. The value to the firm and to the customer goes up geometrically in these instances. The lesson to be learned is that it
makes little difference what the product or service is. Customers
want to be dealt with fairly and with alacrity, get good value for
the money they spend, and come away with the feeling that
someone within the organization cares for them and did not
waste their time. Such satisfaction comes from a system designed
for today's consumers.

Improving Purchasing Power

Access to repositories of data can provide a means for effective
use of reengineering techniques. Purchasing has proved to be a
fertile area for applying this type of reengineering and a power-
house in enhancing net income. Many firms find themselves in a
global market that requires ever-expanding spheres of sourcing
and distribution. As the circle of action increases in size, so does
the opportunity to aggregate the purchasing that supports manufacture and distribution. Innovative firms such as Tenneco and
Allied-Signal have used their immense buying power to assist their
suppliers and customers by pooling resources, thereby cutting the
costs of goods, services, and supplies.

The improvement process begins by drawing information from
the immense data bases that most corporations have today, which
document what is being purchased, by whom, and for what purpose. The first surprise usually is finding how many sources and
people are involved in placing orders. Both numbers are typically much greater than anticipated. Consolidating suppliers
and limiting procurement are the usual first cuts, but the real

results come from reengineering the sourcing process with the key strategic partners. Armed with accurate data on purchased goods and services, from the largest to the smallest sources, the firm is in a position to look at global opportunities for its sourcing. It can also consider pooling its needs with other firms to get further advantages.

Tenneco went so far as to determine that major purchases offered the firm a chance to establish a profit center (Tully, 1995). The Houston conglomerate formed a purchasing subsidiary, TennEcon Services, to negotiate discounted rates on the major products and services purchased across the firm. The subsidiary then marketed the improved conditions to external companies for a fee. When it was determined, for example, that the company was one of the major buyers of phone services and overnight mail delivery, TennEcon negotiated single contracts with MCI Communications Corporation and Federal Express Corporation, respectively. It then offered the use of the contract conditions to other firms, some of which were Tenneco suppliers or customers. TennEcon is able to pass on savings of up to 20 percent and still make a profit.

Purchasing Opportunities

Purchasing operations have proved that they can become profit centers. They do so by redesigning their processes into a global network in such a way that small, remote participants can gain quick access to the system and garner the benefits of the pooled resources. Participants of all sizes can use technology that is integrated into the new process design and gain the position of a much larger entity. They can take advantage of the new information systems and channels of distribution to get needed materials at prices that are usually reserved for only the biggest buyers. Discounts, special delivery options, and service features that are typically applied only to the largest purchasing groups become added benefits of being part of the pooled network. DEC has built a world-class I/T support system to manage its international operations while promoting top-flight contract rates. Enforced with a strong and proactive management discipline, DEC has cut the number of its buyers and enhanced its professional capabilities; in addition, it has saved substantial amounts of money and enhanced service quality.

Having determined where to apply the BPR tool, in the areas cited here or others mentioned later in the book, the next step is to make certain that the information system can keep pace with the revised methods and systems that will be created. A well-redesigned process can flounder if the information system does not support the requirements of the abbreviated and less labor-intensive processes that typically are the product of the new design. From that perspective, it is imperative to approach I/T as the catalyst that will make BPR efforts successful.

Information Technology as the Catalyst

During his seminars, Michael Hammer is careful as he espouses the benefits of reengineering to admonish would-be users to avoid the temptation to "pave over the cowpaths." He uses this expression to caution management against the typical first reaction of wanting to design new systems that copy the flawed processes that need to be changed. Doing the same things faster or with fewer steps is not a guarantee that a better process will result. His advice is to throw out most of the old, weak systems in favor of new, more effective designs. I/T systems can then be designed and implemented to support the improved processes.

Often, we find situations where this advice has gone unheeded—for example, when senior executives gather the I/T group and inform them that they are to go out and purchase new systems that will force reengineering to happen within the firm. With many organizations anxiously waiting to fill orders for software and hardware, such a commission can quickly be satisfied. Unfortunately, the purchases may or may not satisfy the real organizational needs. The I/T group is typically separated from the CEO by one or two layers, so care must be exercised to control such messages or major investments will be made in information systems that do not fit either the needs of the strategic plan or the corporate intentions of the CEO.

A core belief exists that by enforcing executive will on the organization or adding sufficient capital funds to the I/T budget, the organization will somehow reinvent itself and become prepared to function in changing market conditions. The facts belie the potential of such a strategy. The policy of superimposing expensive hardware and software over old, worn processes has proved that the usual result is a more expensive bad process. By automating the work to be done, an organization may simply become more efficient at doing things the wrong, or less effective, way. Until management flushes the ineffective portions of the business process out of the systems and stops rationalizing the desire for quick and easy fixes, the returns from such improvement efforts will be minimal.

The problem is that the roots of performance difficulties lie in the work processes themselves; these areas must be analyzed and changed to be effective in current market conditions. It is not always the organization that defines those new processes. Often, it is the interactions of suppliers, producers, distributors, and customers working together to define the redesigns needed to create advantageous systems. To return to an earlier point, a large percentage of reengineering efforts have failed. These failures have resulted from trying to jump too quickly at easy solutions that actually should have had far greater up-front analysis before being initiated. This same admonition can be applied to the need for effective I/T support. The needed redesign should come first, and then the enabling and enhancing technology.

I/T is the most powerful weapon for breaking established business paradigms that are no longer appropriate for market conditions. Used in a proper fashion, it can cut cycle times, reduce or eliminate errors, eliminate inventories and increase turns, and reveal an enormous number of ways to find savings. But it is not a total panacea. It must be well understood, managed, and utilized.

A number of success stories describe better utilization of I/T as an enabling factor in achieving world-class results. A few of these will highlight ways in which technology played a key role in the successful implementation of improvement efforts.

Timberland

Timberland Co. is a New Hampshire shoe company that was featured in a special *Business Week* report (McWilliams, 1993). As the story reported, Timberland had "in the past measured their productivity by the size of the delivery, so priority was given to department store orders rather than those from small retailers." Although that historical focus had proved successful, management recognized that changes in the market were occurring that had to receive attention, or future results could be jeopardized. The report stated, "Managers of the $291 million company began to realize that small boutiques were a growing chunk of their business" (p. 59). As a result, management developed a strategy to change their emphasis in routing orders to meet the changing market conditions.

Timberland began by making internal changes that allowed the company to schedule multiple shipments to each customer each week, instead of making single large deliveries. With more flexible manufacturing capabilities, order size became less of a factor in profitability. Scanners were employed as technology was applied to track inventory and create shipping bills, in a manner that handled the increasing smaller orders as well as the former larger orders. These techniques made the firm competitive with both types of orders and gave it an opportunity to expand its customer base. Timberland is also using I/T to interact better with customers. "By letting stores transmit orders automatically to its computers," the report relates, "the company expects to double sales volume for every 25 percent increase in its sales force" (p. 59).

This firm chose to design a new route to get to the changing market. In the process, it reached out for the necessary technology to enable its strategy to be implemented. What we want to emphasize is the natural sequence that was employed. The design of the new system should precede the design of the enabling technology. That is the proper order in supply chain improvement.

Agway

Agway Corporation, a major supplier of farm supplies, recognized that a market change was having an important impact on its activities and took the necessary corrective action. The small farm, a mainstay on Agway's customer's list, was undergoing dramatic changes. One out of eight small farms has disappeared during the last decade. Replacing them was a much larger, more sophisticated customer who required sales qualifications that were not available in the existing Agway system. The six-hundred-store company found it necessary to rethink its entire business strategy.

During the early 1990s, the Agway executive team found themselves facing several years of losses without having a concrete plan for recovery. Retailers such as Wal-Mart were nipping at their traditional market in everything from cattle feed to tools for the garden. A further complication was that their ordering process was a jumbled and expensive web in which customers ordered from a store, with delivery often coming from a mill or warehouse. The management team knew that they had to radically alter the existing methodology.

As they explored the options and considered the use of reengineering, management found many alternative ways to conduct business. The problem was the difficulty they encountered as they tried to develop a consensus. In the words of the senior vice president of planning and operations, Bruce Ruppert, "At the beginning, when we asked where Agway should go, all the top executives said different things" (Stewart, 1993, p. 43). With some executives ready to champion new procedures, Agway could have thrown I/T at several existing processes. Instead, it persevered and elected to promote a two-pronged approach to its changing market, developing a commercial farm and a retail business. This became the strategic imperative and the basis for the new business design. Agway then designed the necessary processes to reach these two different markets, tailoring its services to meet the needs of its customers. More important, before it began the reengineering effort, it first established a strategy.

General Electric Credit Corporation

GECC is a well-recognized arm of one of America's most successful firms. It built its original business around servicing the consumer market with credit to buy GE white goods—refrigerators, stoves, washers, and so on. As the financing arm developed, it elected to offer private-label loan services on myriad other non-GE products, ranging from jewelry to mobile homes. In the early 1980s, as the cost of lending money became erratic and significantly more risky as a result of extraordinarily high interest rates, high delinquency, and defaults on loans by consumers, GECC found itself on a decision path that led toward exiting this business.

A special team of business executives and an advanced technology group were formed to determine if there was a way to manage the business so that it could be returned to profitability. Through a radically reengineered method of collecting past-due accounts and the application of advanced-state telephone technology, GECC discovered that it could reduce its existing collection personnel by a ratio of 10 to 1. This change provided the impetus for reducing the number of sites from over three hundred to fewer than twenty, taking twenty-five million dollars per year out of the cost structure. This landmark process redesign and adaptation of I/T provided the basis for a number of other efforts that assisted GECC to become a premiere nonbank organization.

The Return on Information Technology

Over recent decades, businesses have spent more than a trillion dollars to buy computer hardware, software, and services. Until recently, management experts such as Peter Drucker have claimed that a negative productivity gain has been the result of such investments. Over the last three to four years, however, a radical shift has taken place. Significant returns are now becoming the order of the day. The difference is management's insistence that technology should only be applied after solid business processes have been designed and implemented. Although reductions of 10 to 1 in the work force sound impossible, a growing number of corporations have been able to achieve this kind of result. The right kind of vision combined with the right technology partners can break the old paradigms and create the new ways business should be done.

With I/T well placed in the role of enabler and enhancer, firms next build on the platform provided, capitalizing on the expanding technological capability in order to wring values from their supply networks. They do this by combining technology with the types of data interchanges that they know are becoming necessary.

The Technology–Data Interchange Connection

In the days before the forced divestiture order imposed on AT&T, before communications became readily available at reasonable rates, it probably made little sense to expend much effort on capturing data in a standard format. Standardizing the wide variety of forms and standards existing in each work area, both within and between organizations, would have required too much costly processing to be of much value beyond local applications. With the landmark decision, competition in the communications industry added momentum to a major business revolution that was under way, the movement associated with access to cheap computing power. Industry after industry learned that it would be much better to enter data once, in standard format, allowing the information to be communicated not only locally or within a single plant or division, but throughout the organization and eventually across an entire supply chain. EDI has grown out of these joint movements and has provided the means to advance this reporting and communication ability to a fine art, as optimization is sought across these supply networks.

EDI probably had its roots in the railroad transportation industry, which learned its lessons many years ago. Using pre-computer technology, that industry used communications systems that led to setting standards associated with the gauge of railroad tracks. Pioneering new agreements across an industry in those times was difficult, yet the participants were able to seize the moment and create the agreement necessary to establish the coast-to-coast network of railroads. They were able to give birth to a tool that is only now beginning to fully exercise its potential. As retail consumption moves to a global environment, with customer preference a dominant feature, bringing industry communications to high levels of standardization becomes an imperative. Indeed, we see the movement gaining such momentum that those who fail to embrace the technique will be left out of participation in the emerging markets.

Often, practitioners overly complicate such an issue and in doing so become overwhelmed by the size of the task. That tendency should definitely be avoided as EDI is considered. In its most simple terms, EDI is nothing more than the electronic replacement of paper documents by electronic methods that are used in subsequent transmission of information in standard business transactions, such as purchase orders, acknowledgments, invoices, shipping notices, and remittances. Companies that utilize EDI do so on one of many private networks, running over a standard protocol developed specifically for the application, called X.12.

The advent of industry consortia and X.12 has addressed the most critical issue that in the past prevented companies from speaking to one another electronically—standards and compatibility. With agreements struck among the majority of users to maintain these elements, the largest barrier associated with EDI has been removed. Some firms still wish to use noncompliant methods of addressing other companies, but they have become the exception. EDI, based on agreed-upon standards, has now become the uniform method of exchange of business information in most industries.

The largest gains can be achieved with this tool when EDI is used in concert with other technologies and methods, such as electronic mail, BPR, work flow software, and business system applications. For example, streamlined operations and shorter cycle times can only be achieved when the up-front design of new work flows is consummated around the access and speed associated with EDI transactions. By allowing computers to receive data directly into the existing business applications rather than having to rekey it, organizations find that the work processes can be redesigned to remove the errors and time-wasting steps of normal data entry and analysis. As time delays and nonvalue-adding work are removed, customer satisfaction increases and savings are generated. Coincidentally, it has become apparent that reliance on the improved methodology begins to permeate the new relationships.

The gains related to most of the redesigns that have resulted from EDI interactions have been so outstanding that many experienced users have begun to enforce a policy in which they contractually require their suppliers to set these transactions in place. Wal-Mart and the Kroger Company have been particularly insistent in this area. Beginning with order entry, the movement has been to eliminate incoming purchase orders and acknowledgments on paper. Billings quickly have become a second application. Now the interacting parties are looking at all of the paper that moves between entities, with each piece being a candidate for elimination. Advance shipping notices are rapidly becoming common practice; they speed notification of goods transfer and eliminate the need for traditional paperwork. One major retailer, Sears, is moving toward using these electronic documents to pay vendors, rather than creating an extra step and using paper in the payment process. Electronic funds transfer completes the cycle as errors and conflicts are eliminated and invoices are no longer necessary. Funds move into the right accounts after receipt of goods via the electronic connection.

The ultimate application of EDI is the complete elimination of paper documents. Some of the leaders in the movement have taken the step of opening their networks and procedures and allowing their business partners to exchange data without any forms or documents. Some of these manufacturers, like Procter & Gamble, Motorola, and Ford, have identified substantial reductions in their costs as a result of these interchanges. When Ford looked at the typical cost of fifty to sixty dollars to process a purchase order, it applied that number to the annual orders needed to keep its system going and decided to make a move toward EDI. Ford actually allows many of its parts suppliers to dial into the network and create their own orders. While they are engaged in the network, Ford will download data on its production volume and current parts demand. The suppliers will then use the data to actually ship replacement parts or assembly parts where and when they are required. In essence, Ford has outsourced the management of parts inventory and control to the suppliers, who have accepted the responsibility for maintaining production schedules in exchange for what is often an exclusive supply position.

The Ford example is not unusual in the EDI scheme. Other firms have decided to outsource entire functions on the upstream side of their supply chain using electronic connections. One major manufacturing organization has outsourced its packaging to a select group of prime sources that have passed all the necessary quality and delivery specifications. Under this new system, the company no longer needs sales and purchasing interaction. Its packaging requirements are automatically conveyed via the EDI network; the chosen suppliers are responsible for having the required packaging goods at the point of need, without excess inventory. High levels of reliability are part of this system, which functions without paperwork or the need to negotiate pricing on every item. The possible need for any safety stock is at the discretion of the suppliers, but this has proved not to be necessary. Because of the electronic linkage, the demand information from the manufacturer is significantly more accurate and timely than traditional forecasting; this enables the suppliers to schedule more precisely and not incur the usually unrecoverable costs that resulted from making numerous scheduling changes because of the limitations of the previous forecasting system. The former sales and purchasing representatives have not been displaced. They are busy working on further system savings that can be developed on a joint basis.

As the use of EDI continues to accelerate, so do the number of applications that are found. A complete listing would be beyond the scope of this text, but an ever-enlarging menu of items that can be a part of the interchange is being documented by professionals in this area. EDI is one of the key ingredients of a supply network. It improves the flow of necessary information, eliminates the tiresome errors that are so much a part of existing systems, speeds reaction times as cycles are cut to the bare minimum, and allows people who were previously focused on manual overrides to pay attention to future improvements.

Action Study: Tenneco Packaging

·····································

Tenneco Packaging is a two-million-dollar division of Houston-based Tenneco, Inc. Tenneco Packaging produces a wide variety of packaging products, including corrugated boxes, folding cartons, molded fiber products, aluminum and plastic containers, and the primary paper known as linerboard and corrugating medium. Among the first excursions by Tenneco Packaging into reengineering was a major effort in the molded fiber division.

The time was the summer of 1991, and the locale was Tenneco Packaging's largest molded fiber plant, in Red Bluff, California. At this site, Tenneco Packaging manufactures a variety of products such as produce carriers for apples and molded paper plates. It also produces a significant number of molded fiber egg cartons. In fact, Tenneco Packaging is the dominant supplier of that product on the West Coast. During this time, the company was facing a dilemma. Demand for the molded cartons had increased dramatically compared to the competitive product made from blown polystyrene foam. Both products would carry the eggs from the producer to market, but the more environmentally acceptable recycled paper product produced by Tenneco Packaging had come into greater favor. The rapidly increasing customer interest in this type of product led to significantly greater demands on the production capability of the Red Bluff plant.

Numerous manufacturing improvements were employed to increase capacity during this period, but demand seemed to keep outstripping supply. The process is not overly complex. The raw material is recycled fiber, primarily old newspapers, that is repulped and drawn onto copper dies for forming into the familiar dozen-egg carton. Unfortunately, Red Bluff's ability to add additional lines was limited by space and capital, so the problem became how to extract more output from the existing facilities. In spite of sizable improvements, demand continued to run ahead of supply and customer satisfaction was slipping. As Bill Haser, then plant manager, said in describing the situation, "When you have to ship 5 million cartons the next day, and you only have 2 million on hand, that's a problem."

By the fall of 1991, the problem had become a crisis. Customers were becoming increasingly dissatisfied with Red Bluff's ability to meet the order requirements. "Life was chaotic," related Linda Thoennes, customer service manager. "We spent all our time putting out fires. We were filling orders for whoever screamed the loudest, even if it affected other customers." From the customer's perspective, it was impossible to have hens laying eggs and not have packaging to transport those eggs to market. In the absence of cartons, the egg producer had no choice but to send the product to organizations known as "crackers," which supply separated eggs to bakers and industrial firms that require eggs in their manufacturing. This latter market is less economically attractive to the egg producer.

In spite of continued efforts to meet the demands of the customers, shipments had fallen to all-time lows in terms of on-time delivery and fill rates. Relations continued to deteriorate as Tenneco Packaging made a valiant effort to keep customers supplied, to the point where several large customers threatened to form a cooperative venture and produce their own molded cartons. The division's general manager at the time, Rob Gluskin, recalls that, during this period, he spent 60 percent or more of his time simply trying to mobilize resources to get more product and to mollify an increasingly aggressive and upset clientele. One sign of the depth of the problem was the constant presence of Federal Express trucks in the plant parking lot. Given the limitations of the situation, Gluskin elected to pilot a reengineering effort at Red Bluff in an attempt to correct the condition before a competing plant appeared nearby. To Tenneco Packaging, BPR was an untried process, but the crisis rallied quick support.

A particular condition associated with the production of egg cartons is that two distinct seasonal variations must be covered. Demands peak sharply just prior to the Easter and Christmas seasons. Typically, inventories are prebuilt to cover these peaks, but with the plant running at full capacity, it had little opportunity to continue that practice. The BPR effort was started late in the year, with the executive caveat that the processes had to fully satisfy the Easter peak at the increased demand levels. This objective was tantamount to saying that the effort could not come close to failing. Indeed, it had to be a roaring success, in spite of information available at the time that more than half of all BPR efforts did fail!

During the course of the initial analysis of the as-is conditions, it was quickly determined that the existing processes of order entry and verification, planning and scheduling, and logistics and transportation were hopelessly burdened with manual steps that added little value. These processes also took an excruciating amount of time to complete. The processes contained an enormous number of steps that the analysis team quickly targeted for removal. According to Haser, the order-processing system that had been in place for years had too many duplicate steps and not enough procedures to keep up with high-volume business. As the implementation team reengineered and automated the work flow, and as each new process design was developed, the team also documented substantial opportunities for cycle-time reduction. They clearly saw that the accelerating demands could be met with existing manufacturing capacity if the changed systems could be properly assimilated.

True to the radical nature of most of the early BPR efforts, Tenneco Packaging had to make some difficult decisions. The new processes demanded a dramatic shift in the way information was received and handled. The process steps from order to delivery were reduced by over 35 percent, because the team included only steps that brought accurate order information into the system. Correct specifications, pricing, delivery requirements, and actual usage were required or automatic entry was denied. Personnel involved in handling orders had to learn entirely new procedures and disciplines, and the plant had to adjust to the greater accuracy and timeliness of the orders. As the new procedures were documented and tested, cycle times were reduced but another problem appeared: the computer systems could not accommodate the new processes. An entirely new I/T platform had to be designed and installed rapidly. With the new technology, more steps were taken from the process, resulting in a total reduction of over 60 percent of the involved steps.

The Easter season was met, with outstanding results. The redesigned processes stood the test, as customers received their orders on time, and the possible consortium scrapped its plans for a competitive operation. In addition, other key results were achieved. The number of customer service calls to the plant dropped from a high of 60 percent to less than 1 percent. The inability to find inventory to meet the burgeoning demand ceased to be a problem, and Tenneco Packaging had proved its ability to implement a tool as complex as BPR without the usual first-time difficulties.

The effort put forth by this plant showed that it could find the right solution using BPR. It also demonstrated that it could use I/T to meet both its internal needs and the external needs of the changing market. The plant manager and the division manager also used the effort to break down the functional silos that had previously held onto outdated processes, allowing them to meet and exceed customer demands. It was a win-win-win application.

Summary

BPR is a much-praised, much-maligned, and often-misunderstood tool in the business improvement arsenal. It has proved its ability to deliver radical, positive results, but it fails more than half the time it is used. It is not a magic potion, a panacea, or a technique for easy success. It is a tool that has to be carefully applied to applications that need a dramatic change to meet altered market needs. Like so many faddish practices that are embraced by corporations looking for quick fixes, its use must be approached with caution. To do otherwise is to risk a failure that impinges on further use of the tool. The success stories we have related are intended to be an incentive to use the tool, advisedly, as a powerful means of improving supply chain networks.

Chapter Seven

Advanced Partnering

• •

Supply chain processing can be optimized. Some firms are making decided progress in that direction. These firms begin with a serious dedication to achieving success and then keep the effort alive as part of a continuous improvement process. To guide their journey, they employ a model that has relevance across their particular network of supply with a focus on the market of choice. These organizations exhibit a willingness to accept advice, criticism, and resources from all of the constituents in their supply chain in order to build a better system to create and move goods and services to the ultimate consumer. Using the best improvement tools and techniques in the appropriate locations in the chain, they and their partners redesign current processes to achieve the quantum enhancements that gain a competitive advantage for the supply network.

By adding an understanding of the importance and role of appropriate information systems and technology in supporting any supply chain improvement initiative, these firms implement systems and procedures that truly define the new way of doing business in a supply network. They then work tirelessly to enhance their advantage by seeking innovations that define new method-

• • • •

ologies for satisfying the ultimate consumer while driving the cost of that satisfaction to the lowest possible denominator. Those on the front edge of accomplishment have succeeded in defining new methods of doing business and have supported those methods with equally advanced information technology and systems.

In the previous chapters, we outlined a framework for keeping pace with these front-runners, emphasizing the concept that partnering is the essential ingredient in attainment of real, long-term achievements. In this chapter, we turn our attention to a higher plateau—the advanced techniques that are being developed to move beyond the formation of early, mutually beneficial alliances. The focus will be placed on ways to fit the continuous improvement effort into an action plan that defines the roles and purposes of many concurrent activities, involving the use of cross-organization partnering teams to achieve further enhancements. The goal of such a plan is, of course, to come as close to optimization as possible. As with most partnering efforts, preliminary actions of an advanced nature should begin on the inside and then expand to external areas with suppliers and customers.

Beginning Inside the Organization

Most of the organizations with which we have worked on some type of supply chain initiative have gone through serious downsizing. This has usually yielded short-term benefits by reducing fixed overhead costs. On the positive side, bloated departments have been reduced to a more appropriate level of staffing. Other areas have been sized to match organizational needs. But when we review the one-time write-off costs associated with these downsizings and their later effect on the desire to achieve quantum improvements, we reach two conclusions.

First, we have serious doubts about the long-term payback and validity of such drastic reductions. We fail to see how the organization is stronger overall. Selected areas become more agile. Layers are removed that used to inhibit decision making. Job responsibilities become more defined and a youthful vigor appears.

Following the downsizing, however, we see an absence of the key learning and understanding needed to develop the innovations and techniques that build leading-edge supply chain practices. The remaining employees become so concerned about the possibility of future downsizing that they split their focus between what could be done to attain the desired improvements and just keeping their jobs. The result is far less intensity than the leaders believe exists.

In one organization, a manufacturer of home improvement products, an intense effort to reduce the head count was followed by an equally strenuous effort to find savings that would reduce unit costs to more competitive levels. The people within this firm volunteered or were assigned to improvement action teams that were to find millions of dollars of savings. The charters for the teams were oriented around finding these savings to ensure the firm's survival. In spite of the rhetoric, the attention in these teams' meetings was divided between working on the specific action and discussing rumored further downsizing. The effect was a dramatic slowing of what could have been rapid progress in designing useful changes. We were left wondering if the exercise in reduction accomplished the intended objectives, or if the firm would have been wiser to redeploy the people to appropriate assignments based on the type of prioritized opportunity lists we have referenced previously. The choice can become to do what was being done before with fewer people or do more with the people who are there. We prefer the latter strategy.

Second, we see a hoarding of the important resources that are needed to carry out the many initiatives required in order to reach optimization in a full supply chain network. Talented resources are needed after a head count reduction to fill out teams so that they can find the next level of enhancement that creates, and sustains, the competitive advantage so fiercely desired in today's business arena. But the best talent is carefully guarded by managers who want to have the resources ready when they find a hot project.

In one company we analyzed, a powerful executive had virtual control over all of the engineering talent, which was supposed to be available to the total firm. Unfortunately for the company, this executive insisted on placing the best of the engineers on assignments that only affected the portion of the firm that was directly under his control. The balance of the organization had to scavenge for resources for projects that could have had a major positive impact in other areas. The fact that the company suffered because of this hoarding of resources had no effect on the executive, who showed absolutely no concern for the other sectors.

Under these circumstances, the challenge is to find hidden resources that can be accessed to pursue the list of prioritized opportunities that await the firm seeking competitive advantage. Our thesis is that such resources reside inside the supply chain network, waiting to be mobilized on focused actions. In spite of dramatic downsizing, the first area of such resources can be found in the internal organization among the army of people who can still rise to a special effort when given the proper motivation. They do this especially well when they become part of a focused effort that contains tangible improvement targets of a significant magnitude and impact on the firm.

To access these hidden resources, the first step is to stop focusing on organizational "right-sizing" and identify the driving factors that will gain a competitive edge, in whatever arena the firm focuses on. This exercise establishes the focus for the improvement effort. Most firms have taken the time to develop a survey or benchmarking effort that uses customer input and data-base information to define the elements that drive customer satisfaction in a particular market. From this information, they develop a list of key drivers, usually oriented around profit, customer satisfaction, quality, cycle time, and productivity. They then focus the improvement effort on exceeding benchmark measurements in these drivers to gain the sought-after advantage. They begin this effort inside the organization by describing what the internal needs of the organization might be to meet the customer drivers, and they expand to defining the roles for people, departments, and areas within the firm. The firm moves next to analyzing how members of the internal groups treat each other. Nothing less than a totally frank evaluation takes place in this step, as the various internal constituents assess what is needed and how the supporting service or product is provided across areas of responsibility.

In one instance, we worked with a technical department that

had been reduced in size and was under scrutiny for a further reduction. Although the workers' internal attention was diluted by
the concern for job security, we were able to use internal partnering to prove the need for a redesign of functions to achieve higher
levels of customer satisfaction. The technical group was brought
together and asked to seriously consider the job being done for the
internal customers. Then selected internal customers were asked
to evaluate the job being done for them by the technical services.
The results were so widely different that the technical group
dropped back and redefined their charter. They determined that
they had been very busy supplying services that were not necessary for the well-being of the organization. With the help of the
key customers, a new charter was drawn up to define what the
group could do to add real value. When the exercise was over, it
was discovered that the smaller number of technical members
could accomplish this twice as effectively, as rated by the internal
customers, as before the downsizing.

Successful organizations seriously attack their guarded turf
areas and build a true team effort, thereby tapping the full synergism of their pool of talent. As we studied these groups, we found
a consistent use of a matrix type of management system or shared
resources, which applied the appropriate talents to the highest-
priority actions. Most of the firms that want to gain leading-edge
performance hire, promote, and challenge talented people. The
best go a step further and assign this talent to the most important
actions, regardless of organizational appointment.

To organize and begin such an effort, we recommend the
building of a performance matrix similar to the one described in
Figure 7.1. The key internal drivers are indicated in the first column. For any particular organization, these drivers represent the
factors that are traditionally a part of the continuous improvement process and that have been developed as a result of serious
customer surveys and benchmarking efforts. In a manufacturing
firm, we find such categories as changeover time, line efficiency,
and percentage of returns. These factors relate to the desire to
have a flexible manufacturing system that responds quickly and
without mistakes to changing customer needs. Lost time and work-
men's compensation are finding their way onto these matrices, as

FIGURE 7.1. Matrix of Potential Value: Best in Class Internally.

| | Locations | | | | | |
Key Drivers	City A	City B	City C	City D	Internal Best	System Value
Changeover (Hours)	12	6	10	8	6	$xxx
Line Efficiency	91	92	88	94	94	xxx
Shrinkage (%)	8	12	5	10	5	xxx
Shipping Cost/Unit	$24	$28	$27	$30	$24	xxx
Labor Hours/Unit	1.4	1.2	1.5	1.1	1.1	xxx
Returns (%)	1.5	.92	.75	2.1	.75	xxx
Lost Time Rate	2.2	1.6	1.7	.8	.8	xxx
Workmen's Comp.	$558K	$1,200	$475K	$1,430K	$475K	xxx

Internal Best—Total System Value $xxx

companies also seek to cut costs in areas that are usually given a second level of attention. Service organizations could list reaction times to customer inquiries, number of service responses per employee, favorable ratings for services, number of complaints, and so forth. The idea is to build a matrix that will help to define how to get the best practices in the most important areas.

Companies with multiple locations can array the various sites across the top of the matrix. The illustration in Figure 7.1 has been drawn for a manufacturing operation, but a similar matrix could be developed for a service organization, placing the key service centers across the top. Within the matrix, we have depicted a possible listing of current performance measurements. The observer gets a quick fix on what a total grouping has been doing in the key areas. On the right, the best internal performance is selected from the columnar listings. For example, City B has the lowest changeover time, so six hours is the internal best for that category. City C has the lowest shrinkage factor, so 5 percent is the internal best in that category. By comparing current performance at each location against the best in the category, a firm can quickly determine the opportunity that exists to bring all sites up to the best levels. The column headed "System Value" is intended for entry of the organization-wide savings that would accrue if each location was at the internal best performance level.

Most organizations have this information available and access it in some form for their improvement effort. Few take the time to make a simple array like the one in Figure 7.1 to bring focus to areas where the best practices can be found. The usual disclaimer for not using the array is that differences in the various sites or service centers detract from the usefulness of the data. This reaction overlooks the possible improvements that can be gained by seeking the best practices, which are then reflected in better performance data.

Differences in site characteristics can be allowed for by eliminating certain categories or making adjustments based on legitimate local factors. The purpose is to get a solid fix on what has been accomplished in the key categories at the best locations, and what the immediate value to the firm would be if that performance could be driven across the entire operating system. When these numbers are developed and totaled for all locations, the opportunity is usually quite significant. In one example, we arrayed the information for a seven-plant division of a major food manufacturer. When the best practices were determined and an evaluation made of what the impact would be of getting all locations to those levels, the potential savings for a seven hundred-million-dollar group was found to be close to thirty million dollars annually.

Most leading firms are now willing to also look outside to determine how their performance compares to the best in the industry or the best in their category. Figure 7.2 illustrates a performance matrix that can be developed to find the highest benchmarks for each driving category that can be proved to be attainable anywhere in the industry. This matrix can be used to develop meaningful benchmarks in the key areas, with the focus on competitors and on firms that operate in similar industries or have similar characteristics. This means looking for the best in class in each category, regardless of the business. The final column becomes the potential value of bringing all sites up to the best-in-class level of performance. The grand total for this column is typically quite impressive and can establish the basis for a multiyear improvement effort, as actions are oriented around the highest-value categories in a prioritized system. For our food company, expanding the matrix to best-in-industry benchmarks led to identification of potential savings of nearly fifty million dollars.

As organizations use this type of performance matrix to develop action improvement initiatives, they invariably begin within their organization, developing internal best practices before going to the outside for further improvements. By starting on the inside, they bring existing operations to the best level that can be achieved with current technology and equipment, or with a careful redeployment of people, equipment, and selected new investments. Typically, they find that most of the desired improvements can occur without resorting to major capital investments, as long as the supporting information technology is available. They then benchmark against the best in class, regardless of the industry, in the areas critical to success and competitive advantage. With this information, they set out to exceed the benchmarks and establish new norms for the competition to pursue.

FIGURE 7.2. Matrix of Potential Value: Best in Class Externally.

			Locations						
Key Drivers	City A	City B	City C	City D	Internal Best	System Value	Industry Benchmark	System Value
Changeover (Hours)	12	6	10	8	6	$xxx	.5	$yyy
Line Efficiency	91	92	88	94	94	xxx	98	yyy
Shrinkage (%)	8	12	5	10	5	xxx	4	yyy
Shipping Cost/Unit	$24	$28	$27	$30	$24	xxx	$15	yyy
Labor Hours/Unit	1.4	1.2	1.5	1.1	1.1	xxx	.8	yyy
Returns (%)	1.5	.92	.75	2.1	.75	xxx	.25	yyy
Lost Time Rate	2.2	1.6	1.7	.8	.8	xxx	.20	yyy
Workmen's Comp.	$558K	$1,200	$475K	$1,430K	$475K	xxx	$100K	yyy
				Internal Best—Total System Value		$xxx		$yyy

A simple example would be an organization that wants to have the highest possible customer satisfaction rating in several key areas that are known to differentiate companies in a particular business. Suppose one of the areas identified on the performance matrix as being a weakness is number of customer complaints. The organization applies resources to diligently seek the benchmark that only the absolute best performers can achieve in this category. It then establishes a reasonable goal, at or beyond that level, and sets cross-departmental action teams into motion to develop the means to achieve a new level of performance and a new benchmark. To do so, the firm pools the best talent and focuses intense effort on an action plan that will close the performance gap and set the new benchmark. Typically, it achieves the new targets and immediately begins looking for the next area of competitive advantage. Firms like Motorola, Hewlett-Packard, Toyota, Rubbermaid, Canon, Lands' End, and Xerox stand out as leaders that have parlayed this type of effort to bring their internal operations to unprecedented high levels of performance.

The key is that these leaders take a relentless attitude toward finding the most effective means of doing the necessary work of the business. They look closely at the benchmarks and the identified performance gaps. Care is given to selecting early, high-priority, achievable improvement actions to add impetus to the effort and to show the significance of the potential savings. Because the first efforts are internal, they allow for the complications of chasing best practices in the more controversial areas; they start with initiatives that can test techniques for digging out how certain locations can achieve superior performance in normal operating areas.

With an area selected, such as line efficiency, the team proceeds to make a flowchart of exactly what happens within the organization, both for typical machines and at the best-in-class location. The differences that show up in this early analysis begin to indicate the reason for high and low performances. The variations in some of the areas we have studied have often been extremely large. Similar machines running similar products can result in variations of 40 to 50 percent. When the standard practices that were set for those machines are reviewed, we find a large amount of operator override, which results in wide differences in actual procedures.

Using the flowchart analysis, the team now proceeds to search for the underlying procedures, practices, and local variations that will explain the difference in the level of results. It is crucial in this step to have team members who possess good interviewing techniques and an ability to draw out the people who operate the machines or directly serve the consumer—the ones with the true knowledge of what is happening on the shop floor or in the service center. By probing carefully and doing a lot of analysis and discussion of the findings, the team comes to a determination of the best procedures to be applied across different locations, machines, and crews. New standard procedures are documented, tested, and approved. With diligence, a successful implementation brings the action teams to the best-in-class practices inside their organization across the array of categories shown in the performance matrices.

A key requirement is testing and completing a few internal exercises before venturing outside for advanced partnering opportunities. The firm should move outside only when the technique has been proved successful and team members are comfortable with at least a modified version of what we are suggesting. The internal house should be in order before attempting to build external alliances for competitive advantage.

The secret we have discovered from studying the leaders is that they are impatient with excuses from individual locations, oriented around local conditions. Allowances are made for age of equipment and product mixes, but their drive is to find the best practice and quickly spread that information across the organization. For the leading firms, this means that they have established a means of relentlessly pursuing any idea within the organization that can help at multiple locations. In lesser firms, we find a lot of conversation that implies great cooperation in sharing ideas, particularly with anything of a breakthrough nature or best practice. On closer inspection, however, we find a curious paradox. In spite of the presence of mechanisms for communicating these improvement techniques, a significant percentage of what we define as better practices never gets through these systems. When a particular operation discovers a breakthrough practice, the people sit on the information rather than sharing the news and spreading the benefit across the organization. Whether this happens because of peer pressure to keep the ideas for personal advantage or simply because of the lack of time to communicate the information, the fact is that the firm suffers because beneficial insights are left at individual sites.

The actual entries in the performance matrices have to be of importance to the customers of the firm, internally and externally, and the length of the matrix should depend on the number of key drivers the organization can pursue with current resources. Chasing too many initiatives, especially in the beginning, has already been cited as a pitfall. It is better to be choosy at first and expand with success. As the organization becomes adept at improving the internal drivers with significant results, the performance matrix can be expanded to include additional categories. Figure 7.3 shows the type of additions, usually made for a firm delivering products through a supply chain, that pick up on external customer feedback. By adding these categories to the matrix and developing the order-of-magnitude value of bringing all sites, departments, and locations up to the internal best in class, the firm gets a quick view of what the potential value is for the supply chain improvement process. This is another way of determining what can be added to profits by bringing all parts of the company up to what has been accomplished somewhere in the industry.

As mentioned, the expected caveat for those who oppose this type of exercise will be that all locations are different, as indeed they are. Our experience has proved, however, that they are generally far more similar in basic techniques than is typically accepted. Customers and equipment are different, levels of technical support vary, and skills are widely divergent, but the processes are often quite similar even though they do not show elements of consistency in practice. Each location tends, over the years, to develop a best practice for that location. Improvements across sites are rarely shared, unless this is forced by senior management. We find when we make assessments that bringing visiting members onto the improvement team from other internal locations always leads to identifying better practices unknown to those at the

FIGURE 7.3. Matrix of Performance Value: Best in Class for Customer Drivers.

Locations

	City A	City B	City C	City D	Best-in-Class	System Value
On-Time Delivery	90	88	91	92	92	$xxx
Fill Rate	91	86	85	88	91	xxx
Load Time (Days)	22	15	7	18	7	xxx
New Product Index	2	7	5	4	7	xxx
Quality Index	87	94	88	91	94	xxx
Number of Complaints	42	31	25	46	25	xxx
						$xxx

investigated site, but generally practiced at the visitors' site. By studying all sites to isolate these better techniques, a focused assessment process can result in best practices across the network of sites.

In one example, a major firm offered us the opportunity to look at a particular location in a six-plant system. In this group, the only difference between the plants was the volume; similar materials and machines were used to produce products with similar labels. As part of our normal procedure, the visiting team included experts from the firm, selected from locations other than the one being studied. The firm initially objected to bringing members onto the assessment team from the other plants. Management felt that there would be little difference in the practices, because for a long time the plants had been producing the same products. When we insisted, they reluctantly agreed to bring in what we considered to be key participants from three other locations. These individuals were selected for their particular skills in the areas identified as having the greatest impact on performance (the high-priority categories selected from the performance matrix). As is typical in our assessments, these three outsiders made major contributions to the better procedures that could be practiced at the evaluation site. The order-of-magnitude potential savings from this initial appraisal were five hundred thousand dollars annually at the selected site.

The improvements generated by this type of sharing can be very significant and usually do not require major capital expenditures. By recording simple measurements in the matrices shown in Figures 7.1–7.3, management can quickly highlight where resources should be applied to have the greatest impact on overall performance. The total of the values in the right-hand column of each matrix will also provide an order-of-magnitude number for the total potential for finding the internal best practice. That number varies by the size of the firm, but it typically runs into millions of dollars.

As the organization starts to develop best practices across the organization, advanced partners begin looking for other resources to go even further, to changes that will sustain and enlarge the lead they create over competitors. They start to look outside of the organization to find further possibilities for improvement. They might seek joint improvement projects, look for potential joint investments in machinery and equipment or a focus facility, or develop a world-class information technology system that sets new industry standards. Very little limits the thinking of the frontrunners in using any and all available resources to gain a competitive advantage.

Expanding to Suppliers to Find Resources

With an understanding of what the customer needs and how to bring the producing and servicing sites to the point where they are approaching best practices, the firm is prepared to enlarge the performance matrices presented earlier. Now suppliers are brought into the discussion to evaluate how they can help in reaching the benchmarks identified in each category of importance. The value being sought is that of using the supply base to reach high-priority process improvements more quickly and effectively.

A great deal of effort has been expended in developing help within the supply base. Some results of these efforts were presented in Chapter Four, when we discussed how organizations are using partnering techniques to develop key suppliers from the total supply base. For the purposes of this chapter, we will consider how a few organizations are moving to more advanced arrangements. To provide valuable assistance with this phase of supply chain improvement, we usually suggest that those who are responsible for purchasing and procurement analyze the existing supply base and make a sort, as illustrated in Figure 7.4.

In this triangle, the firm typically arrays the suppliers from bottom to top, starting with the "tolerated" sources. We use this term to refer to the suppliers who enjoy a long-term relationship, but for small- to medium-sized purchases. Most organizations have worked hard to downsize this base in an attempt to save purchasing time and to reduce variation in the products received. Several firms talked to us about reductions of 40 to 50 percent in the number of tolerated sources. Upon closer inspection, however, we found that many of the sources supposedly eliminated from this

FIGURE 7.4.   Typical Supply Base.

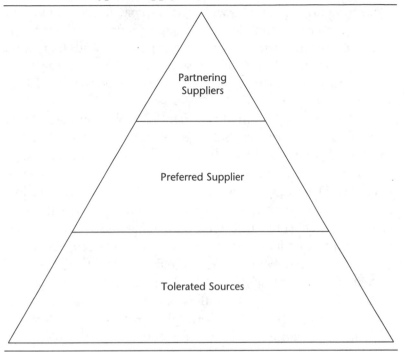

lower supply base have found their way back. When a listing was prepared of all the suppliers that received checks in the previous twelve months, many names showed up that were supposed to have gone. With fewer purchasing personnel and more empowerment, many people are doing buying today, and old sources have a way of finding the means to get back on the supply list. A more important factor to us is that this supply group has little impact on the kind of improvements being sought by most companies chasing today's objectives and probably has less impact than the cost of the reduction effort. For the purposes of supply chain improvement, the lower group can be ignored.

We prefer to move up the triangle to the "preferred supplier" category. In this sector, the firm lists the sources that have satisfied the quality criteria to attain the preferred status. They have verified some criteria that meet minimum quality standards of supply. They have also met all the requirements of the buyer's specifications so that special inspection and checking have become unnecessary. They have demonstrated a willingness to participate in joint improvement efforts and have a history of some significant contributions to the buyer's improvement process. With this group, selection is made of the truly key sources that should be given the opportunity to participate in the highest category, that of partnering supplier.

Within the top portion of the triangle, most companies find a small number of sources that together make a major impact on the cost of goods purchased and the needs of the firm in producing their own products. A firm that has several thousand suppliers overall will have fewer than a hundred in this category. Selections should be made from this grouping of companies that can have a significant impact on costs and performance. Measures of capability and compatibility of vision and business strategies should also be considered before making the final choices. With a list of potential partnering suppliers, the firm next asks for the participation of key executives from these suppliers, in a discussion on how partnering concepts can be implemented for the betterment of both organizations. Typically, a meeting is arranged near the headquarters of the buying group in which senior executives get together, share some of their strategy and philosophy, and agree on how a preliminary relationship can be initiated.

Following such a discussion, we generally see a nearly unanimous agreement to participate by the key suppliers, as long as a reasonable chance exists that they will be treated fairly in partnering with the buying firm. The arrangement next leads to focused meetings, where the attention is placed on initiating joint efforts that will have a high potential payback. With a prioritized list similar to the one we have been discussing, augmented by the suppliers' input, team assignments are made with cross-organizational participation, and process improvement begins in earnest.

Motorola has stood out as a leader in this area by developing leading-edge practices with key suppliers. This firm allows suppliers to take an active role in the design of new products, recommending changes and innovations that will bring already high internal performance levels to new benchmarks that are well beyond current competitive capabilities. Engineering advice is not only accepted; it is sought as the firm allows suppliers to take an active role in suggesting any type of improvement that will enhance performance and cost.

At Honeywell's Golden Valley, Minnesota, plant, selected suppliers have not only been invited to participate in key initiatives; they are also given space inside the building from which to operate. These in-plant suppliers, like forms maker Standard Register and Packaging Corporation of America (PCA), are allowed to create their own orders based on analyzed needs, most of which have been redesigned for better quality and cost. This plant site has fifteen representatives from ten such suppliers, ranging from printed materials to electronics. They occupy cubicles near the production floor, where they work on new product designs alongside the Honeywell teams and modify existing products and procedures to enhance productivity. In time, these on-site, loaned resources begin to think of themselves as extensions of the Honeywell work force.

The *Wall Street Journal* has reported on this type of activity; it cited an interesting variation on the above practice by Apple Computer (Bleakley, 1995, p. A1):

> When Apple Computer Inc. set up partnering deals with suppliers last year to reduce inventories, it gave them production and forecast data they previously didn't have. But "too many people running around would filter information they wanted to hear to get mixed signals," says Shaun Connolly, who designed the system.
>
> So instead of giving suppliers space at its Fountain, Colorado, plant, Apple built a warehouse 12 miles away and arranged for a third party to manage it. The warehouse keeps suppliers' inventory on consignment and tracks shipment on the move, so that Apple has one system to contact if it wants to schedule a production change. Otherwise, Mr. Connolly says, "Everyone has different ways of showing and receiving numbers. We'd have to have five people managing five suppliers." His system, which is saving the plant $10 million a year in inventory costs, will be rolled out at other Apple factories as well, he says.

Purchasing and procurement are areas within most business organizations that are undergoing a dramatic shift in focus, based on the new partnering techniques. A typical manufacturing organization will spend fifty to sixty cents of every dollar of revenue on purchased goods and services. By contrast, within high-efficiency plants today, most firms have reduced labor cost to under a dime, and overhead to similar levels. Under these conditions, management has finally realized the great leverage that a purchasing group can have over total costs. By reducing purchased goods by 5 to 10 percent, a firm stands to make much greater profits than with a similar improvement to labor and overhead. More important, leading firms have learned that key suppliers can make contributions far beyond charging lower prices on their deliveries. They can become major allies in the search for ways to move performance levels to and beyond the benchmarked goals illustrated in the previous action matrices.

At AT&T, the purchasing chief, Daniel Carroll, calls this new initiative "creative collaboration" (Tully, 1995, p. 76). The idea is to help key suppliers "manufacture more efficiently and thereby hold down prices." That is the win situation for AT&T. But in the vein of partnering, AT&T allows these suppliers "a share of the savings." That is the win for the suppliers. One expert, Jack Barry, a former purchasing specialist with Electronic Data Systems Corporation's A. T. Kearney consulting division, predicts a favorable future for those pursuing this type of effort. Barry states, "As we move to a seller's market, companies win by treating suppliers not as adversaries but partners" (Tully, 1995, p. 76).

Logistics has proved to be an extremely fertile area for gaining help from the supply base, and Chapter Eight will be devoted to an analysis of the role this function plays in supply chain optimization. For the purposes of this chapter, we note that suppliers and customers are working diligently to find novel ways of cutting extraneous actions to reduce the inventory, handling, freight, storage, and stocking costs associated with typical supply chains. So many options are developing in the logistics area that only a networking focus will bring about the optimal solutions. Otherwise, local improvements will take place that may simply pass a large part of the logistics cost to other members of the network. Advanced partners always look at this critical area in terms of removing unnecessary costs. The Goodyear arrangement previously cited is one example of firms that have formed joint efforts to reduce handling and delivery costs. Many more stories are developing that demonstrate the savings that can be generated by looking for every possible way to keep handling to a minimum and truck utilization at peak levels.

The partnering techniques that do the most good do not have to be complex. In one recent example, National Semiconductor of Santa Clara, California, worked with a supplier of silicon wafers, Siltec, to cut expenses (Tully, 1995). The case involved the conservation of packing materials. As described by Shawn Tully, "At National's plant in South Portland, Maine, workers on the loading dock used to discard the expensive plastic cassettes the silicon wafers arrived in. Now a giant box sits on the loading dock, already inscribed with the address of Siltec's plant in Salem, Oregon. As workers unload the wafers, they chuck the cassettes into the box. When the box is full, a driver from UPS tapes it shut and carts it off for return to Siltec, which passes to National the resulting savings: more than $300,000 a year" (1995, p. 79).

A firm that stands out as a leader in the partnering field is Allied-Signal. This supplier of automotive, aviation, and other industrial products began its supplier partnering effort by selecting key sources from among its very large supply base. Admittedly, it leveraged its large purchasing power to extract favorable pricing, often in exchange for a sole sourcing position. More important, Allied-Signal did not stop there; it formed joint improvement teams with many of its key sources, to go in search of other savings that could be shared across the relationships. In a typical situation, Allied-Signal would form a council that concentrated on a specific area like packaging, metal parts, or fittings. These councils would be staffed with representatives from within Allied-Signal and the suppliers, who were focused on developing a charter that resulted in the formation of action groups to pursue improvement opportunities in the focus area.

The packaging group, for example, developed a lengthy list of opportunities that came from such focus areas as productivity, quality, engineering, and finance. Figure 7.5 illustrates the format used to develop proposal ideas. Armed with this type of form and the desire to find improvement opportunities, the joint teams would visit a particular site or gather at a mutually agreed-upon location and discuss improvement possibilities together. The best ideas would find their way onto this type of record and were forwarded for review by the joint steering group. With approval, the teams would execute the implementation plan and track the savings. At all times, the emphasis was on how to save money for Allied-Signal. At the same time, as the process matured, the suppliers became adept at suggesting ways to find mutual savings, and Allied-Signal became equally willing to develop these types of initiatives.

Another firm that was involved in advanced partnering long before it became the vogue is Corning. This New York–based manufacturer of glass products has for many years been the absolute leader in developing and succeeding with alliances. Even though its focus was strategic in nature, Corning was forging long-term alliances with the Dow Chemical Company, Owens-Illinois, Asahi Glass Co., and others to meet market needs long before many of the other leaders became interested in developing mutually beneficial arrangements with supporting organizations. These arrangements were made to build on Corning's strong research and development practices, while concentrating on core strengths. The partnering firms brought selling and marketing strengths that enhanced the mutual relationship. Out of these alliances came a willingness to look at any partnering arrangement that made sense, even if it was necessary to share profits. Risk sharing, an ingredient that keeps many large firms from pursuing such arrangements, was always a part of these deals. Along the way the lesson of trust, which is held in the highest regard by Corning, became the key ingredient holding the alliances together. This element has to be cultivated by organizations that want to make partnering a part of their survival arsenal.

The purchasing literature continues to document a growing awareness of the powerful impact that using suppliers wisely can have on a firm's profits. As these stories appear, an increasing number of them demonstrate how the normal leveraging of position for volume is giving way to a more enlightened approach in

FIGURE 7.5. Improvement Opportunity Format.

Allied-Signal/PCA
Cost Reduction Proposal

Allied-Signal Location: _____   Date Submitted: _____
PCA Location: _____   Submitted by: _____

Current Situation:	Proposed Improvement:	Approved:
		Division _____
		Plant _____
		Supplier _____
		Rejected: _____
		Comments _____
		Further Review: _____

Cost Information:

	Current	Proposed	Initial Investment	Estimated Cost Savings:
• Material	_____	_____	_____	Material: _____
• Labor	_____	_____	_____	Labor: _____
• Process	_____	_____	_____	Process: _____
				Total _____

Implementation Plan:

• Necessary Actions: _____
• Person(s) Responsible: _____
• Estimated Date of Implementation: _____
• Actual Date of Implementation: _____

Note: PCA = Packaging Corporation of America.

which business organizations seriously look at the supply base as an extension of their internal resources. With a willingness to listen to this added resource and share the fruits of a joint effort, they are going out selectively to key suppliers to look for ways to enhance productivity, quality, cost, and service to the ultimate customer. This is the logical first step in advanced partnering.

Becoming Proactive with Selected Customers

With the network working well internally, and with a cadre of key suppliers helping to find and implement further savings, the firm is ready for advanced partnering with customers. Now members of the upstream portion of the supply network look over the customer lists to find the select group of key customers to whom they want to offer opportunities for enhancing relationships. Specifically, they go in search of potential long-term partnering accounts where mutual advantages can be developed.

Suppliers at the very front end of the network might select manufacturers that have a strategic fit. A producer of grain like Cargill might select a food manufacturer such as Sara Lee Corporation, Pillsbury, or General Mills as having the potential for a long-term strategic fit. Aluminum Company of America selected Anheuser-Busch Companies, the world's largest user of aluminum cans, as a strategic partner. Du Pont has worked for a number of years with Milliken & Company to develop partnering arrangements that made sense for both firms.

A manufacturer might select a distributor or retailer as a strategic fit. The alliance between Procter & Gamble and Wal-Mart has been well documented in this area. Other alliances have included Bo Rics Beauty Products, Inc., and Kmart, and Starbucks Coffee and Dominick's Finer Foods. The concept is to find customers who both provide the chance to establish long-term working relationships that help the strategic plan and provide the opportunity to find significant supply chain savings. A special preference can be given to finding retailers who offer space in which a manufacturer can go directly to the consumers, as in the Bo Rics and Starbucks cases.

As relationships develop, interesting opportunities to share resources appear. For example, a small number of firms are finding beneficial results by joining forces to make joint sales presentations. Manufacturers have been successful in using this technique, which includes helpful suppliers, to enhance their presentations to key accounts. A plastics manufacturer might include a supplier of resins and styrene, in order to discuss the best possible formulations and materials to meet a particular customer's needs. The manufacturer may also suggest a totally new material or a means of forming products that is based on knowledge gleaned from experience in a foreign country. PCA used this technique successfully with representatives of the Dow Chemical Company. A metal or plastics supplier could participate with an appliance manufacturer to discuss design innovations and improvements that might result from changed specifications, or a novel application that was successful in another industry.

When Whirlpool was under a short time constraint to present a new line of refrigerators to a major customer, Sears, it enlisted the help of a software supplier. Together, the group made a presentation that used virtual reality techniques to demonstrate the new line on a computer network. The buyers at Sears were regaled with a show on the interactive computer network they were watching that took them into a kitchen to use the innovative features contained in the new line of products.

Subassembly suppliers may participate with manufacturers to help customers consider engineering changes or product innovations that can enhance the final product. By meeting together, they save the usual third-party communication that invariably includes filtering and selectivity in message transmission. Cycle times are also improved, because the parties that will be involved sit together and review exactly what the best way is to get products through the supply chain and meet ultimate consumer demands.

The real purpose of customer partnering is to find, as closely as possible, the best way to meet current market needs. An advanced partnering firm might use the resources available in the supply-to-manufacture network to extend its relationship to selected customers. Together, the group searches for further enhancements in the spirit of mutual advantage. Scarce, talented resources are shared in high-priority improvement opportunities for a specific customer or market segment, and the resultant savings are also shared, as an incentive to find more opportunities.

Advanced partnering can be conducted in many ways, and the book is still being written on successful efforts. Following are some of the techniques we favor:

- Valuable engineering and design talent is shared, with a focus on projects having a clearly defined market advantage. This sharing goes beyond the typical electronic linkages available through computer-aided systems. It includes joint identification of development and improvement projects and the assignment of joint resources of the highest caliber to work out innovative and salable solutions. The automobile industry is becoming very adept at making use of supplier talent to design and engineer features on new cars.

- Joint training sessions are held in which the most skilled trainer conducts the program. Problem solving, the latest business planning techniques, skills applied to planning and scheduling tools, and use of logistics capabilities are a few of the potential subjects to be covered at such sessions. Here the cost is spread over a larger group and the skilled facilitator conducts workshops designed to create interactive skills and foster joint activities when the sessions are concluded. The foremost purpose, however, remains the development of techniques through which the parties share valuable resources to search out opportunities that have meaning to the final customer. The Atlanta Consulting Group stands out as an organization adept at conducting these joint partnering activities between suppliers and customers.

- Joint executive overviews are made that focus on leading practices that could benefit both parties. The supplier and the customer arrange high-level briefing sessions on what they each know to be the best practices they have observed or used. Such sessions can also contain data on leading-edge concepts that might be pursued on a joint basis. We have personally conducted such overviews for major clients who wanted a periodic review, to keep pace with what other organizations were doing to sustain a competitive edge and to benchmark their current practices against global best-practice activities.

- Pilot studies intended to test improvement ideas are usually avoided because of the difficulty of arranging and funding them. But under conditions of advanced partnering, the firms can quickly set up a test to find the real benefits of an idea. The test, or pilot model, can provide invaluable insights about the real potential for introducing an innovative solution and can test out unproved ideas.

- Joint investments in focused facilities or specialized equipment are a natural means of capitalizing on an advanced partnering arrangement. We have seen original partnering efforts that focused on improving packaging costs lead to an investment in leading-edge machines to bring packaging speeds and efficiencies to levels that were double or triple the previous best performances. The cost of the new machinery was shared, as were the savings from the new results.

- Experiments using qualified third-party organizations can be set up to test new technologies or systems. As firms involved in supply chains look, for example, at finding the most effective EDI techniques, partnering arrangements allow the supplier and the customer to involve third parties who have the hardware and software knowledge and capability to arrange test sites, with the proper planning and experimental equipment. These arrangements can then be used to test a wide variety of potential enhancements.

One technique that has been particularly useful in developing high-return cooperative efforts is putting together an abstract list of activities that could be improved through joint effort, with order-of-magnitude paybacks for the effort. The purpose of such a list is to stimulate the supplier and the customer to think about the actions that offer the most value. Figure 7.6 is an illustration of what we call an "order-to-cash" model, which can be used to develop such an understanding. Across the top of this chart is an order fulfillment cycle. This process can contain the elements noted or can be modified for any particular business. This example is a typical one for a manufacturing organization.

FIGURE 7.6. Order-to-Cash Model.

Order Fulfillment Cycle

Identify and Forecast Market	Generate Orders	Enter Orders	Procure Materials and Manage Inventory	Schedule Production	Manufacture and Fabricate Components Process Orders	Manage Inventory	Assemble and Test Product	Package Warehouse and Ship	Invoice and Collect	Customer Support and Warranty
Identify New Business Opportunities	Forecast Analysis	Order Entry	Forecast Material Requirements	BPICS MRP I MRP II SAP	Stage Materials for Manufacturing Order	Release Manufacturing Order	Assemble Product	Kit, Pack, Crate and Process Documents	Invoice	Manage Warranty and Returns
Forecast and Manage Customer Orders	Negotiate Price	Establish Correct Pricing	Procure Materials	Planning Capacity Utilization	Build Units and Components	Sequence "Pick" List	Test Product, Quality Review	Manage Freight and Distribute	Accounts Receivable (A/R)	Post Sales and Service Field Application
Respond to Customer Requirements	Obtain Orders	Track Report and Expedite Orders	Set and Meet Quality Parameters	Perform Setup and Changeover	Inspect Parts	Pull and Pack	Troubleshoot	Manage Shipping Documents	Collect	Respond to Customer Requests
Data-Based Marketing Assistance	Manage Goodwill	Resolution of Order Issues	Coordinate Specifications	Emergency Changes	Troubleshoot	Inventory Reduction Plans	Feedback to Product Development	Ship Products		
Key Account Analysis	Sales Support	Change Existing Order	Expedite Critical Items	Expedite and Troubleshoot Orders				Manage Finished Goods		
Competitive Analysis	Credit Verification		Accounts Payable (A/P)							
	Agents: Broker Orders		Supplier Partnering							

BPICS = Business Process and Inventory Control System
MRP I = Materials Resource Planning
MRP II = Materials Requirement Planning
SAP = Systems Application Processes

The process begins with identifying and forecasting the market. It could start with product design or development, but we generally choose to start by looking at the market. Each element in the process is then subdivided into the key supporting activities, listed below it, that are necessary for the element to be done effectively. Such areas as forecasting and managing customer orders are listed as key parts of the first element in this cycle. Performing a key account analysis and analyzing the competition are also listed. These lists can be as long or short as necessary for each element in the process cycle, although the items should be specific to the type of business being studied.

The next step in this model is to generate orders. Under it, we include such activities as performing a forecast analysis, negotiating pricing, obtaining orders, verifying credit, and providing sales support. Again, the items should be specific to the needs of the customer to whom the proactive partnering support is being offered. The actual matrix should never be completed in isolation; instead, it should be codeveloped, with a great deal of input from those deeply involved in the various activities.

The process cycle continues, through order entry to customer support and warranty. Under each element are listed the activities that are important to performing that element, as well as areas in which current improvement initiatives are under way. The use of this tool then progresses with two assumptions:

1. Any firm of any size has a number of important initiatives already started, in various stages of temporary completion. It would be hard, and deemed inappropriate, to divert attention away from the best efforts, so joint initiatives should be focused on building further enhancements.
2. No organization has all of the resources necessary to complete all of the valuable initiatives at the present time.

With this understanding, the partner-to-be approaches the customer on the basis of sharing resources through the partnering arrangement to help implement the model. The first step is to eliminate activities in the matrix where sufficient resources are already being applied, where the current work has shown definite signs of being dramatically improved, or where extra resources would really get in the way of successfully completing the current improvement effort.

It is a waste of valuable resources to focus on areas that are already on the way to significant improvement. Rather, the focus in using joint resources is on important areas of potential improvement where limited or no resources are now being applied. If customer partnering is to have real meaning, the joint effort has to fit some sort of overall plan or model and have a direct match with strategic intent. The order-to-cash model is one way to focus the collective thinking and ensure that a critical fit is being developed.

Now the crucial step is to establish the potential savings to be derived from joint actions in the areas selected for a joint improvement effort. As the matrix becomes filled, certain areas will be deemed to have so little value that they will be relegated to the lowest priority. The participants are seeking the few areas of highest potential and highest priority where it makes sense to focus scarce, key talent for a joint improvement effort.

Building a Total Supply Chain Experiment

When a serious partnering group has completed a preliminary analysis to isolate the actions with the highest potential, we always suggest setting up a total supply chain experiment to test the working relationship and the partnering techniques across the supply chain. Using the interenterprise model, we have helped several organizations to arrange partnering pilots that begin with raw materials or primary supplies, proceed through the manufacturing phase, pass on through distribution, and reach the retail outlet for purchase by an ultimate consumer.

The parties sit together and draw up process maps of the flow of forecasts, goods and services, and important data between their organizations. They then look at how savings opportunities can be created across the full network. A wealth of material is discussed and shared with the other parties in the linking chains. The caveat is that they must be prepared to share as much as they receive. This is the essence of advanced partnering.

A typical first session is very tentative in such relationships, but selecting the right participants usually leads quickly to sharing existing improvement techniques. From this point, the groups can escalate to drawing up some sort of prioritized list of potential joint actions. A few special actions are selected from this list that could result in significant benefits from participation across organizations. Key talent is then allocated to these actions, again on an experimental or model basis, and action plans are drawn up, with timetables and order-of-magnitude savings. By tracking the results of the model, the participating organizations should be able to determine rather quickly if the joint effort has real potential.

The Need for Customized Solutions

Each network is unique and requires the development of solutions that meet its specific needs. We strongly advise that any actions that are taken to develop optimized solutions to a network system should focus on developing customized answers from the redesigned processes. In this manner, the actual needs of the network will be met and a competitive advantage created that will be difficult to duplicate. More generic solutions are too easily copied, and the advantage gained is fleeting.

For example, customized solutions require that any supporting technology be designed to fit the new processes and solutions. The tendency we see most often is for networks to jump to the use of existing hardware, and particularly to off-the-shelf software. While some very powerful programs are available, we have seen very few that can be plugged into system networks, particularly those that have recently been reengineered, and still work at high levels of effectiveness. More often, we find that remedial help has to be sent in to do the customizing that is necessary to make off-the-shelf software work as intended.

An area that is especially prone to this type of oversight is that of planning, scheduling, and logistics. An abundance of programs exist that are intended to help manufacturers improve their efficiency in these sectors. Programs intended to improve forecasting accuracy, plan material resources needs, develop production plans, schedule operations with multiple machining capabilities, and arrange for warehousing and distribution stand out as ones that often are not customized for the problem at hand. We have found that some of the greatest demand for remedial help is to clean up the messes that have been generated in these sectors and get the systems to work as planned.

Action Study: The Dominick's Experiment

Beginning in November 1993, we participated in a series of meetings with Nick Ciaccio, vice president of logistics for Dominick's Finer Foods. Dominick's is a Chicago-based grocery firm with over one hundred stores within a thirty-five-mile radius of the city of Chicago. The firm is noted for its leading-edge position among its peers in the industry and its willingness to look at initiatives that will build improvements into its systems.

The initial meetings centered on how a new initiative could be generated that would be low in cost to Dominick's, build on its existing effort to develop efficient consumer response techniques, and span an interenterprise model specifically designed for the retail grocery business. Because of progress Dominick's had been making, Ciaccio was particularly interested in building onto the existing initiatives rather than forging totally new systems.

By March 1994, a decision had been made to attempt a pilot effort based on the interenterprise solution. Using that model, shown in Figure 7.7, PCA was asked to participate on the supply side; Sara Lee Corporation's bakery division was invited to participate as the manufacturer. Dominick's agreed to supply resources from its own distribution center and to let its stores be the retail focal point. Letters of invitation to participate in a pilot effort were sent to appropriate individuals in each of these companies, and acceptances were received.

On March 23, 1994, a "supply chain proof of concept" was formulated to add potential discussion topics, and sent to each participant. (See Figure 7.8.) This format was used, in conjunction with a questionnaire that asked for objectives and expected deliverables, to solicit preliminary ideas from the group as to the validity of the pilot and the areas that should be explored together.

FIGURE 7.7.   The Interenterprise Network Solution.

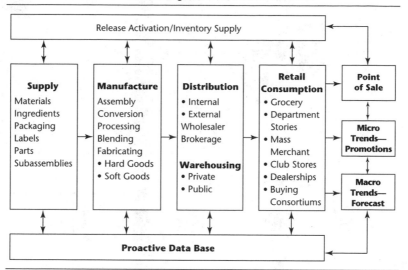

On May 5, 1994, participants from each company met to discuss the pilot. Consensus was quickly received on the validity of the exercise, and the group set about to draw a process map of the interconnecting relationships. A brainstorming session led to the creation of over fifty potential improvement areas. These possibilities were distilled into twenty-nine key issues, and five action teams were proposed. These teams were subsequently reduced to three as functions were combined. The primary teams were formed to (1) develop a flowchart for the order-handling process and analyze it, (2) develop a flowchart for the forecasting and planning process and analyze it, and (3) develop EDIs that would benefit the pilot members.

Team assignments were made, timetables were established, and the group set about to find savings across the full network. A list of preliminary benefits was developed that included reduced inventory, transportation costs, and administration costs and improved service levels and cash flows. A list was formulated of process data that were deemed to be available, including product, packaging, quantities, dates, price and cost, promotional impact, and customer or consumer characteristics.

When the teams met to develop their proposed actions, each team developed a high-level map of the process it was considering. Some of these maps were extremely lengthy, but for the first time, the players vividly saw the interconnection of activities needed to supply the product to the stores.

FIGURE 7.8. Interenterprise Supply Chain Proof of Concept—Issues.

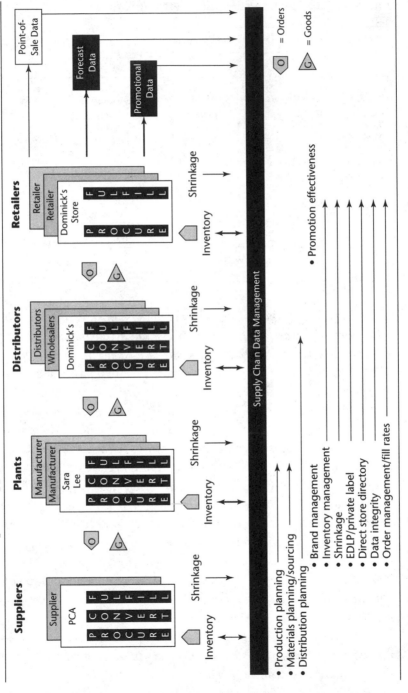

Note: EDLP = everyday low price.

The length of some of these cycles proved to be the first area of enlight-enment, far exceeding the perceptions brought to the exercise. Some of the key areas for improvement that surfaced fairly rapidly were:

- *Fill rates of less than 100 percent, in spite of the presence of over one hundred days of inventory*
- *A lack of consistency in measuring fill rates*
- *Products that were handled in the system a large number of times*
- *Redundant or unnecessary inspections*
- *Too much paperwork between participants*
- *Too many out-of-stock items*
- *The need for improvements in handling promotional items*
- *The need to define and implement the most beneficial EDI transactions*
- *The need to reduce damage spoils, shrinkage, overshipments, and ma-terial system wastes*
- *The need for a more effective system for handling reconciliations, or making them superfluous*
- *Elimination or better use of duplicate infrastructures in the distribu-tion network*
- *The need to improve the flaws in POS data and use this information for stock replenishment*
- *Increasing the accuracy of distribution center forecasting*

From these possibilities and others, the teams developed the list of ac-tion team deliverables shown in Figure 7.9. The product selected for the actual study was pies, to keep the sku's to a manageable level, and to cover a product that had seasonal variations and high inventory costs, due to the need for freezing the manufactured product. Each company supplied resources to each team, and review steps were established to monitor progress and offer advice to the team leaders. A typical format for pursu-ing the team assignment is illustrated in Figure 7.10. From these joint meetings came a defined scope for the action, a list of specific objectives, a time line for completion, recommended improvements, and a cost-benefit analysis that always included the order-of-magnitude payback for the ac-tions and a means of measuring progress.

A sample output from one of the teams is depicted in Figure 7.11. The team that was forecasting and planning flow determined from its mapping

FIGURE 7.9. Action Team Deliverable Contents.

- Description/Scope
- Objective
- Activities/Work Plan/Approach
- Resource Needs
- Milestones/Key Dates
- Next Steps
- Order-of-Magnitude Savings
- How Savings Are Shared

FIGURE 7.10. Interenterprise Supply Chain Proof of Concept—Approach.

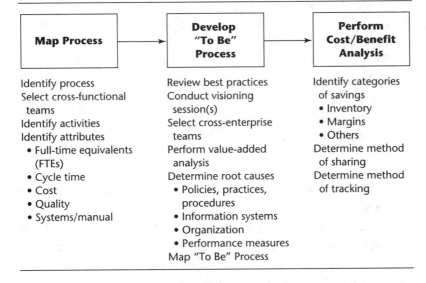

Map Process	**Develop "To Be" Process**	**Perform Cost/Benefit Analysis**
Identify process	Review best practices	Identify categories
Select cross-functional	Conduct visioning	of savings
teams	session(s)	• Inventory
Identify activities	Select cross-enterprise	• Margins
Identify attributes	teams	• Others
• Full-time equivalents	Perform value-added	Determine method
(FTEs)	analysis	of sharing
• Cycle time	Determine root causes	Determine method
• Cost	• Policies, practices,	of tracking
• Quality	procedures	
• Systems/manual	• Information systems	
	• Organization	
	• Performance measures	
	Map "To Be" Process	

exercise that 158 days of lead time were required from the beginning to the end of the cycle to get the packaged pies onto the shelves at the Dominick's stores. With this type of information, the teams also prepared a to-do list of actions that was intended to redesign the process for beneficial results. Among the key findings from these joint actions were the presence of three weeks of safety inventory, to cover inadequacies in the existing network, and the need to make costly changes to the Sara Lee manufacturing schedules because of variations caused by promotional activities.

FIGURE 7.11. Interenterprise Supply Chain Proof of Concept—Forecasting and Planning Flow.

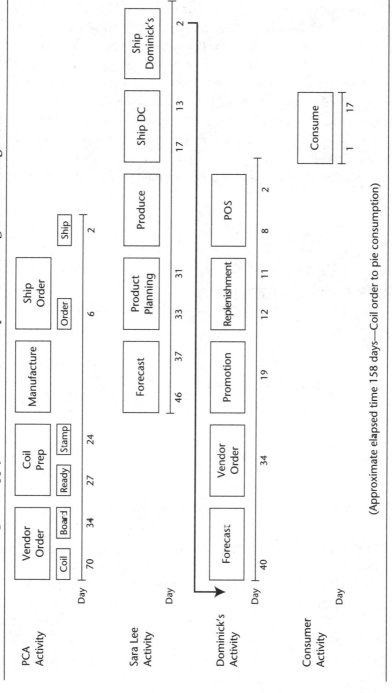

(Approximate elapsed time 158 days—Coil order to pie consumption)

Note: PCA = Packaging Corporation of America; DC = distribution center; POS = point of sale.

The latter situation was particularly relevant. In essence, the manufacturing response necessary to make the promotions work caused variances in the production schedules; these schedules, which had been established on the basis of earlier forecasts, were overridden by promotions that introduced significant extra costs. It was discovered that a much closer liaison could be created between the parties to feed back information on the promotions and mitigate the need to make so many adjustments. The variations could be lessened or eliminated by closer coordination of data on the timing of the promotions and feedback on how the promotions were progressing.

Following the analysis and recommendations, these preliminary results were identified:

- *The opportunity to eliminate one week's inventory per firm, a reduction of three weeks' inventory*
- *Cycle-time improvements of 40 to 60 percent*
- *Elimination of paperwork and redundancy*
- *Better promotion management and a decrease in manufacturing variability*

More important, PCA, Sara Lee, and Dominick's have established a strong working relationship, built on a new feeling of trust, that can be expanded as they seek other areas of potential improvement together. This is the essence of their advanced partnering exercise. The cost was kept to a minimum, and with the potential savings, future work together now takes on a self-funding characteristic.

Summary

With virtually every company involved in supply chain networks chasing continuous improvement, a wide range of enhancements is possible. Unfortunately, most of these improvements are developed in isolation. We have demonstrated how the potential that resides in the possible pooling of resources and ideas can be drawn out to extract a total supply chain solution. We also have illustrated how much deeper the analysis can go and how synergistic action can lead to savings that will exceed those of even the best of firms working only with internal resources.

By forming the kind of teaming efforts described, previously aloof or adversarial participants find numerous ways to share resources, focus their efforts on mutually beneficial innovations, and, together, redesign the way their supply chains function. The results can be savings far beyond those achievable with current initiatives. Implementation of these efforts can also lead to a network advantage that will be hard to replicate by organizations working in isolation.

A better way to find systems improvement does exist. It begins with the selection of key allies and the development of a pilot model to test the ability of the alliance to work out custom-designed, mutually beneficial solutions. Success is then measured by the enhancements that are developed and the savings that are shared across the relationship.

Chapter Eight

Logistics as the Driving Force

The process of approaching optimization in a supply chain begins when an organization decides to pursue improvement across its full supply network, using whatever resources are appropriate for gaining a competitive advantage. As companies find that they can reach out and partner with willing suppliers and customers, they discover a wealth of resources that can be focused on serious improvement actions. For organizations that have followed this course, one lesson appears to take on special significance: logistics is an area that offers a sure route to improvement opportunities.

Once the area of responsibility of those charged with keeping transportation costs as low as possible, the field of logistics has matured into an important business practice that should be placed only in the hands of skilled professionals. The logistics revolution started nearly a decade ago. Fueled by a few visionaries who insisted on increasing emphasis on what was typically a subordinated effort, logistics is now producing the levels of earnings enhancement predicted by those early advocates. The field is now beginning to proliferate with individuals eager to enter the arena and seek even further enhancement. Donald J. Bowersox, a noted expert on logistics from Michigan State University, states, "There have been more changes in the process of logistics during the past ten years than in all decades combined since the industrial revolution" (Bowersox, 1995).

From its former position as an afterthought of senior management, logistics has taken on a new importance. Corporations are learning how to tailor their logistics network to provide new delivery systems for their products and services. In the process, they have discovered that logistics can be a valuable tool for increasing customer satisfaction. An article in *Harvard Business Review* identifies logistics as having the potential "to become the next governing element of strategy as an inventive way of creating value for customers, an immediate source of savings, an important discipline on marketing, and a critical extension of production flexibility" (Fuller, O'Conor, and Rawlinson, 1993).

The Role of Logistics

Logistics is the nitty-gritty operation of packaging, unitizing, loading, unloading, transporting, moving, storing, sorting, and reloading products. It also includes keeping track of these actions, providing valuable data on location and storage, and finding ways to constantly improve on handling, inventory, warehousing, and transit costs. Logistics took on a cost in 1993 of $670 billion, or 10.5 percent of the U.S. gross domestic product.

This basic business requirement has recently been the subject of serious study by supply chain organizations. When Kurt Salmon Associates was engaged by the major grocery manufacturers to study costs embedded in the supply chain (discussed in Chapter Two), they concluded that a significant portion of the potential thirty billion dollars of savings was to be found in eliminating unnecessary logistic steps or extraneous inventories. Our own studies determined that basic products sold from the shelves of grocery outlets could take 137 days from the receipt of orders by the suppliers until the goods were placed on those shelves. We found that by focusing the right effort on that chain of events, potential reductions in cycle times and inventories ranged from 30 to 75 percent. With possible gains of this magnitude, we expect that the rate of interest in logistic opportunities will continue to accelerate.

To reap the potential benefits from a deep scrutiny of logistics in a supply chain, the traditional ways that companies linked in those chains interact must be reconsidered and redesigned under the scrutiny of a total system model. Traditional methods, procedures, and processes must be studied with the intention of finding full-network benefits, rather than suboptimizing the whole for the benefit of a single player.

A better way of handling logistic needs is to seek the savings potential in concert, using the combined resources of all the parties in a supply network. Organizations that are bound together by the chain of events from supply to consumption combine forces to determine how they interact now. They then redesign the total process to become the most effective system possible. The extracted savings are shared across the chain, and all parties benefit, including the ultimate consumer.

The technology necessary to implement these redesigned systems is readily available. It resides in the minds of skilled practitioners and their information technology supporters, who can take the reengineered processes and custom-design the supporting hardware and software platforms. The real limiting factor is getting parties to fully participate in a total system effort. In our discussions with many senior managers in the retail sector of the supply chain, we found the overwhelming attitude to be that potential logistics savings are large and real, but limited by the lack of cooperative efforts beyond those that benefit a single entity.

We have asked many in this group of executives, "If you had a trillion dollars to purchase an entire supply chain, would you still manage the group of operations as if they were independent companies?" The response we consistently receive is, "Of course not. I would act as if it were one organization." Jack Welch echoes this sentiment as he continues to forge the General Electric attitude. As chairman, he has focused his organization on managing the total supply chain, from the initial supplier through to the ultimate customer, as if the total entity were owned by GE. In the culture of this multinational company, not treating the other players in the supply chain as part of the same company is considered a serious act of impropriety. This is the way participants in a supply network looking for serious improvements in logistics have to treat each other. Anything less leads to suboptimization.

Satisfying Customer Demand with Optimal Costs

Trying to move toward optimal costs by compressing logistic processes that transcend the boundaries of multiple companies, as well as by dealing with the ever-increasing size of geographic networks, is far easier to formulate than to execute. But with the immense payback available through reengineering intracompany systems, the rewards are definitely worth the effort. Through a redesigned system that illustrates the possibilities of using logistics as a profit and service enhancer, Global Computer Parts, Inc. (GCP) (a fictitious name) has been able to make dramatic gains. Its story relates more to using logistics as a driver than to advanced partnering, but it serves to show the potential in this key area of business practice. The results of GCP's improvement process include cutting standard delivery time by 45 percent, reducing the cost of distribution by 2.5 percent, and increasing sales by 35 percent. The company achieved these results by taking a hard look at its total logistics network. It closed six warehouses, previously deemed important to distributing their products, and now airfreights its microchips to customers worldwide through a new 150,000-square-foot facility in Hong Kong.

GCP, headquartered in Burbank, California, is the fifth largest U.S. computer parts company, with annual sales of $2.0 billion. In a twelve-month cycle, GCP will ship 2.5 billion semiconductors and 3.5 billion transistors and diodes to 4,000 worldwide locations. GCP's supply system is shown in Figure 8.1. Through this network, the firm does 45 percent of its business in the Americas, 20 percent in Europe, 10 percent in Japan, and 25 percent in Southeast Asia.

GCP had concentrated for some time on improving costs and quality across its supply network, and it made substantial progress

FIGURE **8.1.** Market Channels.

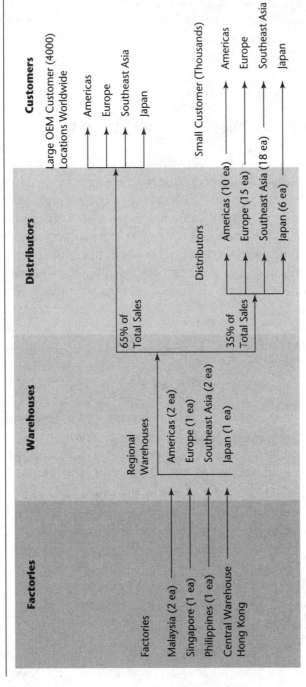

OEM = Original Equipment Manufacturer

in those areas. As the firm went into the 1990s, it determined, with important input from its customers, that the next level of improvement should come in the areas of time and systems integration. To enhance performance in these areas, GCP drew a model of the order-to-delivery process, depicted in condensed form in Figure 8.2. A percentage of the total time to complete the normal cycle was indicated for each segment of the process. An analysis was then started to determine how to shrink the total time and improve the effectiveness of this process. The original purpose was to increase customer service, but financial opportunities quickly appeared.

In 1994, GCP's worldwide semiconductor sales were $100 billion. Semiconductor customers retained forty-six days of inventory, valued at $12.5 billion. GCP calculated that if inventories could be reduced to seven days, the industry savings would be $2 billion. This level of savings would provide benefits for everyone involved in the improvement process and would enhance GCP's position with the customer base. The challenge was how to transform the existing manufacturing-to-delivery system, shown in Figure 8.3, into a more effective system that would approach the seven-day target. Figure 8.3 outlines the six fabrication sites, the six assembly locations, the original five distribution centers, and the customer regions through which the finished product was shipped. The difficulty with the original network is shown in Figure 8.4. Products could flow from fabrication to assembly through thirty-one channels, or "lanes," thirty-two lanes were present between assembly and distribution, and an undocumented number existed between the distribution centers and all the end users.

To expedite the delivery system, air delivery was used for many shipments, but with a cycle that was longer than desired. Figure 8.5 illustrates the original air delivery system. It had a six- to fifteen-day range for transfer of product from the factory to the distributor, and a one- to six-day cycle to move the goods to the customer. Not only was this cycle considered to be too long; it had many inconsistencies and did not meet customer expectations. Factors such as order completeness, accuracy of items ordered, and administrative quality caused an excessive amount of controversy and reconciliation.

FIGURE 8.2. Order-to-Delivery Process, Showing How Time-Definite Logistics Dominates Quick Delivery.

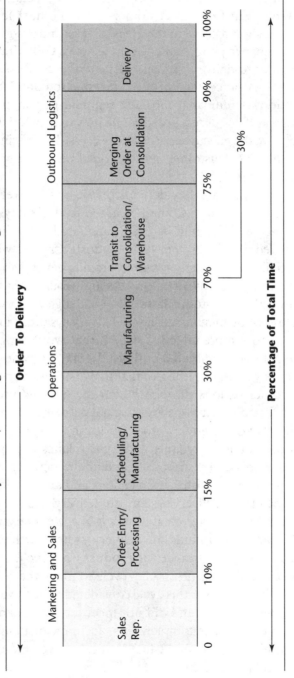

FIGURE 8.3. Original Manufacturing-to-Delivery System.

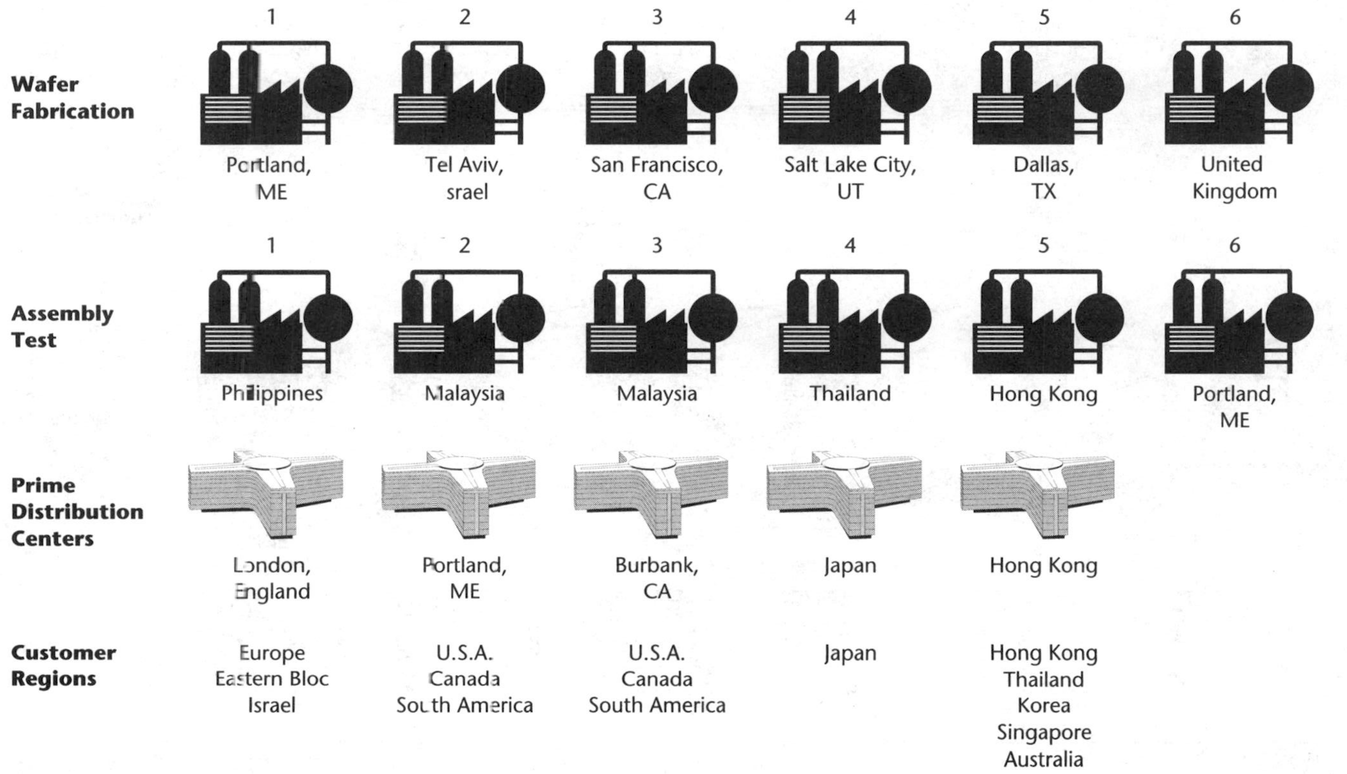

Wafer Fabrication

1	2	3	4	5	6
Portland, ME	Tel Aviv, Israel	San Francisco, CA	Salt Lake City, UT	Dallas, TX	United Kingdom

Assembly Test

1	2	3	4	5	6
Philippines	Malaysia	Malaysia	Thailand	Hong Kong	Portland, ME

Prime Distribution Centers

London, England	Portland, ME	Burbank, CA	Japan	Hong Kong

Customer Regions

Europe Eastern Bloc Israel	U.S.A. Canada South America	U.S.A. Canada South America	Japan	Hong Kong Thailand Korea Singapore Australia

FIGURE 8.4. The Challenge

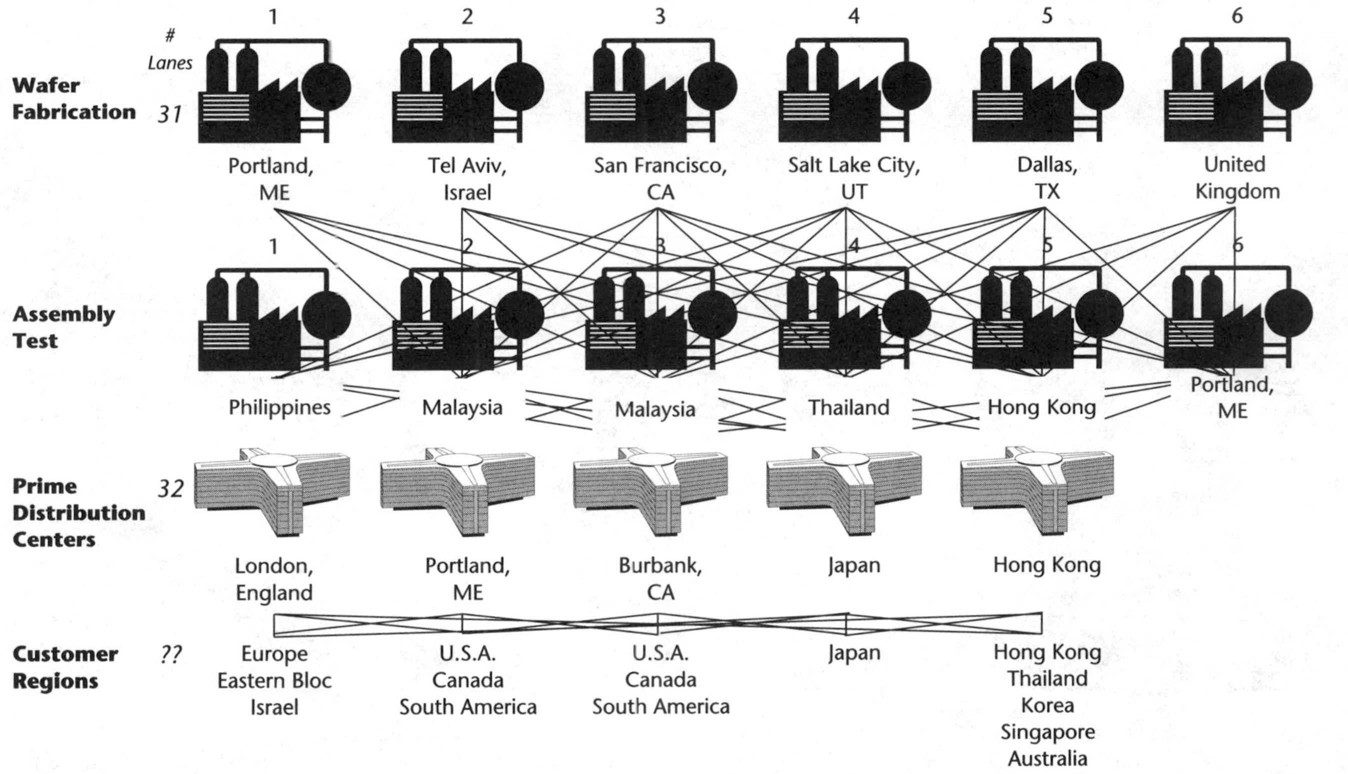

	# Lanes	1	2	3	4	5	6
Wafer Fabrication	31	Portland, ME	Tel Aviv, Israel	San Francisco, CA	Salt Lake City, UT	Dallas, TX	United Kingdom
Assembly Test		Philippines	Malaysia	Malaysia	Thailand	Hong Kong	Portland, ME
Prime Distribution Centers	32	London, England	Portland, ME	Burbank, CA	Japan	Hong Kong	
Customer Regions	??	Europe / Eastern Bloc / Israel	U.S.A. / Canada / South America	U.S.A. / Canada / South America	Japan	Hong Kong / Thailand / Korea / Singapore / Australia	

FIGURE 8.5. GCP's Current System.

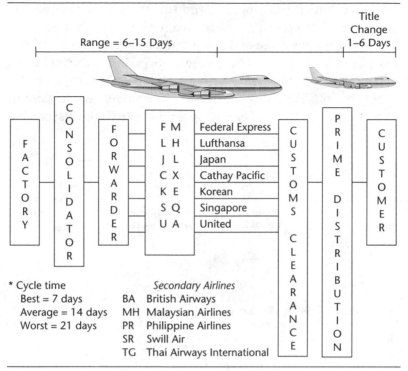

* Cycle time
  Best = 7 days
  Average = 14 days
  Worst = 21 days

Secondary Airlines
BA British Airways
MH Malaysian Airlines
PR Philippine Airlines
SR Swill Air
TG Thai Airways International

GCP determined that the process had to be redesigned and improved. The desired state would have to meet these criteria:

- A simpler process
- One integrated operating scenario
- Highest levels of service satisfaction
- Lowest overall customer service costs of logistics
- Reduced inventory levels
- Logistics cycle reduced to greater flexibility and response of two business days

The logistics team developed a logistics evaluation process to guide the improvement effort they anticipated would be necessary. This guide is shown in Figure 8.6. The year-long project began with a clarification of strategy and goals; went through baseline development and recommendations for improvement from suppliers, customers, distributors, and transportation experts; and concluded with acceptance of the team recommendations.

The areas considered and the way the team reached its conclusions are shown in the matrix in Figure 8.7. Here the team looked at options regarding possible changes to the distribution part of the supply system. The options considered were to remain the same or to consider several ways of having a third party take responsibil-

FIGURE 8.6. Logistics Evaluation Process.

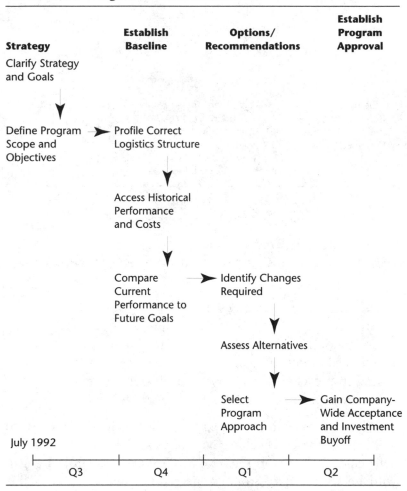

FIGURE 8.7.   Options Matrix.

Expectations	Status Quo	3rd-Party Warehouse	GCP Warehouse Integrated 3rd-Party	Total Integrated 3rd Party	Ship from Work in Process 3rd-Party Source
1. Consistent—100% on time	0	+	++	++	+
2. Short cycle time—1 to 2 days drives toward theoretical best	0	+	++	++	+
3. Flexibility, deliver to line— hourly delivery	+	+	++	++	0
4. Visibility—EDI tracking	++	++	++	++	++
5. Responsiveness feedback (demand change, communications)	+	+	++	++	+
6. Seamless process					
7. Total cost (inventory, investment, profitable)	0	++	+	++	++
	+	++	+	+	+
8. Samples—2 days	0	+	+	+	+
9. Special—Pack/combines	+	+	+	+	+
10. Reduce inventory	+	+	+	+	++
11. Quality—Zero defects	+	+	++	++	+
Administration	+	+	++	++	+
Standardization/Systems					
Totals	9	15	19	20	14

+ = Positive capability   0 = Neutral capability

ity for this function. A "+" on the matrix indicates a positive capability in meeting the expectations from the change exercise. With this type of information, the team selected the option with the highest capability. It was recommended and approved, and a decision was made "to create a third-party customized, high-quality, totally integrated distribution system that exceeds GCP's cost and service expectations while providing our customers with a competitive advantage."

To implement this decision, GCP went through five phases of change:

1. It redesigned the global logistics process and established a pilot warehouse in Hong Kong, as the most logical site for a single distribution center.

2. The Hong Kong warehouse was developed into a state-of-the-art centralized distribution center, and the goods in the other plant warehouses were consolidated into this center.
3. Systems were developed to move products directly from the distribution center to the customer's dock, with most products going by airfreight.
4. GCP consolidated what remained of the regional warehouses under the third-party management.
5. The distributors' inventories were consolidated and transferred to the third-party organization.

Figure 8.8 describes the redesigned and reconfigured system and lists some of the important results. The key feature was a cycle time of less than four days and nearly forty-eight hours from factory to customer dock. The major program expectations were achieved, as indicated in Figure 8.9. Additional features and advantages included the following:

FIGURE 8.8. GCP's Future System (Program Phases 1–4).

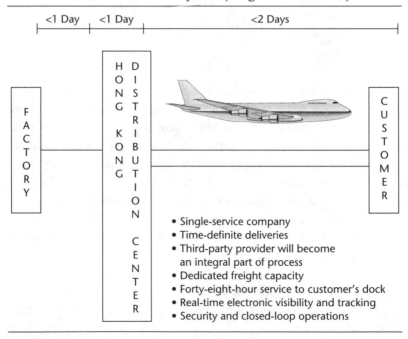

|<1 Day | <1 Day | <2 Days |

FACTORY

HONG KONG DISTRIBUTION CENTER

CUSTOMER

- Single-service company
- Time-definite deliveries
- Third-party provider will become an integral part of process
- Dedicated freight capacity
- Forty-eight-hour service to customer's dock
- Real-time electronic visibility and tracking
- Security and closed-loop operations

- A global integrated supply system was established.
- Time-definite delivery was a feature of the system.
- Consistency of delivery was greatly improved.
- Cycle times were dramatically reduced.
- Supply chain logistics were considerably simplified.
- The new network was supported with a state-of-the-art information system.
- GCP's vision to be the best in class was achieved.

To make such dramatic strides generally requires a change of paradigms for management in which logistics is moved to the forefront of important initiatives. This type of focus has proved fruitful for most of the firms we have studied, especially companies like GCP. In the past, shipping, warehousing, inventory levels, and their associated costs were more or less overlooked, because they were driven by production needs and not customer demands. With an insistence on cost reduction and quicker response, the

FIGURE 8.9. Major Program Expectations.

Key Indexes	Program Start 1992	Current Progress 1994	Program Expectation (End 1996)
Administrative Quality Parts per Million	700	200	5
Days: Average cycle time 98th percentile cycle time	14 21	7 14	3 4
Distribution Cost as a Percentage of Sales	3.0	2.0	<1.6
Distribution Employees National FLS—Federal Express	831 0	379 192	181 225
Sales per Year	**$1,400M**	**$2.0M**	**$3,000M**

emerging focus in logistics is on areas that help the total supply network, including:

- Measurement of raw materials, work in progress, and finished goods
- Palletizing and pallet costs
- Labor and cost of moving to and keeping in storage
- Unloading and receiving
- Order picking and loading
- Packaging and wrapping
- Paperwork and data integrity
- Handling throughout the system
- Warehousing
- Transportation
- Forecasting accuracy
- Planning and scheduling
- Order status and expediting data
- Promotional response

From work in these important areas has come the desired cost savings that promote the drive for further improvement. With customer satisfaction appearing as the ultimate scorecard for measuring success, the effort is now becoming synthesized and expanded into key initiatives, with joint efforts concentrating on advancing the enhancements that a logistics assessment can develop across a full supply network. Leading firms have serious efforts under way in several areas of focus.

High-Integrity, Error-Free Systems

The one factor of paramount importance to the retailers with whom we have had discussions is that manufacturers and distributors should have the correct priorities. Upstream constituents should know at all times what product they have and where it is in the system. They should also be able to make fail-safe commitments concerning supply. An inability to get the goods they want upsets retailers less than having to rely on unfulfilled commitments and false promises. It is better to know that a shipment

will be late or will not be delivered than to be waiting to fulfill a
retail promise without having the goods in the correct amount at
the time of need. Some emerging logistics systems are being built
to be very flexible and to make commitments that can be accomplished with integrity and without errors. To do this, a system is
needed that provides instantaneous information of a highly accurate nature on what is in the pipeline.

Minimal System Inventories

"Cut my inventories; keep them until I need them!" has become
a battle cry in supply chain networks. Fulfilling that request allows the retailer to reduce a burdensome need for working capital, but it does little to extract total system costs. When leaders
work together across previously adversarial lines, they remove the
need to keep anything but minimal safety stock in inventory. Designing a system that has the necessary information flow and
works smoothly between constituents allows inventory to be dramatically reduced across the network, while still maintaining
high customer satisfaction ratings; it also reduces the network requirement for working capital invested in inventory. The process
requires interaction of all the supply chain participants, focused
on optimized conditions. This is the essence of network savings.
The alternative is for manufacturers to accept the push-back from
retailers to cover inventory costs, and for the retailers to find out
later that they are still absorbing these costs in the prices of their
purchases.

Short Cycle Times

The move to more flexible manufacturing systems began over ten
years ago, when a few firms saw the potential advantage of being
able to meet the demands of ever-changing markets without over-
inflating the cost of this quick response. By working diligently to
reduce setup and changeover times and to install innovative systems and procedures, these companies created a communication
network that was in close, accurate touch with real customer
needs, achieving new, shorter lead and response times. This trend

has progressed to the stage where it has become a basic requirement for supply chain interaction to have some way to react to demands for short cycle times. To react to the needs of retailers, it is essential to have a flexible supply system that can match the movement of products with fickle market conditions, a constant flow of promotional deals, and the need to meet the more concise requirements of micromarket responses to local constituencies. A major portion of the emerging logistics effort is focused on bringing to the absolute minimum the time from packaging the goods to placing them on display.

Utilization of Investment

"Use that equipment or get rid of it!" That is another battle cry, as organizations in the supply chain seek to maximize the return on their invested capital. Funds for new infrastructure are always at a premium, because of the many choices for investment. Most firms have a request list that greatly exceeds their available capital. An area where particular emphasis has been placed on utilization of equipment is transportation. Historically, firms relied on their own fleets of tractors and trailers to transport materials and products to their customers. Now they are questioning the costs embedded in acquiring and maintaining these fleets and are asking how effectively they are used. This investigation begins with a thorough assessment of truck utilization. Every part of the empty trailer is an opportunity waiting to be filled. This requires taking a hard look at unit loads, palletizing, loading, and mixing loads. Clever options can be considered to mix loads in order to keep equipment as fully utilized as possible. This consideration also opens the possibility of pooling loads with suppliers and customers. By enlarging the number of products that can go into a trailer, the logistician can increase the possibility of filling the cube inside the trailer. Computer software is available to assist this effort.

Fleets are shared and back-hauls (where loads are solicited to put into otherwise empty trailers returning to home depots) are used fairly extensively by supply chain optimization leaders to take advantage of available equipment. The most dramatic move is outsourcing. In this instance, one or more members of the supply chain call in a third-party organization that has recognized expertise in the transportation area, which then takes charge of the function. Tight demands are typically placed on such arrangements, but the savings and the ability to free the manufacturer to concentrate on other, core issues usually make such alliances feasible. Warehousing has become another area in which these third-party arrangements are gaining in popularity. A costly part of the logistics system is placed in the hands of an outsourcing firm that is more capable of performing at nearly optimum levels, while freeing the manufacturer to concentrate on higher-priority improvement actions.

Innovations

At the center of the emerging focus on logistics in the supply chain is a consistent emphasis on the need to be innovative. The old ways of getting materials, supplies, products, and goods to market have to be challenged to find new, better ways. So many of the existing systems are steeped in traditional practices that it is difficult to transform a network. It has become almost mandatory to inspire a transformation by demonstrating innovations that change one segment of a typical network. Only a few years ago, networks introduced the idea of cross-docking, moving products across loading docks without having to put them into storage first; this captured the imagination of a few innovators willing to try what was then a novel innovation. Now many firms in supply chain activities have some portion of their products moving across loading docks without having to be put first into storage. Direct store delivery is also gaining in popularity as modern versions of the idea are introduced, and now the innovation is being tested by an enlarged base of potential users.

Service Through Enhanced Transportation Networks

One industry that has seen a win-lose mentality applied to logistics is the transportation sector. An indispensable part of the system for moving goods to consumption, the industry has gone through many changes as deregulation has affected the way deliveries are made. At the same time, most manufacturers were seeking reductions in their internal production costs, so many of them looked at transportation as an area that might offer sizable savings. By comparing their internal costs against the potential of using outside carriers, which were now free to charge whatever rates they chose, a number of firms elected to transfer their transportation needs to outside organizations.

The trend has continued, but recently it has taken a more sophisticated approach: firms are now looking for ways to use transportation as a tool in their drive to find an effective supply network that also offers customer satisfaction features. To find advanced methods, they have gone outside the box that normally defines logistics and transportation to focus their delivery methodology on using transportation as a competitive tool. Those that moved quickly established a leadership position that will be difficult for their followers to meet.

Federal Express and United Parcel Service serve as examples of organizations that have used guaranteed delivery to create an entirely new business service environment. IBM felt so secure with this type of service that it now allows Federal Express to warehouse and transport maintenance parts to locations all over the world. Roadway Services, Schneider Logistics Inc., Yellow Freight System, and other transportation firms are developing the next state-of-the-art methods and systems to use transportation as a vehicle to enhance supply chain effectiveness.

As this type of service increases, transportation service firms are finding that it takes more than offering new delivery features to succeed. Electronic capabilities have to be exploited to speed delivery and ensure accuracy of information. EDI has become the key enabler. This use of electronic data has been one way that Roadway Services has achieved what it terms an EDI "maturity model." The model consists of four states (Csvany, 1994, p. 4):

1. *Internal EDI:* This feature provides the ability for employees to electronically gain access to order status anytime. Voice response can be used to send valuable information on freight rates, routing information, and the location of shipments to

anyone who has a touch-tone telephone and the correct security password. Without such accessing and monitoring ability, significant loss of productivity becomes a critical issue.

2. *External EDI:* This feature allows Roadway and its customers to share information via EDI connections. Transporters and their customers typically use their own proprietary systems, which do not communicate with each other. Roadway has shown partnering customers that, by adopting existing industry standards, they can easily communicate with little to no investment in new equipment or software development. Now the network goes beyond tracking trucks and orders to expediting, changing, and setting routes. End customers can be linked into this network to provide full system access to communication.

3. *Sharing information:* This stage is different from step 2 in that information passes in both directions. It also takes EDI to a higher level; transportation firms share their developments to the point of offering software that helps in the exchange of data to improve logistics tracking and analysis.

4. *Leveraging information sharing:* This stage brings the interchange to the level of partnering, where joint efforts at reengineering the processes can be engaged in for mutual benefit.

EDI, of course, is only successful when the process changes that are necessary to create an efficient system are worked out in advance. If this is not done, the result is just a sloppy system that works more quickly. Schneider, another major national transportation firm, has been at work in this area, particularly with Spartan Food Services, the large Michigan-based distributor, wholesaler, and retail grocery chain. These two organizations began by questioning how they could develop the most efficient transfer of products from Spartan's many manufacturing suppliers into their distribution centers. This alliance differs from most of those developed in the supply chain because it focused on upstream interactions from the manufacturer to the distributor. The organizations took a hard look at the as-is condition and isolated several nonvalue-adding activities. The first target for improvement was the delay time associated with loading and unloading; they then looked at pallet exchange and "touch freight," the amount of time spent handling loads. Their interaction is an example of what can be accomplished when traditional adversaries learn to cooperate and diagnose areas of potential savings.

During their diagnosis, they made certain assumptions that ran counter to traditional logistics thinking:

- Drivers are not free labor, so their time should be effectively spent delivering loads.
- Drivers have a schedule that needs to be kept.
- Drivers are not second-class citizens, but valuable assets in the logistics chain. They should be used to the best advantage in their position in the supply network.

The allies next selected some issues that would drive their process redesign. They challenged unloading allowances, the use of slip sheets underneath the loads to assist in pallet-load handling, customer pickup practices, the use of driver assistance (particularly the practice of using "lumpers," or free-lance help), and transfer delays. The analysis led to several pertinent redesign conclusions:

- All carriers should be unloaded on time. This requires a strong discipline for both the shipper and the receiver.
- Quality standards should be met on every shipment, eliminating the need for incoming inspection and facilitating the unloading process.
- Customer pickup allowances must be consistent in relation to prepaid freight rates, so time is not wasted in nonvalue-adding arguments.
- Suppliers should be accountable for being on time for scheduled docking times, to smooth the flow of incoming and outgoing movements at the distribution centers and to avoid delaying other parties in the typical unloading queue.
- The receiver should be accountable for unloading the trailers; the driver should be responsible for driving.
- Carriers should notify the distribution center of any late arrivals prior to their scheduled dock time, so that unavoidable adjustments can be planned rather than forced.
- At the distribution center, these times should be set for unloading: palletized freight, 45 minutes; slip sheet freight, 75 to 90 minutes; and floor load freight, 120 to 180 minutes.

Applying operating procedures that derived from their redesign, the allies worked the joint handling and transportation
system down to such tight standards that turnaround times are
among the lowest in the industry. Thirty-minute unloading se-
quences are not unusual within the new system. Communication
links are state of the art as Spartan insists on meeting docking
slots, charging for late arrivals, and maintaining nearly perfect
loading conditions. Spartan has assumed the responsibility for all
unloading features, spending its time and effort to create the most
efficient conditions possible at its distribution centers. It also
places high expectations on carriers such as Schneider to do their
part to make the transfer of goods as efficient as possible using
today's technology. No margin is allowed for sloppy practices in
the system; this is an acceptable premise for both parties, because
the result has been the achievement of targets and a dramatic improvement in service levels.

Other industries are making equally impressive gains. Compaq
Computer Corporation has built a reputation for creating state-of-
the-art equipment in a market where product life cycles continue
to dramatically decrease. It has been able to keep pace with
growth in its business without making major logistic expenditures.
Since 1991, Compaq has multiplied its production and kept up
with delivery demands without adding any new factory or warehousing floor space. The company has sustained or increased
service levels without major capital investment by constantly redesigning its logistics network to meet revenue growth. Laura
Ashley, the well-known producer of ladies' garments, turns inventory roughly ten times each year, a rate five times greater than
the rate three years before, since installing new information technology solutions and consolidating its warehouses. The Saturn division of General Motors, known for its world-class logistics systems, links suppliers and factories so that information flow is
facilitated across the full network. The result is that dealers turn
their inventories over three hundred times a year.

In Japan, where space is at a premium, a customer who wishes
to purchase a bicycle goes to a store that literally has no stock, not
even a floor model. Instead of the traditional approach of placing
the individual on several floor models to identify likes and dislikes,
at these retail locations the customer is placed on a machine that

measures and records relevant data regarding leg thrust, weight, and certain other preferences. The machine designs a custom order that is reviewed instantaneously with the customer. When the customer agrees to purchase the bicycle, the order is automatically transmitted to the factory for manufacturing.

Outsourcing as an Effective Concept

Organizations that lack the core competency, resources, or inclination to study improvements to their internal logistics system have another alternative. Within the logistics networks many applications of outsourcing can be found. Firms are questioning why they must try to develop leading-edge practices in every area when some areas are better left to organizations with specialized capabilities. By outsourcing, they can apply their scarce resources to strengthening core expertise. In the transportation arena, many firms have begun to outsource their transportation needs. In many instances, firms decided that their core competency was manufacturing, and not handling a fleet of tractors and trailers and dealing with unionized drivers.

From these successes, transportation firms turned their attention to other areas in the supply chain where using outside sources seemed to be a reasonable choice and offered the chance to get a fresh insight from another firm's best practices. They determined what core competencies should continue to receive internal support and where an outside partnering firm could do other functions more efficiently and effectively, without jeopardizing the firm's long-term interests. The result has been a streamlining of functions, built around keeping the most important activities in the hands of qualified internal resources, with peripheral work being performed by external sources. Firms using this technique have outsourced accounting functions such as accounts payables, call center customer service, credit analysis, and billing. After a close look at distribution channels, other companies have engaged third-party firms to handle warehousing, delivery, and restocking. Now organizations are receiving their information technology, telephone and communication services, and other noncore functions from external firms that complement the organization strengths. Firms that have done this analysis and decided to keep all functions in-house still agree that the exercise of benchmarking their practices against those who specialize in these functions was beneficial.

As an example of the value of outsourcing, some innovators are helping to improve supply chains by taking an intensive look at reducing the size of the inventories that support supply networks. In the grocery industry, where mass merchandisers and club formats have captured more than a fourth of the total market, the ability to find alternative ways to provide efficient store replenishments, without excess inventory and safety stock, has become a core issue. As the desire to remove nonvalue-adding activities from interactions becomes more intense, manufacturers, distributors, and retailers have turned to innovative companies that offer cost-saving alternatives.

Earlier in this chapter, we spoke of the relationship between IBM and Federal Express. IBM recognized that it was not in the transportation business and that although transportation was vitally important in delivering service to its customers, this was not a core function of the company. IBM also recognized that it obtained little value from having IBM personnel move products from one location to another. On the other hand, they saw several businesses that performed these tasks continuously and did them in an exceptional manner, providing excellent service at a profit.

This made sense and became the impetus for a review of outsourcing. We find that this scenario is generally present when decisions are made to move functions to an external source. Organizations review a particular area to see if performing that function internally:

1. Adds value to the core products or services supplied to their customer base
2. Is or is not a core competence of the company
3. Could be assumed more effectively by another firm that has developed an exceptional practice in the considered area
4. Requires costs that could be improved by using an external resource to perform the function more effectively

With answers to these questions, a firm is in a position to decide whether outsourcing is the right thing to do.

Effectiveness of Direct Store Delivery

Once the decision has been made to keep a portion of the supply chain functions inside or pass them on to outside professionals, a few areas can still be considered for further improvement effort within the supply chain. One area that offers potential is that of direct store delivery (DSD), which extends the manufacturer's role in the supply chain beyond the normal production cycle. Under DSD, the manufacturer takes responsibility for the delivery and merchandising of products in the retail outlets. Originally, this concept evolved to meet the needs of products with a short shelf life like bread and snack foods, but it has been extended to include products where the manufacturers control distribution. The manufacturers ensure sales by providing direct deliveries that they control, and the retailers eliminate the cost of pickup and delivery and of stocking shelves, while receiving a consistent, fresh product.

Once they gain a foothold in the stores, DSD manufacturers soon learn how to use their position to merchandise their product through direct use of the retailers' shelves. It is a labor-intensive effort, but the result is generally justified on the basis of the sales position it secures. DSD adds as much as two to three times the cost of conventional deliveries to the supply network through the use of special delivery trucks and route sales representatives and through the cost of the restocking. Nonetheless, it is a prevalent practice that is much in need of reengineering to reduce the cost to the system.

This improvement can start with the paper transactions that surround DSD arrangements. A typical grocery retailing system, for example, may have more than three hundred DSD suppliers; they make up fewer than 20 percent of all suppliers, but they generate almost 90 percent of all invoices that must be processed. Although these suppliers will create 60 to 70 percent of the deductions that must be tracked, they still account for only one third of the product moved through grocery systems.

What are the typical steps in this system and how can they be improved? Giant Food, the large grocery retailer, has worked out a model that sets a leading-edge standard for others. It developed its improved system with the help of such partnering manufacturers as Frito-Lay, Coca-Cola, and RJR Nabisco. Giant determined that paper invoices in its system were exceeding 1.5 million per year, more than 30,000 per week. All of these invoices were being processed manually. Handwritten invoices with poor legibility were prevalent, creating significant levels of incoming errors in the system. Invoice corrections and extensions were also done manually, a labor-intensive, nonvalue-adding practice. Unauthorized products were getting into the stores through DSD. Invoices were lost in the stores or en route, requiring a lot of manual retracing and reconciliation, and no standards were in effect for handling credit merchandise. Also, many of the invoicing disputes were not identified until after the billing cycle.

For these and many other reasons, Giant decided to attack the amount of paper in these arrangements and design a better system. To do so, an electronic invoice trail was established. Route drivers were equipped with hand-held computers that could be connected with store computers, creating an EDI system for invoicing. Adjustments to receiving quantities were quickly verified and automatically updated in the system, and acknowledgments were sent back to the route person via computer. With this improved interchange, the accounts payable system validated invoices overnight. All EDI invoices were then uploaded at the headquarters site at the end of the day. Invoices were verified, posting was done to the general ledger, and remittance advice was prepared and sent to the supplier. To close the transaction loop, an electronic funds transfer was authorized, with invoices held electronically for easy access and audit purposes.

The savings came from many areas. Paper flow from the many mail rooms was dramatically reduced and the need to prove that deliveries had been made was eliminated. Error-prone manual systems and procedures were automated in a virtually error-free environment. Discrepancies were dramatically reduced, and deductions were minimized. Eleven suppliers worked in the paperless system, eliminating over 450,000 paper invoices. Giant continues to look for additional partnering accounts within its DSD network to achieve the critical mass that can dramatically improve the overall costs of a DSD network. This partnering effort with

DSD suppliers has been successful in improving a very traditional system, illustrating the kind of improvements that can be generated with an inspired joint effort.

Summary

If one thing is clear in the field of logistics, it is that the world as it was known will never be the same again. Too much has positively affected this area. Participants who were early in applying new paradigms and redesigning their logistics networks have found an advantage over the slower competitors. These leaders are forging further advantages through new techniques, information technology, and partnering concepts. The need to meet shifting global priorities and customer demands does not pose a problem for them.

The emerging issues that will dominate the future logistics landscape and offer the next opportunities are:

1. How to achieve standardization, simplification, and compliance in an environment that is becoming increasingly structural and operationally complex
2. How to negate years of operating under the win-lose mentality that has hindered progress toward more effective systems, and how to move to a network built on trust and mutual benefit
3. What structure to put in place to manage a logistics system in the new environment of increased demands for speed, accuracy, and quickest response
4. How to shift those who manage the logistics function away from shipping and transportation to a holistic approach that includes forecasting, purchasing, planning, and selective outsourcing of services that can be done better externally

These and other questions must be answered as consideration is given to the supply systems of the future. Logistics must play a key role in these systems. It has become a link to the process improvements that have been conducted primarily inside organizations. These improvements must now be chained together with suppliers and customers in a partnership in order to obtain the best overall supply network. Logistics is the major catalyst around which to build that partnering effort.

Chapter Nine

Creating the Virtual Network

· ·

As firms seek to gain an advantage over their competitors in the future through optimization of the supply chain, management has to consider the trends in all the major segments of its supply network. Our studies and interviews strongly suggest that two major scenarios exist, creating a business dichotomy for the future. Organizations will have the choice of being significant global players, meeting all the risks with the ability to conduct business on a large international scope, or of being in a strong niche position, where particular advantages create a specific customer base that keeps them viable. Organizations trapped in the middle of this dichotomy will find it difficult to sustain their future in the pressure to achieve outstanding competence in one of these two areas. Additionally, without the presence of competitive strength based on leading-edge supply capabilities, preeminent customer satisfaction, and the best possible supporting linkages across the full supply chain, their future will indeed be at risk, regardless of what strategic position they take.

Potential customers and suppliers span most of the globe. Each year, the opportunity increases to engage in commerce in new nations. Firms are now spending significant time and resources to study these new markets and to find out how to integrate them profitably into their existing supply and distribution systems. They must understand a wide variety of cultures, track important economic and political trends, monitor competitive action, and design supply networks that optimize the activities contained in the system of choice. This requires them to meet current needs while building the supply network of the future. We see this network emerging as a seamless system of competing organizations in which a virtual network has been created—spanning full supply, from raw materials to consumption—supported by nothing less than a proactive, real-time information technology system, with a focus on delivering unprecedented high levels of customer satisfaction. This represents a radical departure from the silo mentality practiced by current organizations. Firms that are linked together in this manner will command a distinct advantage in the markets of the future.

In this chapter, we will focus on how these virtual networks will develop for both types of business situations, global and niche, and on the elements of success they will contain. Some of what we discuss has already been implemented, but opportunity still beckons those who want to create a system with the greatest competitive advantage. An enormous opportunity exists for organizations to build supply networks that contain features far beyond those available in most current global and niche systems.

The Supply Chain of Tomorrow

Many business organizations are already at work creating what is being termed the "virtual organization," a seamless system of interacting parts spanning multiple organizations that work together so well that the firm establishes a competitive advantage by providing the ultimate in customer satisfaction in the shortest possible cycle times. In the process, these firms are building strength in their core competencies and contracting out noncritical functions they have found other organizations can perform better, faster, and at less cost. They are not admitting incapacity, but rather recognizing that some skills are better acquired than developed. Also, because of technological changes in some noncore areas that are vital to success, they are viewed as being better suited to development by others who are more directly in contact with the areas of expertise being considered. The continuing evolution of communications technology, for example, makes that area a prime target for outside assistance, for a firm to remain on the front edge in terms of speed, features, accuracy, flexibility, and cost. Future business organizations will be this type of hybrid association, with a core strength unit surrounded by interacting entities focused on necessary support functions. To the customers, such an organization will appear as a seamless system providing the goods and services they need.

As firms create their virtual organizations, they also concentrate on building total network strength by partnering with other firms to address the market opportunities of the future. These alliances can be temporary or long-term, but they are built with the intention of sharing resources to solidify a competitive advantage into the future. An example of a short-term arrangement would be the collaboration between Apple Computer, IBM, and Motorola to develop a microprocessor and operating system for the next generation of personal computers. A long-term example would be the alliances formed by Corning that have been in effect for many years and that still serve as a means of jointly sustaining a market position.

A midrange alliance might focus on the core competencies of organizations across a supply chain; partnering arrangements could be worked out to let the best units perform the necessary linked actions, instead of each unit trying to do its own. Having external specialists perform, within a seamless network, the functions in which the main industry player does not have a core competency makes sense in the effort to build strength into the network. Such functions as accounting, logistics, transportation, fleet management, and administrative services can be performed by others while attention and valuable resources are focused on the core business, thereby bringing the best value to the customer. This type of partnering should be particularly appealing to the niche players, who can never build the same kind of departmental strength as larger firms. Instead, they must concentrate on the areas of expertise that set them apart and establish their advantage over larger competitors. For these organizations, alliances with third-party groups, which provide necessary functions that cannot be supported internally, are beneficial. However, they must avoid being so dependent on these third-party providers that losing their priority with them puts their customers' satisfaction at risk.

The longer-term emphasis, and the one most likely to dominate advanced supply chains, will be on the virtual network. With computers of the correct size and configuration to fit the exact needs of the users, and with enabling software at the heart of the system, all the communications needed to support the chosen customer base at the highest possible levels of satisfaction will be built into this network. Short cycles with the most rapid responses will prevail. The network will be seamless: all constituencies will know how and when to react to create a customer-friendly network, virtually free of errors and waste, with the highest-quality standards maintained as a natural way to do business. Size will not be an inhibiting factor; the niche players will use the same techniques to focus their network toward the customer base that needs their particular product or services. Pioneering work is being conducted in this area by Xerox, Motorola, Canon, Bell Canada Enterprises, GTE Corporation, and other forward-looking organizations. Their focus is on defining clearly what the customer of the future will consider valuable and then creating the system that best satisfies that demand. Smaller firms are building an equally strong base of operations by establishing niche positions in computer software, logistics and warehouse handling, and a host of support functions for banking, health, and other service industries.

Firms operating the global and niche supply chains of the future must build this virtual network. It is a necessary business strategy that creates the appropriate alliances to produce, in a proactive manner, the products, services, and processes that most correctly satisfy ever-changing market demands, complete with the enabling technology to sustain a leading advantage. The volume and accuracy of information needed to sustain that supply chain can be overwhelming, whether the chain is large, multinational, or niche-oriented. The right partners focused on the right functions with the right information are the keys to making it all work effectively. We envision such chains developing in the next three to five years.

Niche firms are building their networks with an eye to sustaining a focused role in segmented parts of future supply systems. Wholesalers are especially hard at work finding solutions that will enhance their ability to survive in an era when their very existence is considered an extra step in the supply chain by most manufacturers and retailers. Early tests show a preference for innovative and open systems environments that accurately speed communications to widely dispersed cultures. In this manner, the smaller, niche-oriented firms become more nimble than larger and more ponderous competitors, making the smaller firms a natural choice for markets that need quick responses.

The supply chain of tomorrow will be a virtual network, whose members share as a primary business objective the ultimate satisfaction of selected customers and markets, on a global or niche basis. These customers and markets will have been established through analysis of the enormous troves of data that are now being accumulated at the point of purchase. The transactions that must occur to satisfy these customers and markets will be analyzed with activity-based costing systems to see how they fit with the business plan, resulting in a true strategic application for conducting business within these sectors. At the heart of the selected supply network will be functioning systems operated by skilled partnering organizations that will use the latest technology and interpersonal skills to create an unbeatable competitive advantage. From these networks will come changes in the philosophies that have supported the old way of getting products and services to consumers. Some of the more obvious new features follow:

- The simple transfer of products and services will be supplanted by supplying products that satisfy a real customer need, supported by all the necessary information on these products and their intended use. Instead of providing a full line of products to a customer, including some that sell well and others that do not, data and costs will be shared so that the best-selling and most profitable items are included in the selection and moved to the consumers.

- Perceived value will be measured in terms of direct customer satisfaction and not by the value to the manufacturer or the retailer. Reward systems will be based on achieving high performance on these measures.
- The funding necessary to support the network and to sustain its competitive advantage will derive from continuous improvements and from sharing the savings that are developed across the full network.
- Waste and errors within the system will be reduced to minimal levels that are as close to perfection as possible with the current technology.

Figure 9.1 illustrates a focus mechanism we have used with organizations in the consumer products arena to analyze future improvement opportunities. It shows some of the ways in which the seamless network of the future will operate, and how functions can be linked and enhanced. The top of the diagram illustrates the core processes that must occur in a successful consumer products business. Beneath the core processes, we list some of the support processes for each area of focus. New product development, for example, is critical for a strong core process that takes new concepts to market in the most effective manner. Below the support processes are listed the services that are likely to have an impact on the process. Finally, we list the strategic enablers that can make process improvement a success.

It is necessary to constantly bring out new concepts to create a feeling of innovation and freshness in the product line. Today's consumers insist on these characteristics and expect product leaders to have very short cycle times for introduction and replenishment of products. This requirement puts pressure on the research and development department to create the desired flow of new items. Marketing also has to be involved in this critical beginning function to keep the flow of innovation synchronized with perceived market needs and trends. Together these functions create the opportunity to design new processes and techniques that can give the firm an advantage in the chain from concept to market.

Next, firms must go from product design to order production, moving the products from development into the manufacturing

FIGURE 9.1. Consumer Products Focus.

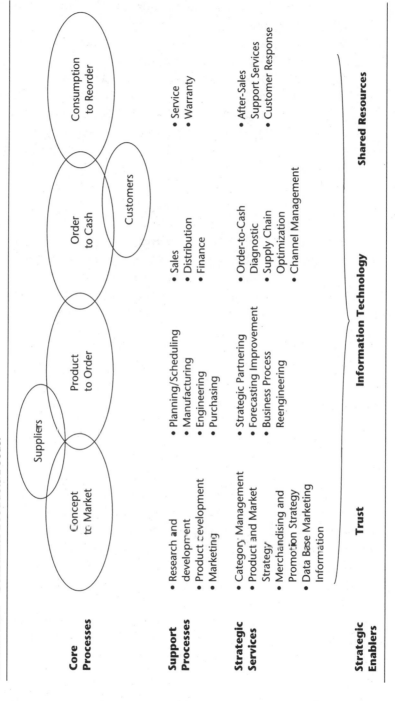

Core Processes

Suppliers

Concept to Market — Product to Order — Order to Cash — Consumption to Reorder

Customers

Support Processes

Concept to Market:
- Research and development
- Product development
- Marketing

Product to Order:
- Planning/Scheduling
- Manufacturing
- Engineering
- Purchasing

Order to Cash:
- Sales
- Distribution
- Finance

Consumption to Reorder:
- Service
- Warranty

Strategic Services

Concept to Market:
- Category Management
- Product and Market Strategy
- Merchandising and Promotion Strategy
- Data Base Marketing Information

Product to Order:
- Strategic Partnering
- Forecasting Improvement
- Business Process Reengineering

Order to Cash:
- Order-to-Cash Diagnostic
- Supply Chain Optimization
- Channel Management

Consumption to Reorder:
- After-Sales Support Services
- Customer Response

Strategic Enablers

Trust — Information Technology — Shared Resources

system in the most efficient manner possible. Purchasing works out supplier partnering arrangements and alliances that ensure that the raw materials and incoming resources are of the highest possible quality as well as being supportive of the conversion systems that follow. The planning and scheduling functions become deeply involved here as they interface with the engineering and manufacturing departments to develop the internal systems that most effectively get the products made and on their way to distribution. Reengineering efforts have been especially fruitful in this area of the business.

Next, a leading-edge order-to-cash system is needed to enter error-free customer orders for new and old products and services into the system, process these orders swiftly, guide the products and services through distribution and delivery, and move into finance for payment. In a modern system, the sales, distribution, and finance functions have to combine their expertise to analyze the process that turns an order into cash and to look at opportunities to move toward supply chain optimization. Cross-departmental teams are vital here to make certain that all unnecessary and redundant steps are eliminated.

Finally, a consumption-to-reorder sector makes certain that the order is properly fulfilled, after-sale services are performed to the satisfaction of the ultimate consumer, and replenishment is handled. Closely allied with the latter two functions is the need for a partnering loop with key customers to make certain that the system is achieving high levels of satisfaction. A particularly important feature is direct linkage and feedback from key customers who agree to monitor the network's effectiveness, so that further enhancements can be introduced. Most leading firms today have an established customer advisory panel that helps them to adjust processes so that they remain current with customer needs.

The support processes associated with this type of focus are listed under the major sectors of the model. A sample of the services that are allied with these support processes is arrayed in the next horizontal listing. The operating system of the future will have, for example, a strong category management system that supports and drives changes in product development and marketing.

Information will flow back from the interaction between the products on the consumer shelves and the consumers, and a stream of new products and enhancements to long-term stable items can be matched with true consumer demands. In the future, merchandising and promotional strategies will be tied much more closely to development and marketing sectors to make the best use of all resources and to maximize the impact of these efforts. The ever-increasing data warehouses will provide the information needed to prepare the success strategies of tomorrow.

Strategic partnering will be very visible as products are brought into the manufacturing and conversion parts of the system. From design and initial purchases through engineering of the manufacturing processes and into forecasting, planning, and scheduling, alliances will be formed with organizations that can be trusted to take a sincere interest in the success of the total network and to make a continuous contribution to sustaining an advantage over competing networks. As the orders flow from entry to cash, diagnostics will be conducted to make certain that the best practices are present, supply chain systems have been optimized, and distribution channels are being managed effectively. Once products and services reach the consumption stage, appropriate after-sales support will be present to ensure satisfaction and the continuation of the sales and consumption cycle.

The future supply chain will be optimized for all the various channel possibilities, such as grocery and retail stores, warehouse clubs, convenience stores, specialty merchants, and mass merchandisers. Each segment along the supply chain will be the best possible, because members of the virtual network will have shared their best ideas. Figure 9.2 shows how this optimized network will function. Each network will have its own value chain, consisting of the manner in which market information and experience are transformed into a flow of products and services to the distribution channels of choice. From value chains that have been brought close to optimization, products and services flow into the specific consumer channels that are best for each network. Each channel is specific, however, and the needs of the consumers in those channels will require customized solutions to meet needs in an optimized manner.

FIGURE 9.2. A Typical Value Chain Optimized for Each Different Channel.

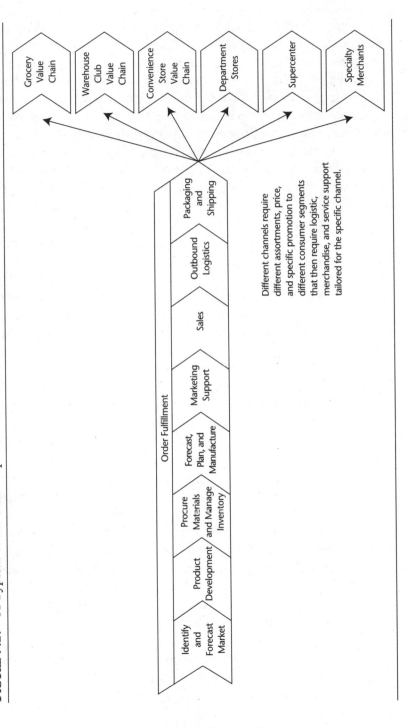

Figure 9.3 (which appeared earlier as Figure 7.6) is a larger illustration of the typical value chain for a network that begins the cycle with market information and development of products and services. Similar chains can be constructed for networks that begin with established products and orders. The purpose of this figure is to describe some of the supporting initiatives that are always candidates for continuous improvement. Leaders in future networks will be looking at these and other functions as opportunities to sustain front-edge positions and to define the ultimate chances for future optimization. From this array of opportunities, partnering activities will be working on the currently most important functions to sustain the advantages gained from past practices. For example, a firm that is very good at identifying the market and generating orders, but feels weak in order entry, could circle that area and look for help in improving its existing processes. Another firm might select inventory management or invoicing and collections.

The matrix will be kept current and accurate, with an emphasis on benchmarking against major competing networks. The network will never let down its guard against the competition by assuming that the perfect system has been created. As a member of the supply network discovers an improvement technique in one of the model areas, it will be quickly communicated and implemented in the network. Continuous evaluation and improvement will be the order for tomorrow's leaders. Following are some of the features that will distinguish these leading practices:

- Order entry from agents, brokers, and direct sales personnel will be absolutely accurate and free of errors, with pricing that is not under debate or in need of reconciliation. These orders will be processed without paper or acknowledgments in the shortest possible cycle times. Electronic entry will be the system of choice.
- Forecasting will be based on historical data-base information and current POS transactions in a manner that gives these projections reliability. Promotional activities will be integrated into this flow of information so that planning and scheduling can be based on pull-through activity without the need for large safety stocks of inventory.

FIGURE 9.3. Order-to-Cash Model.

Order Fulfillment Cycle

Identify and Forecast Market	Generate Orders	Enter Orders	Procure Materials and Manage Inventory	Schedule Production	Manufacture and Fabricate Components Process Orders	Manage Inventory	Assemble and Test Product	Package Warehouse and Ship	Invoice and Collect	Customer Support and Warranty
Identify New Business Opportunities	Forecast Analysis	Order Entry	Forecast Material Requirements	BPICS MRP I MRP II SAP	Stage Materials for Manufacturing Order	Release Manufacturing Order	Assemble Product	Kit, Pack, Crate and Process Documents	Invoice	Manage Warranty and Returns
Forecast and Manage Customer Orders	Negotiate Price	Establish Correct Pricing	Procure Materials	Planning Capacity Utilization	Build Units and Components	Sequence "Pick" List	Test Product, Quality Review	Manage Freight and Distribute	Accounts Receivable (A/R)	Post Sales and Service Field Application
Respond to Customer Requirements	Obtain Orders	Track Report, and Expedite Orders	Set and Meet Quality Parameters	Perform Setup and Changeover	Inspect Parts	Pull and Pack	Troubleshoot	Manage Shipping Documents	Collect	Respond to Customer Requests
Data-Based Marketing Assistance	Manage Goodwill	Resolution of Order Issues	Coordinate Specifications	Emergency Changes	Troubleshoot	Inventory Reduction Plans	Feedback to Product Development	Ship Products		
Key Account Analysis	Sales Support	Change Existing Order	Expedite Critical Items	Expedite and Troubleshoot Orders				Manage Finished Goods		
Competitive Analysis	Credit Verification		Accounts Payable (A/P)							
	Agents: Broker Orders		Supplier Partnering							

BPICS = Business Process and Inventory Control System
MRP I = Materials Resource Planning
MRP II = Materials Requirement Planning
SAP = Systems Application Processes

- Manufacturing systems will be flexible and efficient, providing a supply of products and services at the point of need, at the appropriate time, and in the amounts necessary for the short replenishment cycles that will be in effect.

- Financial systems will be swift and accurate. Accounts receivable and accounts payable will be handled electronically in an error-free environment in short cycles. Funds will be transferred via this medium to expedite the process and ensure accuracy.
- Logistics systems will be handled through a network of supporting parties in a way that minimizes delivery cycles, utilizes equipment to the best possible levels, and minimizes handling and storage throughout the process. Supporting inventories will be as close to zero as possible.
- After-sales support will be visible and proactive. Consumer information will be used to engender the continuous improvement that sustains a network advantage.

With these features, future leaders will have created an advantage over other networks, mired in the paradigms of the past, that have a false sense of security because they think that their network has superior features it really lacks. The spirit of trust and cooperation that virtual networks will require and establish will be their mark of distinction. These networks will move ever closer to optimization by using shared resources for mutual advantage. With this scenario as a backdrop, we can discuss the internal features of this network, beginning with how it will function without the need for a pyramid of supporting paperwork.

Paperless Systems

In the future, cooperating networks will test all of their current ordering, tracking, reporting, and reconciling systems to determine if they truly add value or just create costs. Among the functions that add little value are receiving incoming purchase orders, returning acknowledgments, maintaining price schedules, applying prices, manually tracking and recording, reconciling price arguments, editing price changes, reporting exceptions, mailing reports and change data, and copying, storing, and retrieving of reports.

As future networks are reengineered for advantage, these paper-intensive functions will be eliminated. In their place will be practices that set new standards of effectiveness, supported by the most current technology. A sampling of these practices includes:

- EDI systems that contain accurate transactions
- Pricing that is accurate, flexible, and specific to clients, volume, geography, weight, terms, and so forth
- Effective promotional administration that connects firms in the full supply chain to ensure optimum results with minimum deductions and inventories
- Impeccable accuracy of order entry and expediting from agents, brokers, and direct sales personnel working in an electronic network; accepted responsibility from these representatives for deductions resolution and pricing
- Proactive, coordinated customer service that delivers consistent results at the highest performance levels in the market
- Flexible manufacturing systems based on accurate forecasting, using leading-edge planning, scheduling, and production processes, with an indifference to lot size because the shortest possible changeover times are used
- On-line, accurate reporting of the full system inventory, with all loads, trucks, pallets, or cases clearly identified with scannable uniform code information
- Automation of routing and delivery based on customer need and use of the most effective distribution technique
- Electronic communication of shipping data for tracking and meeting special requirements
- Automated billing and payment systems that include electronic funds transfer

With these effective features, the virtual networks will lead the competition because customers will want to work within the umbrella of their services. From an external perspective, these networks will be making optimum use of the international communication systems that will support future commerce and building an advantage that will extend their markets to consumers in the emerging nations.

As we look at this future of electronic, rather than paper-intensive, interchanges, we could pose many questions. How extensive will the move be to a paperless system? How far-reaching will electronic connections and interactions be in the next five to ten years? What will the effect be on supply chain activities? What will the connections be in the future between the global data linkages of Internet and consumption habits? How will these habits affect distribution systems? The answers to all of these questions point to changing consumer practices that will increasingly be linked to data interchanges on a global basis. The consumer of tomorrow will find it just as convenient to order a sweater from Ireland, suits from Hong Kong, or shoes from Italy and have them delivered as if they were purchased at the local superstore or from a domestic catalog service. The dreams of the most avid computer specialist will most likely be exceeded as the coming generations of consumers utilize their tool of choice, the personal computer, to do their shopping.

The implication of this scenario is that firms should be planning now for their supply systems, with a focus on how the Internet will change the consumption habits they are now satisfying. Paper products will always have a market because consumers insist on maintaining a reliance on the printed page. At the same time, they want their buying experience to be as easy as possible, a desire that can best be accommodated by computer purchasing. Newspapers, books, and magazines will still provide information and advertising to the harried traveler. Paper packaging will still transport most of the world's products to market. Personal care will be enhanced by the wide variety of paper-based materials we use in our hygiene. Trees will continue to be harvested and replanted to satisfy the demand for paper, though most likely with an ever-increasing amount of recycled fibers.

In the world of marketing, selling, and communications, however, the role of paper will shift from the primary data source to a secondary support function, behind electronic capture, delivery, and effective utilization of value-adding information. We are only in the infancy of this transformation from the printed page to digitization of information. Growth in the number of connections and users will be the catalyst for this explosion of applications and use. The mushrooming expansion of interconnected consumers will have a direct impact on supply chain interactions. Future consumption will become inexorably linked with our love of computers, television, and the latest electronic wizardry. Behind most of us is an advancing army, an entire generation of new consumers, who are receiving their basic training in computer systems. To exercise that training, they will forge new habits in the world of buying and selling built around electronic communication—a world replete with exciting possibilities, but one that functions with digitized information instead of paper.

For a moment, let us take you on a stroll through the future shopping experience, using technology that is already in use. We will use a current success story to describe what is yet to come in the world of supply chain activities. Our walk begins with a look at what is presently available in the grocery shopping arena, through interactive systems being used at Safeway stores in California and Jewel Food Stores in Chicago. The medium being employed is a combination of interactive technology and an understanding of human engineering, all delivered through a personal computer. The experience comes courtesy of a company named Peapod LP, based in Evanston, Illinois.

Using a personal computer through the Peapod network, customers can eliminate the physical trip to their Jewel or Safeway store. Peapod has created software to enable the consumer to build a virtual supermarket of their own design. Consumers interactively use the personal computer in a way with which they are comfortable. They can request, for example, a list of ideas by category (snack foods), by item (potato chips), by brand (Frito Lay), or even by what is on promotion on a particular day. Within each category, consumers can have items arranged alphabetically, by brand, package, unit price, or nutritional value. As prospective buyers pass through what would be displayed on the various store aisles, they can select items or request specific information found in a format identical to that printed on the package.

When a certain meat is selected, the program may also suggest a complementary wine or vegetable. A couple can tour an entire store from the comfort of their den or living room and make selections at their leisure, with the order delivered to their door within hours.

With an initial software acquisition fee, consumers gain access to Peapod's on-line network. Peapod teaches its customers to shop more effectively in its virtual supermarket, so most subscribers feel they save money through the effective use of coupons and better comparative shopping. Consumers also save the time and cost of making trips to the store.

The people at Peapod also gain valuable customer data as the interaction is conducted. By asking consumers about the shopping experience before signing off, they get instant feedback from about 35 percent of the people using the service. Following the receipt of instructions from the consumer, a Peapod employee, called a generalist, does the actual shopping and pays for the groceries. The order is then taken to a holding area in the supermarket, where a deliverer picks up a set of orders and makes the deliveries to the customers. Coupons are credited, if appropriate, and picked up at the time of delivery. The service has reached 13,000 customers and has benefited from an 80 percent retention rate. At the stores where Peapod is used, Jewel and Safeway report that 15 percent of the volume goes through this service. Imagine for a moment the extension of this service to a center that has no supermarket, but rather a simple replenishment area where the orders are filled from a warehouse type of stocking facility. This could be the shopping medium of the future. Reliable sources project a $4–5 billion dollar potential market for interactive home shopping by the year 2000.

The computer-literate shopper of tomorrow is going to have many of these services available to enhance the shopping experience. The venue does not have to be local, either. In the not-too-distant future, the ability to shop globally will be as real as the ability to get groceries from a local store. Marketers who want to be on the leading edge in the future have to begin making plans now. They should be evaluating their supply chain networks to determine how to redesign them to take advantage of these future buying habits. The features that will react best to tomorrow's consumers are being created today.

To continue our futuristic stroll, let us proceed to that burgeoning area of the new supply chain, the global Internet. Our stroll continues by simply switching on the personal computer to access one of many Internet links available. As we make this connection, we remind ourselves that we are about to experience only the tip of a gargantuan iceberg that is yet to be created. What is available now is only the beginning of the future of interactive marketing through global electronic linkages.

Our connection can be to Prodigy, CompuServe, America Online, or other services that have electronic mail gateways to the Internet. At present, over fifty thousand of these networks are in place in nearly one hundred countries. Currently thirty-five million users participate, a number that is growing at a rate of 8 to 10 percent per month. Such a trend cannot be sustained indefinitely, but at this rate, it will not be long before most global consumers are connected to the Internet. As they become participants, certain consequences can be anticipated:

- A future, dynamic global network will exist, through which consumers can make selections without proceeding to the actual retail outlet.
- This network can work for the multinational participant or the leading-edge niche player who develops the mechanisms to adapt marketing strategies to fit this medium of purchasing.
- The size of this marketing segment will continue to grow geometrically as the number of personal computers grows and the number and diversity of software programs increases.
- This medium will become a major link to the consumption patterns of the future.
- For those consumers who relish technology-based experiences, computer-to-computer on-line business transactions will become the innovative way to shop. This is a growing segment of the new consumer profile.
- Supply chains that want to sustain a competitive advantage will have to plan in order to meet the order fulfillment requirements that will be spawned by this growing network.
- Such a planned response will require linkages into the right networks and having the modern means to respond, through distribution channels that ensure quick response without creating any discomfort for the buyer.

How extensive will this future network be? Nicholas Negroponte, professor of media technology at Massachusetts Institute of Technology, predicts that by 1999 100 million commercial hosts will be available for would-be marketers through this medium. There will also be an incredibly large web of browsers who are accustomed to "surfing" the Internet. It is already possible to do this, with graphics vivid enough to tour the Louvre in Paris, if desired. Participants can go from asking a manufacturer to look up a part number on a data sheet to going directly to an order in less than two minutes. This is quite a change from the current retail shopping experience. The trend is unstoppable and will result in unprecedented levels of interactivity, through an ever-increasing number of on-line communication systems that very shortly will include the home television set. Markets and consumers are going to be tied together by an international network that will make conducting global business as easy as buying in a local area.

Commercial uses of communication may currently be limited on the Internet to advertisements for products and services, customer services, and some limited purchasing options, but present systems already provide great opportunities. Today's Internet player can call up information down to the details of the chip in a Sony electronic device. Tomorrow's player will have an incredible array of options that have to be anticipated to maintain a competitive edge. A new shopping experience is on the horizon, geared to the coming generation of buyers. This is the opportunity that has to be seized by players in the commercial supply chains.

One set of experts in this arena, James Morehouse and Donald Bowersox, predict this future scenario: "Consumers [in the future] will buy globally via computer networks and electronic catalogs. They may choose to buy directly from suppliers in various countries, bypassing entirely the classic importer, distributor, wholesaler and retailer sequence in the supply chain. Delivery may be from efficient global overnight carriers that did not exist in 1990" (Morehouse and Bowersox, 1995).

The point to stress is that the future world for consumer products is not for the timid. One has to be proactive. The future winner will anticipate the paperless regimen of consumption and the addiction of future generations to the personal computer. The leaders will be on the front edge of building the information technology systems and linkages that support their supply network so that it does not fall victim to more imaginative competitors. These leaders will make their virtual networks seamless in interactions and in communications with tomorrow's consumers. The players who build the virtual network for the future have to cooperate extensively on what they learn and develop to meet this growing affinity for computer-oriented shopping. Computers all over the world will be linked, transferring information and possibilities to the consumer with undreamed of potentials and response times. Alliances formed now to react to this coming change will set the benchmarks for satisfying these consumers. Potential participants should be working on the levels of trust now that will be needed for future success.

The Quickest Response

Can you sell a product on Tuesday and have it back on the shelf by Wednesday? If your answer is no, then you should be determining now how to make this type of replenishment part of your supply system; otherwise, you are not following the trends of the current leaders. Examples are already being established by firms seeking a lead in future markets. At the core of their strategy is the belief that the time is already approaching when, as a consumer leaves a store after completing a purchase, an information circuit will be providing information on the sale to all the key partners across the virtual network. This is tantamount to saying, for example, that the large cooperative farming system that harvests the crops that become breakfast cereals will know about consumption trends as rapidly as the retail outlets where the cereals are bought. In this type of system, today's heavy reliance on forecasts, which typically are useful only as a starting point for replenishment, will have been merged with actual consumption data to create the pull-type arrangement that has been in the development stages for many years. This newer, more effective system will rely on information that relates to the specific purchases that require replenishment, information that will be shared across the full supply network.

A few examples will illustrate how supply chain improvements create a faster response. One of the intense competitions in the garment industry is for cotton denim jeans, a favorite of the modern consumer. As the trend in office clothing becomes less formal, jeans and cotton slacks are very much in demand. In addition, emerging world countries that become more consumer-oriented rank jeans and cotton slacks high on the list of hot items. Although many manufacturers compete in this market, two of them, V. F. Corporation, with its Wrangler and Lee labels, and Levi Strauss and Company, are the market leaders. Their competition offers an interesting insight into preparation for tomorrow's markets. Levi Strauss probably has the most recognized name and marketing position, but it seems to have trouble matching the sophistication of V. F.'s communication network, and it remains in the second position in this segment of the apparel market.

Working with a key customer, Wal-Mart, V. F. has been able to reduce its replenishment time for jeans to a matter of days, sometimes as short as three days. Levi Strauss generally has a much longer cycle, typically measured in weeks. V. F.'s system operates with a state-of-the-art computerized market response system that has been developed for its key accounts. Pull-through POS information is gathered and sent to V. F.'s order replenishment center, where replacement orders are dispatched. The mark of distinction is the electronic networking that has been created and the alacrity with which the replenishments are arranged. Levi Strauss is moving in the same direction, but it has not yet matched the capability of V. F.'s satellite-connected system.

To maintain a competitive stance with a different approach, Levi Strauss has embarked on developing another version of quick response. As it opens more of its own stores to deal directly with consumers, Levi Strauss is planning to offer an unprecedented service. All jeans do not fit all figures exactly the same, regardless of a person's closeness to a standard size; in the store of the future, a customer will be measured for a custom-fitted pair of jeans, which will be delivered within twenty-four to forty-eight hours.

This will be a quick response that will be very hard to beat—a custom-fitted pair of jeans on an overnight basis.

V. F. remains hard at work to sustain its edge, however. As a competitor, in another market segment, of Sara Lee Corporation, the large hosiery and undergarment manufacturer, V. F. used its electronic capabilities to quickly respond to an innovation that might have left the company with a disadvantage. V. F. watched carefully when Sara Lee launched its popular Wonderbra. As soon as American shoppers began to choose this body-enhancing product, V. F. developed a similar version, but it launched it with a state-of-the-art communication and distribution system. As a result, V. F. preceded its competitor in a nationwide rollout by several months (Weber, 1995). V. F. used its futuristic communication system, developed by working closely with Wal-Mart and J. C. Penney Company, to get its version of a hot-selling product onto retail shelves faster than its innovative competitor. As one analyst has said about their networking capability, "VF's computer nerve center looks more like a Star Trek set than the heart of a fashion company" (Weber, 1995). Clearly, V. F. is one of the benchmarking firms that have to be studied to keep pace with the response demands of the future.

Existing cycle times from order to replenishment are often still measured in weeks, but this will change soon for most consumer products. The new benchmark for such products as food, beverages, and apparel is being honed to seventy-two hours, with some firms closing in on twenty-four to forty-eight hours for high-turnover items. Some niche players are also finding a way to fill custom orders in one to two days. Service organizations, too, are hard at work, relentlessly pursuing ways to deliver better answers to customers in less time. Banking institutions have become very adept at shortening their cycle times and increasing the information that can be delivered to their customers.

The limits to this type of quick response seem to be oriented around the size of a typical order, the volume of transactions, or the turnover on the product. It is a lot easier to plan for short cycles on a high-turnover product like disposable diapers than for slow-turning spices or special pet products, where a pallet load could be a year's supply or more and where loads usually must be split to make sense. As replenishment systems mature, however, we already see signs of progress with smaller orders. In the future, the quickest response will have to be measured in hours. Responses will be based on actual transactions and forecasts. Promotions that occur within the system will be handled as well as normal deliveries, and what is pulled out of the network by the consumer will be the key link that triggers all responses.

The Retailer's Dream

Minimal inventories will support actual consumer demand in the future buying system, with no out-of-stock conditions or missed sales opportunities. The right people will be managing the retail shelves for maximum consumption. All the benefits offered by the acronyms of today will be realized in the future: ECR, QR, EDI, and CRP will be realities, and most of their projected benefits will have accrued and will be passed on to the retailer's customers. That is the dream of both large and niche retailers.

The question left unanswered by this reverie is not "Will it happen?" but "How large will the transformation be or where will the savings reside when the surviving supply chains have been brought close to optimization?" At this point, the betting is that the major retailers, like Wal-Mart, Sears, Target, and Home Depot, are the ones that will have their dreams fulfilled. Unfortunately, the profit margins in this area may not increase appreciably, because current results point heavily to any savings being passed on to the ultimate consumer. Our thesis is that the consumer will benefit from systemic savings, but a portion of the value enhancements has to remain with the business participants to cover the costs of the redesigns that are crucial for future survival.

To survive in the face of these conditions, the upstream manufacturers and their suppliers have to provide an equally palatable answer to the drive by the retailers for cost improvements, by finding and distributing new savings, or they will face the reality of having to generate supply chain enhancements that will become the domain of the retailers, allowing them alone to determine in what manner these savings should be dispersed. Clearly a solution with more mutuality is desired.

One example of this retail control trend is in the area of managing actual shelf inventories. Should these goods be replenished by the manufacturer (as in vendor-managed inventory [VMI] systems), should particular categories be managed by manufacturers under the direction of the retailer (as in category management), or should these chores remain in the hands of the retailer? The movement toward VMI and category management is under way, foisting most of the responsibility for change on the manufacturer. It is still too early to draw conclusions from the results, but these techniques are clearly favored by large retailers. This reversal of traditional roles looks to us like another technique for cost transfer to the manufacturer, however, and the results are predictably more favorable to the retailer.

The trend today is for the retailer to offer shelf space in exchange for a low-cost means of achieving replenishment, with the cost of change ultimately being borne by the manufacturer. If this trend is extended across the many items being offered in retail stores today, it will be difficult to sustain profit levels for the manufacturer. Partnering offers a chance to find a more palatable solution. It starts with a simple premise and suggests that both parties can have their dream fulfilled.

The fact is that the individual store and its employees know best what will be consumed and what the current consumption patterns may be. This knowledge should be combined with streamlined supply systems, allowing the retailer (at the store level) and the manufacturer to work in concert to replenish purchased products. Working together at a large national chain or in a local niche store with the help of a wholesale distributor, and using the kind of information on consumers and consumption that is rapidly becoming available, this alliance is in a strong position to have the store ready for buyers at all times and to allow both parties to share in the benefits of having higher pull-through. The large merchant has the advantage of a national image, advertising, and scale of purchasing in obtaining the help of manufacturers. The niche player has to focus on a specific area of expertise, but it can use its

supply base and wholesalers in a similar fashion, to provide valuable resources and expert advice on how to stock the store and present the niche goods for maximum consumer impact.

For retailers to satisfy their dream and still sustain a profit, certain requirements must be met. First, the manufacturer has to start
thinking like a retailer and become part of the exercise to secure
the ultimate consumer, without giving all the benefits of supply
chain optimization away at the stores. But note that not every
retailer will insist on supplier replenishment; major player J. C.
Penney prefers to use its own inventory management system.
Those supplying the niche players must understand the specific
targeted market as well as the store owner.

Manufacturers have to anticipate the reaction to special promotions, know how to handle quick replenishment without over-
loading safety stocks, and know how to keep the best-selling items
easily accessible. They have to build a supply network that keeps
turnovers at high levels with innovation and response, not with
profit-eroding costs. They have to redesign existing systems in a
way that brings to reality the many improvements that most supply chain participants know can be developed for their mutual
benefit. Manufacturers, in their quest for survival, have to think of
the stores to which they bring goods as an assortment of small
businesses that they can help to manage.

Decisions must be made daily on space allocation, category
presentation, pricing, and special promotions. Individual categories are managed as in-house businesses; therefore, the focus has
to be kept on the customer, and suggestions to the retailer should
be developed around that concept. If the manufacturer's products
are not performing to target, action should be taken to meet the
customers' current needs. In a longer perspective, consideration
also has to be given to maximizing the category mix that will draw
through the highest volume. Together, manufacturers and store
managers have to work the categories, by assortment, space allocation, and promotions. They also have to consider how to minimize handling and inventory, and how to break cases and do
stocking.

All of these considerations come down to a second task, which
is to recognize the full cost of quick replenishment. Without the

benefit of redesigned processes that remove unnecessary costs of supply, the system will become nothing more than a mechanism for transferring costs upstream to an obliging manufacturer, and the supply network will have gained no competitive advantage. Supply chain alliances must start working together now to enhance value in the virtual network or they face the inevitable prospect of having manufacturers and their suppliers bear the cost of lower cycle times, smaller store inventory, and faster replenishment. Without some type of partnering, the retailer will have the quickest response, but the cost will simply be moved upstream toward a supplier who is trying to recoup lost margins. We predict that these costs will only flow downstream again in a disguised fashion.

Sharing the Values

Our thesis is that the preceding scenario does not fully benefit the retailer, because the supply base will eventually cease to serve up the savings opportunity, through frustration at not being able to reap part of the benefit. We will return to the story of the one-dollar, four-dollar situation described in Chapter One to emphasize that possibility. Unless the supplier who offers the first dollar of savings gets a piece of that dollar, the incentive for finding the other four dollars of enhancement is not present. The retailer would be better served by working out alliances with reliable suppliers to find, together, the large savings that all the analysts know exist in supply chains.

In initiating such a drive for mutual benefit, one valuable tool is a value chain analysis. This tool can provide a depiction of the flow of materials, handling, and services that takes place as products move toward the retail outlet. Figure 9.4 illustrates a chain for a hypothetical brewery system. This figure shows the flow from raw materials through manufacture and distribution. Across the top of the figure is the time frame for current activities. Across the bottom are arrayed the costs for each of the steps. With this type of illustration, a cross-system team can analyze the opportunity areas on a macro basis and identify the key areas of concentration for an improvement effort. The same type of analysis can be used

FIGURE 9.4. Value Buildup Chain for Beer and Alcoholic Beverages.

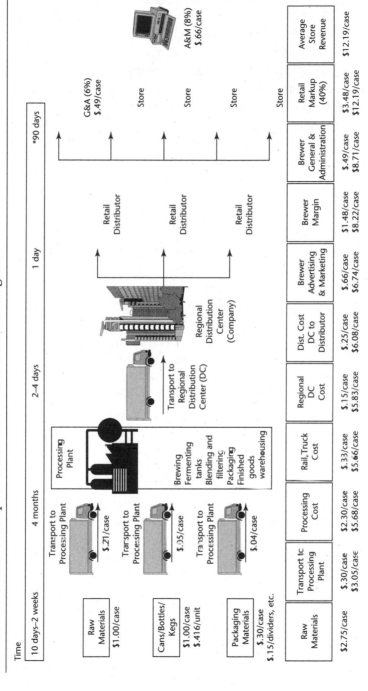

Time

10 days–2 weeks	4 months	2–4 days	1 day	*90 days

Raw Materials
$1.00/case

Transport to Processing Plant
$.21/case

Cans/Bottles/Kegs
$1.00/case
$.416/unit

Transport to Processing Plant
$.05/case

Packaging Materials
$.30/case
$.15/dividers, etc.

Transport to Processing Plant
$.04/case

Processing Plant

Brewing
Fermenting tanks
Blending and filtering
Packaging
Finished goods warehousing

Transport to Regional Distribution Center (DC)

Regional Distribution Center (Company)

Retail Distributor

Retail Distributor

Retail Distributor

Store

Store

Store

Store

G&A (6%)
$.49/case

A&M (8%)
$.66/case

Raw Materials	Transport to Processing Plant	Processing Cost	Rail, Truck Cost	Regional DC Cost	Dist. Cost DC to Distributor	Brewer Advertising & Marketing	Brewer Margin	Brewer General & Administration	Retail Markup (40%)	Average Store Revenue
$2.75/case	$.30/case $3.05/case	$2.30/case $5.68/case	$.33/case $5.66/case	$.15/case $5.83/case	$.25/case $6.08/case	$.66/case $6.74/case	$1.48/case $8.22/case	$.49/case $8.71/case	$3.48/case $12.19/case	$12.19/case

* Shelf life of 90 days after the brewing process

to develop the flows and cost estimates for multiple distribution options such as self-distributing retailers, wholesaler-supplied systems, and direct store delivery. Suppliers, manufacturers, brokers, wholesalers, and retailers can work together with this tool to gain a much stronger insight into the actual interactions and the magnitude of the embedded costs. Our experience has been that virtually every organization that gets involved in such an exercise finds a much greater total cost buildup than anticipated and moves quickly to areas where mutual action can generate improvements.

Armed with the information provided by a value chain analysis or any other technique that isolates the opportunities for a joint effort, the members of a supply chain network can cooperate to find the new savings that remain to be captured. The goal should be quite simple; share the effort, share the resources, share the risk and investment, and share the savings to create tomorrow's advantage.

The grocery industry, through its concerted efforts to find the efficient consumer response savings projected by Kurt Salmon Associates (see Chapter Two), has developed an additional tool that offers value in preparing the potential savings from a joint effort. Figure 9.5 comes from the Grocery Manufacturers of America study, "Performance Measures: Applying Value Chain Analysis to the Grocery Industry." This illustration depicts top-down and bottom-up approaches for developing estimates of the costs related to getting an organization to an effective consumer response system. Used in combination with the value chain analysis, this technique can quickly mobilize an effort in high-potential areas of opportunity. The next steps are to gather the right resources, focus them on the highest-priority items, and begin a process redesign that will improve the current system. Along the way, reviews of progress should be conducted and methods worked out to share benefits across the supply chain.

Typical results of this type of effort include:

- A substantially larger opportunity list than if it were developed in isolation
- Order-of-magnitude savings estimates that secure senior management's endorsement and provide the incentive for the effort
- Enhanced working relationships between the participating companies

FIGURE 9.5. Approach to Estimating Cost Reduction.

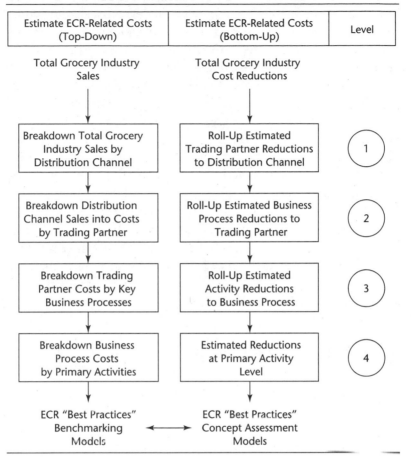

Estimate ECR-Related Costs (Top-Down)	Estimate ECR-Related Costs (Bottom-Up)	Level
Total Grocery Industry Sales	Total Grocery Industry Cost Reductions	
Breakdown Total Grocery Industry Sales by Distribution Channel	Roll-Up Estimated Trading Partner Reductions to Distribution Channel	1
Breakdown Distribution Channel Sales into Costs by Trading Partner	Roll-Up Estimated Business Process Reductions to Trading Partner	2
Breakdown Trading Partner Costs by Key Business Processes	Roll-Up Estimated Activity Reductions to Business Process	3
Breakdown Business Process Costs by Primary Activities	Estimated Reductions at Primary Activity Level	4
ECR "Best Practices" Benchmarking Models	ECR "Best Practices" Concept Assessment Models	

Note: ECR = efficient consumer response.
Source: Grocery Manufacturers of America, "Performance Measures: Applying Value Chain Analysis to the Grocery Industry."

- Creation of momentum to seek further savings in the supply network
- Development of a platform from which activity-based costing analyses can be launched
- Enhanced decision making that is based on factual understanding of the total system cost and value opportunities
- A better understanding of the indirect costs embedded in the network and of ways to assign those costs and begin to reduce them

The process steps for this type of analysis are fundamental. The interested parties across the supply chain develop a steering committee to guide the effort and to ensure that the necessary resources are available. The individual firms then identify and develop internal experts to participate in the process. There has to be insistence at the beginning that the effort will span the full supply chain and that participation will cross all barriers. Process mapping and value chain analysis should be conducted from the beginning to the end of the chain. A comparison of the value-adding features with the nonvalue-adding practices should be included within all team activities and a preliminary list of opportunities developed. The steering committee should participate in prioritization of this list, to let the actual action teams realize the importance of their role and to determine the order of magnitude of the possible savings—in time, cost, or customer satisfaction. Thorough documentation is a natural discipline to include, and considerable encouragement for teams working in new areas always helps to enhance the results.

Ultimate Customer Satisfaction

As extra dollars are retrieved, the real beneficiary will be the ultimate consumer. Even though we have dwelt on extracting savings and sharing them across the supply network, we are cognizant of the need to satisfy the consumer or risk losing the purpose of the network.

As cycle times are driven down, consumers will be able to get responses that were not dreamed of a few years ago. With or without the supporting inventories that sustained the old supply chains, the consumer is going to find the desired item, rather than being put off to wait for the makeup shipment. Product information and help will also be readily available by such services as "800" numbers. Giving the buyer the tools to get a response to questions about the purchase is going to be commonplace in the future. Members of the supply chain have to work out the details to make it happen, but the consumer will be the true beneficiary.

The consumer will continue to be courted by the ever-changing formats of retailers. As the retailers keep searching for the ingredients that will secure lasting loyalty from the consumers, they will extract ideas and initiatives from the supply chain. The virtual network of the future will pass a substantial number of these benefits to the consumers. More important, they will create a pleasurable experience that beats the competing networks.

The Next Evolution in Data Interchange

As the future environment is developing, one premise has to be understood by those who want to participate in tomorrow's virtual networks. Information will be the key enabler for achieving success. The firms that are trying desperately to implement CRP, ECR, EDI, and other process improvements are well aware of the need for high accuracy and timeliness of data specific to the area being improved. Combining this fact with the reality that most of the organizations trying to work the supply chain are more passive than active in their involvement in the type of work that achieves implementation, it becomes apparent that a need exists for a new evolution in data interchange, and that the players who are willing to make an up-front investment will gain the lead.

We do not mean to imply that new equipment or software has to be developed. Indeed, a great deal is available now from which to make choices. We do mean that firms have to work together to gain compatibility in their concept and equipment and to design their system for the future. This evolution requires firms to match systems and understandings and then use data in the most efficient manner possible, so that replenishment and order processing can be handled properly for the satisfaction of tomorrow's demanding consumer.

The logical starting place in this quest is with forecasting. A good supply chain must work with accurate information, using a pull-through system, to bring goods and services to the ultimate consumers. This type of replenishment system should start with an accurate forecast of current demand, so that responses meet real needs. Promotions and special sales efforts will be the most complicating factor in this information flow because they vary from the original forecasts, but they have to be included in the new data interchange networks, and when disconnects occur between expected orders based on the forecasts and actual needs, the system has to respond rapidly to correct them.

One implication in this transition to more proactive response systems will be that the systems will move from using warehouse or distribution center releases to trigger resupply to using the information gleaned from all the technology that has gone into scanning actual store purchases. Information Resources has created a depiction of this evolution, shown in Figure 9.6. This figure demonstrates the move of information power from audit-type informational systems to operational systems based on daily scanner data. In this future scheme, scanner-driven data on actual consumption, with sku movement and promotional responses, will be used to pull inventory and provide input for distribution and material resource planning. These connections will, in turn, spawn a consumption-based supplier fulfillment system that will react to what the consumer is buying and get the necessary replacements into the stores.

Forecasting solutions are available, and they have to be integrated into the supply networks of the future. The growing amount of information in marketing data bases can combine with current product pull-through to make more reasonably accurate forecasts. The seasonal buying that creates peaks and valleys in consumption and manufacturing schedules will not disappear from these projections, but it can usually be explained by captured information and actual distribution data. With today's systems, the involved parties have a much greater opportunity to communicate with each other and make adjustments to the flexible systems behind them, so that response can be efficient without excess inventories.

Integrated solutions that require accurate information from store, distribution, manufacturing, and supply locations are already emerging. In these systems, scanner data are merged with forecasts and the effect of promotions to establish a baseline forecast. Since no retail plan goes exactly according to the predictions, adjustments can be made to accommodate the incremental changes necessary to allow for special sales and promotions. This

FIGURE 9.6. The Evolution of Retail Information Systems.

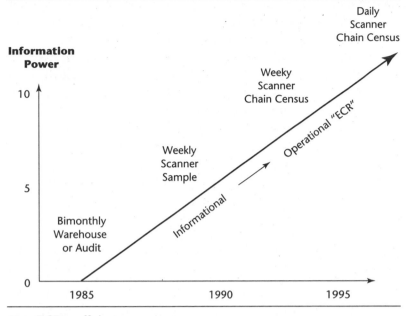

Note: ECR = efficient consumer response.
Source: Information Resources, Inc., 1995.

information is then fed to the manufacturer's planning, scheduling, manufacturing, and distribution systems; orders are processed effectively and the goods are sent to the stores without the need for excess safety inventory stocks. Thus, for any specific product, a first forecast will be generated according to normal expectations, based on substantial data-base information. This forecast will be flexible and will move up or down based on scanned information and promotional issues. On-line review will be available to the parties to facilitate decisions based on actual consumption and unexpected changes.

Suggested orders based on the first forecasts will course through the system, but the flexibility will exist to reduce or enlarge orders to compensate for changes in demand. Many different customer responses can be accommodated by these systems, because the network's response will be based on what the parties have worked out as a feasible solution for virtually any type of consumer aberration.

Supply and demand will be synchronized by the information technology platform and those who are using the information to minimize systemic losses. Deliveries to the individual store sites will be synchronized with store-specific consumption patterns. If a grocery chain finds that a special type of cake or pie is moving in unusually large quantities, this information will be sent through the system to meet the higher demand, without adding so much cost that the manufacturer earns no profits.

An example of working the data evolution is provided by the Black & Decker Corporation, the manufacturer of hand tools and other construction and home use products based in Towson, Maryland. Black & Decker sells 40 percent of its products through large retailers such as Home Depot and Kmart. For this customer base, orders are expected to be turned around on a seven-day "ship or cancel" basis. If orders are not filled in a week, the manufacturer loses them. This requirement created a need for some changes to the traditional manufacturing system, and Black & Decker was forced to take a hard look at the replenishment cycle. The company found that a seven-day cycle was generally feasible and could be accommodated under normal conditions. They also discovered that their existing planning systems were not capable of responding to unexpected changes in manufacturing related to material availability.

In response, the company's advanced manufacturing technology group developed a proactive system called capacity-optimized planning (COP). With this system, when an important part of a unit is expected to arrive later than was originally predicted and the manufacturing system will not be able to respond in seven days, COP informs the other plants that manufacture parts for this unit. These plants are then freed to manufacture other components for future orders. For example, if a plastic housing needed for an electric weed-cutting product that was heavily ordered for summer consumption is going to be late, plants that make the motors or cutting-line feeding mechanisms are quickly notified so that they can switch their manufacturing schedules. The notified plants then make something else that can be delivered in the prescribed cycle time. The customer is notified just as quickly so that adjustments can be made to expected delivery plans.

Because the plants can shift manufacturing schedules and make different parts and products ahead of schedule, a new element of flexibility is introduced. Providing these flexible options maintains plant efficiency, and Black & Decker can quickly make manufacturing time available when the delayed parts arrive. No system is perfect, so Black & Decker has taken the time to design features into its system that allow flexible responses to unfortunate circumstances while still keeping products moving to the consumer in an efficient manner.

Custom Solutions

The final point we would make about the future is that custom solutions, designed for the consumer, will be the order of the day. The members of the supply networks that will dominate tomorrow's markets will have developed such solutions for their key customers. All the suppliers, manufacturers, and distributors will be thinking like the retailer. Their focus will be on the ultimate consumer and on using the supply chain to pull products to that consumer in the most effective manner possible. Because each retailer has slightly different conditions, the supply chain players upstream have to decide on the key outlets for their goods and services and construct a systemic response that is efficient to both effectively supply products and services and meet actual demands in the network.

Because significant costs are associated with developing response solutions and adding information technology enablers, making changes to distribution channels has to be managed as closely as possible to maintain margins. This requires the upstream players to decide which retail outlets make the most sense for them and their infrastructure. Having made that decision, they must design a system that establishes their competitive advantage. We advise building a unique, basic model for the few most important customers and then modifying that model for the balance of the customers.

Three factors drive this need for customization. First is the obvious cost associated with trying to create a system that can be all things to all consumers. Consumption patterns today change too frequently to accommodate such a wide-reaching strategy. Focus has to be the discipline of tomorrow. Sufficient information is available to determine trends and to decide which customer base affords the best opportunity for profitability. These customers will want to feel that their suppliers have taken the time to design solutions that are specific to their needs—a custom-designed delivery system. Economy balanced against supply potential becomes vital in determining which customers should be included in the long-term partnering system.

The second factor is the need for a strong perception in the mind of the retailer and the ultimate consumer that the supply chain of choice offers the best overall value. As we consider this factor, we quickly sense that only by custom-designing a network that efficiently provides a flow of goods and services toward consumers will we have the customer satisfaction necessary to secure loyalty. Today, each consumer defines value differently. The network members supplying those fickle buyers have to work in concert to design a system that meets the buyers' needs without coming apart at every significant change in tastes. A system designed with specific consumers in mind will be flexible and alert enough to make the adjustments needed to stay on top of the market and its current demands.

The third factor is the organization of the firm's technology. The challenge is no longer just how to gather the pertinent information; it is how to apply the data in the growing information bases to gain customers and sales. This problem requires business practices that deliver product value, building cost-effective and satisfaction-guaranteeing systems. We have repeatedly emphasized information technology's role as an enabler in the process. Now we add that this technology has to be customized to prevent others from easily duplicating what gives the network an advantage. When the nonvalue-adding costs are removed from the physical systems of supply and information technology platforms have been designed to perform what were formerly manual processes, the virtual network will keep improving, while also minimizing the possibility of imitation. Time spent customizing technology solutions helps to provide this safety factor.

Efficient consumer response may be a generic tool for eradicating the many inefficiencies that exist in supply chains, but the systems developed by virtual networks do not have to be generic. Time and care spent on solutions that have been designed for a cooperating network and customized for a particular segment help to maintain the competitive edge.

Action Study: Apollo Motors Corporation

Many firms have successfully initiated process improvements by designing their systems for the future. Examples come from industries as diverse as automotive, utilities, publishing, financial, insurance, and telecommunications organizations. Unfortunately, when many of these companies recorded their improvements, they found that 50 to 80 percent of their supply chain activities did not warrant the management attention or resources they were receiving. Valuable resources were being wasted in the improvement effort that could have been more effectively deployed.

One area in particular that has surfaced from this type of attention is what is commonly referred to as MRO, or maintenance, repair, and operating costs, which includes items such as lubricants, towels, gears, bearings, and fasteners. Research has revealed that the cost of acquiring these lower-value, low-risk, high-transaction items often exceeds the cost of materials. It takes more time and money to get these supplies than the individual items are worth. Improving methods of procurement has done little to balance this disparity. It has simply been overlooked as larger procurement areas got most of the attention.

Over the last ten years, much of the focus by procurement professionals has been on improving the quality, service, and cost of strategic sourcing by reducing supplier bases, building partnering arrangements with key suppliers, working on supplier certification, and developing joint improvement efforts. Unfortunately, similar advances were not made in the area of MRO procurement. Most of the prevalent logic counseled that it was not a significant enough area to warrant serious effort. Recent information, however, is verifying that for many firms the acquisition costs for MRO or indirect purchases are higher than the cost of the items, and a better solution is in order. In a survey of one thousand purchasing groups,

MRO made up 10 to 18 percent of total costs and 50 to 80 percent of acquisition costs. Something was obviously out of balance, and the need for improvement was revealed.

Our action study is about a division of Apollo Motors Corporation (a fictitious company) that decided to build a partnering solution for tomorrow around available technology and practices in this area. We use this study because it illustrates the fact that a network has to look at all areas of potential savings to make sure that an important segment is not being overlooked. This study took place at Apollo's assembly operation. At this facility, Apollo's MRO procurement strategy had three key features:

- *One hundred percent use of full-service primary suppliers, selected for their long-term partnering relations*
- *Tracking and accounting for 100 percent of inventory still in use*
- *Elimination of purchasing and receiving functions as unnecessary for effective implementation of the arrangement*

Under their system, Purchasing managed the primary supplier relationships and processed the "kanban" (replacement matched with actual usage) replenishment needs through EDI transmissions. Twenty-two full-service suppliers assumed responsibility for using warehouses located within easy access of the Apollo plant to make kanban deliveries of needed supplies and materials. Second-tier suppliers were included in the network to provide backup supply through the primaries when necessary and to fill out specific product categories. The full-service primary suppliers kept minimal stocks in these warehouses. From a break-bulk facility, which took large-sized shipments and separated them into smaller, site-specific amounts, the actual needed parts and supplies were sent to a team crib (a holding container) for use by the group that actually utilized the parts.

At the foundation of this new system was the development of two categories of suppliers:

1. *Primary MRO suppliers: Apollo has one supplier for each major commodity group, such as cutting tools and abrasives, oils and lubricants, and power transmission. Each primary supplier has an annual contract, which remains in place unless it is canceled by one of the parties, and the primary responsibility for providing the items covered by the agreement.*

2. *Second-tier suppliers: When an intermediate-component item in a primary supplier's commodity category is short, but is not in the primary supplier's end-product line, then the primary supplier procures the item for Apollo from a second-tier supplier.*

Under this customized solution, the suppliers act as an indirect material inventory supply base for Apollo. The suppliers assume the traditional purchasing role with secondary sources and place their specialists in the Apollo plant, where they constantly look for improvements to materials and processing. Purchasing personnel at Apollo are freed to seek further improvements in their area of responsibility. There is twenty-four-hour emergency telephone support. All suppliers provide qualified representatives, matched with people from Apollo's indirect materials group, who meet regularly to discuss continuous improvement activities.

An interesting feature is that Apollo makes it difficult to order from other suppliers that require extensive purchase order paperwork. Electronic Data Systems Corporation designed the customized EDI system that is used to communicate with each of the twenty-two core suppliers. At the heart of this system is an electronic system that tracks and accounts for all inventory from introduction to use.

In the plant, inventory is primarily stored at team stations, with a small amount in the central storage area. It is then tracked until actual usage, with the team held accountable for that activity. Start-up inventory levels are allowed to be slightly high to cover the effects of beginning conditions, but they are expected to shrink to efficient just-in-time needs. Overall, Apollo and the key suppliers are convinced that in this area of focus, win-win situations were created and a network advantage was established.

Summary

In the future, the virtual network that links participants in a supply chain will consist of the members who have proved that they provide a viable function in the network. This linkage could include raw material suppliers, manufacturers and converters, distributors, wholesalers, and merchandisers to the ultimate consumers that survive the changing consumer environment. But the circumstances of change will be unforgiving for those that do not adapt. They will disappear from future networks.

The prevailing networks will be backed with an incredible array of emerging technological enhancements that make data access, with accuracy and timeliness, a key tool in enhancing customer satisfaction. These networks will be synchronized to accomplish such tasks as assembly, packaging, handling, storing, shipping, and receiving. Suppliers and manufacturers will work in such close harmony with actual pull-through consumption data from the retailers that the consumer will be unable to see any problems with supply. The supply functions will be brought into a synchronized and streamlined format to keep pace with advances in information technology and to provide the smooth flows that will be demanded of tomorrow's networks.

Most of the processes that define response, replenishment, and technological enablers and enhancers will be implemented by the turn of the century. EDI, ECR, and CRP will have reached implementation levels that require participation—that is, nonparticipants will be excluded from major networks. The time is at hand to build the finely honed chains of interconnections that will define advantage in the next century. A plan has to be in place or the future is at risk.

Chapter Ten

Bringing the Network to Optimization

• •

                For firms that function within a supply chain system, the choices for the future are quite simple. On the one hand, they can accept the inevitable trend that leads to finding value enhancements within the supply chain and then passively watch as these savings are extracted from supply networks and transferred to eager retailers, for passage to the ultimate consumers. This approach is our least favorite, because it provides no lasting value to the network; it does not provide funds for investing in further enhancements or improve future viability. The time and amount of resources dedicated to this strategy will be quite limited, and the effort will be disguised in a feigned attempt to keep the retailers happy, because the upstream participants receive no real long-term advantage other than keeping a supply position for a while.

    On the other hand, a more palatable approach is to work proactively with selected members of a full supply chain to find the means by which mutual resources can be applied to develop larger system savings, a portion of which will be shared across the total network. This strategy will be difficult to sell in the current environment, where little to no trust exists between the potential

• • • • •

participants, but it receives our strong endorsement. It offers mutual benefits that are an incentive for full and continued participation in ongoing improvement efforts and it provides future investment funds.

Some strategies fall between these passive and active approaches, but they are simply variations of the decisions that position a firm at one of the two extremes. Our posture has been to strongly favor a network solution that is derived with the help of alliances built from the start to the end of the supply chain. The objective of such efforts is to come as close to optimization as possible through the cooperative development and utilization of virtual network resources and the best of current technology. Value enhancements have to be pursued across this network with an eye for survival and gaining a competitive edge, with part of the savings used for the future needs of the network constituents. The ultimate consumer's degree of satisfaction is the central measurement of success for the network, but the profitability of the participating firms is the main goal.

The Necessities of Supply Chain Management

Figure 10.1 shows how optimized performance in a supply chain network can be realized. Foremost in this realization will be advanced partnering characteristics that span the total system. The presence of dominant participants who force cost concessions onto other supply chain members will be absent in successful efforts. Such positions would only foster an atmosphere of mistrust in which the suppliant members of the chain bide their time until market conditions allow them to reacquire all of the conceded costs and more. Under conditions of true partnering, with high levels of trust and accountability, solutions and savings are worked out that benefit the total network as well as the selected market and consumers that the full supply chain is intended to satisfy.

Order management will be a key process for all constituents, with a focus on getting goods and services to the ultimate consumer in the most effective manner possible. The use of refined data bases will be extensive, particularly those with information

FIGURE 10.1. Optimized Supply Network Performance.

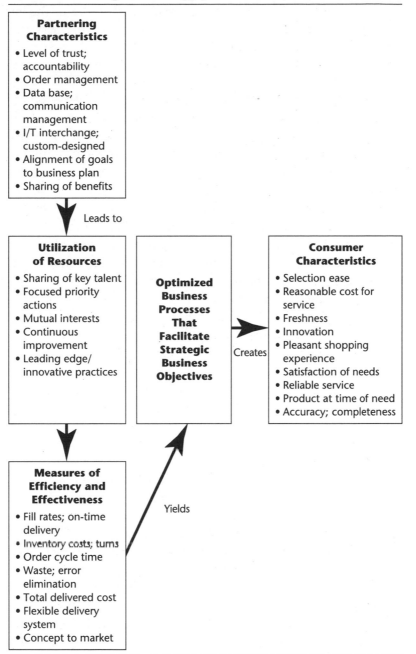

Note: I/T = information technology.

on current, actual pull-through sales, with an emphasis on managing communication between participants and analyzing the implications suggested by the information contained in these data bases. Enabling and enhancing information technology systems will be custom-designed and will be truly state of the art, as a catalyst to gaining a network advantage.

Strategic business intentions and initiatives will be shared among the network's key members, so individual firms can link their strategies together to gain the unbeatable competitive position that every company so ardently desires. And, most important, the senior managers will work out systems for sharing the derived savings, to improve their network advantage and enhance profits for their constituents. These partnering characteristics will lead directly to a determination of how resources will be used in the virtual network. This step is the most important in the evolution of supply chain improvement; it will be the mark that separates the pretenders from the real winners of the future.

The first step becomes the allocation of key talent to initiatives that are surfaced by assessments that generate improvement opportunity lists. If the preparatory homework has been done diligently, the budding network should have a list of possible joint actions, with an order of magnitude of the savings that can be derived from each effort. With these numbers as a guide, the return on talent should be reasonably clear, and key personnel can be made available for the development teams. The important caveat is to make certain that talent is shared, and that one or more members of the network do not take undue advantage of other members who are willing to sacrifice their best people for the effort.

With key talent from all the participants made available, the next step is to focus their actions on the highest-priority efforts. The opportunity list will be created by all participating firms in an effort to select the areas that are best suited for improvement. The team members will then have a clear understanding of how important their work will be and why they have been selected for a particular assignment. Equally important is the need to define clearly the mutual interests that are being pursued. If elements of mutual benefit cannot be found across the full chain, the effort will quickly disappear.

As talent is shared on specific initiatives, the need for continuous improvement must be made clear. The purpose is to constantly seek more efficient methods and procedures and thereby to approach optimization. This need will not be satisfied with a series of one-time improvements. There must be a commitment and a methodology for continuous effort in critical areas to keep the network out in front of competitors who will try to copy what has been gained. Finally, in this part of the effort, action teams must document the best practices that established the innovative features and the leading-edge systems and procedures that distinguish the network from its competitors.

With these functioning characteristics worked out, the next requirement is to develop measures of efficiency and effectiveness that are acceptable to all participating firms and that are clearly agreed upon as the best measurements of success. We have seen too many well-intentioned efforts miss the mark and wither because the measurements were not clear to those driving the process or by those who reward the participants for the effort. The particular measures suggested in Figure 10.1 are simply illustrative. Because a custom solution will be generated, the measures should also be custom-designed, to determine the satisfaction of the consumer and how the individual supply chain members will benefit.

The primary processes will then yield an optimum business supply chain that enhances the strategic business objectives of the participating businesses. This outcome is critical to the effort. Unless a direct link to the strategic business plans exists, support for the effort cannot be expected to continue. Unless the participants want to have their efforts and actions recorded as one-time quick fixes, to be quickly forgotten during the next business crisis, they must insist on seeing how the resulting initiatives are linked to realizing their strategic goals.

Last, a way must be found to determine if the real purpose of the entire effort, that of satisfying the ultimate consumer, has been met. Measures of consumer satisfaction may vary by industry or market, but some criteria measuring consumer actions should be developed that will reflect how the network has gained an advantage.

The measures listed in Figure 10.1 are among the ones we hear most often. Today's consumer is a pampered breed; consumers must be treated well or they will not return. They want selection to be as simple and convenient as possible, with a feeling that the cost, if not the lowest, is at least reasonable in view of the service received. They must find a feeling of freshness in the shopping experience, with a sense that the store has innovative features and products. The shopping experience will be rated as pleasant if needs were satisfied without undue effort and with reliable after-sale service. The products and services desired must be available at the time of need and not put on back order. Overall, the transaction must be accurate and complete. Can these features be measured? They will have to be measured and constantly improved, or the customers will go elsewhere.

Optimization as a Strategy

Optimization, as we have defined it, has to become a strategy in itself. Without such a clear understanding, there is always the chance that the effort will wane under a new management or will be a short-term fix. The objective is to have a strategy that makes the united, synchronous network the supply chain of choice, by eliminating all mistakes and errors, having the best cycle-time contraction, and providing a flavor of innovation surrounding the shopping experience. With virtually every competing network trying to gain the same advantage, the only strategy that makes sense for long-term survival is one that establishes supply chain optimization as the key strategy.

This drive for optimization has to take place within an environment of necessity in order to respond to the forces that are shaping the future of supply chain systems. To give the customer a high perception of value in the shopping experience, sloppiness must be eliminated; that turns today's consumer off very quickly. Customers want error-free interactions, even if they make most of the mistakes. They demand high information content on products, a definitive way to get after-sale service, and, if necessary, a return procedure with no hassles. Under these conditions, extra costs are going to be borne by the supply chain, unless the constituents create such a high-quality network that the consumer receives the perceived value all the time, and there is no need for returns. Such a condition comes only from a network that is close to optimization.

Remembering the Pitfalls

As optimization is pursued, more reasons may be found to stop the effort than to continue. Foremost among the possible pitfalls will be the attitude that supply chain improvement is only for the upstream constituents. Another pitfall is an unwillingness to make scarce, talented resources available for work on intercompany actions. Most firms we studied would prefer to put key people on favorite internal projects that have minimal returns rather than assigning them to joint efforts, where the credit for victory must be shared but could contain five to twenty times the payback on the investment.

The most common pitfall is a lack of trust between potential partnering entities. Many past experiences have revolved around getting the better of the negotiating process, making this obstacle possibly the most difficult to overcome. However, it must be conquered. Our suggestion has been to start with pilot efforts that force the constituents to provide talented players, thereby making the working out of relationships of trust a requirement for success.

The final pitfall that should be anticipated is the internal insistence of those who are concerned with protecting turf and gathering credit for all large-magnitude improvements. Unless the syndrome that insists on maintaining a tubular mentality throughout an organization is stamped out, the quantum improvements the leaders are making will have no chance of being duplicated. Sharing across all areas has to be the byword. The effort begins internally and is then extended outside the firm. The emphasis is on success, with the sharing of benefits matched to the level of effort and the value to the system.

Using the Right Partners

The success of any effort designed to bring a network to optimization depends to a great degree on the ability to pick the firms with which a successful long-term alliance can be forged for mutual advantage. We have recommended that an effort be conducted to find the key upstream constituents who will have the greatest impact on the total network and to conduct with them a search for the key customers on whom the system effort should be focused.

The partners who are selected should have the ability to think like the chosen customers and a willingness to devote key talent to joint efforts. The firm doing the selecting and the partners of choice should have an innate ability to form a joint strategic goal that is oriented around gaining a competitive advantage for the network. It is important to have a creative way of measuring success from the customer's perspective, a dedication to studying the total supply chain as a field of mutual improvement opportunity, and test models and teams for creating initiatives that result in significant results for all members of the network.

Getting Started and Moving Forward

The best way to initiate and to sustain a major improvement effort is to start with a pilot project in an area that has dedicated funding. Logistics can be an early candidate for study. The potential for savings in this arena is so high that any concerted effort should bear fruit. Estimates of potential annual savings run to thirty billion dollars in the grocery industry and twenty billion dollars in service industries. Documentation is also prolific in this area, so it should be easy to provide convincing evidence of the need to get started.

The best beginning starts with gathering sincerely interested supply chain partners to discuss a vision that has meaning across the potential network. With an understanding of the process changes necessary to accomplish that vision, the potential part-

ners are ready to establish a pilot operation in an area of significance, to define the possible enhancements and to establish the
order of magnitude of the returns.

A simple pilot study could include looking at the flow of orders
from the initial raw materials to finished goods in the retail stores.
It could also study the way services are actually developed and
delivered to the customer. With this information arrayed in a flowchart, the participants can develop a priority list of possible improvements, which is then divided into the best potential actions
for the initial joint effort and tracking. Team assignments are then
made that involve key personnel from all the companies in the effort and specific action plans can be developed. By keeping the
first steps within the scope of a pilot project, risks are minimized
and learning is maximized.

As these pilot projects are pursued, a measurement system can
be developed. It is important to make certain that representatives
of the customer base are included in evaluating the results, to meet
the important element of customer satisfaction. Once the pilot
projects confirm the value of the partnering, other areas can be
considered, including the order fulfillment process; the order-to-
cash cycle; product development and time to market; the forecasting, planning, and scheduling processes; and the shipping,
warehousing, and distribution systems. There is really no limit to
how far the effort can be extended. The most important task is to
build on the early successes and nurture the kind of trust that has
to permeate the interactions to gain equality of effort and continuation of management support.

Sources of Help

Many more resources are available to help with supply chain improvement initiatives than is generally realized. Entirely new con-
sultancies have sprung up to offer assistance. The logistics area
in particular is populated with these organizations. Software appears weekly with features that have been proved in test areas.
Three-letter acronyms representing the latest improvement techniques have become too numerous to track. So much potential

help is available that the real need is to sift through the possibilities to find the specific assistance that will help in the development of customized solutions.

The logical order of pursuit is important in this area. The first step should be to seek any existing systemic solutions that may take extraneous costs and errors out of the network and satisfy the ultimate consumer, before selecting software that purports to provide the means to success. We have been involved in many situations where the selected software was indeed thoroughly studied, well designed, and capable of bringing success under the right conditions. Unfortunately, we were brought in to modify that software to fit the specifics of the supply chain interactions and to get the network back into operation. We were there to clean up the mess the firms created by jumping too quickly at a canned solution, rather than taking the time to redesign processes that were in place but badly needed improvement.

Some organizations have hopelessly underfunded their information technology needs for many years. In an effort to make up for lost time—and, usually, lost market position—management jumps quickly at a low-cost bandage, typically in the form of software and assistance in quickly integrating new information technology with other business processes. This approach rarely satisfies the real needs of the firm or its supply chain. More often, it confuses the people seeking a solution to their supply and communication problems by forcing them to use systems and procedures that are not adequately suited to the needs of the current environment.

Outside consultants can provide valuable help but should be carefully screened and selected. It is important to consider how the overall business processes can be improved with the help of critical advice that is frankly delivered and wisely received, in the spirit of building a more capable network.

Prosperity and Strength Through Total Network Alliances

Figure 10.2 shows our idea of how future supply networks will work to satisfy tomorrow's consumers. This figure is an elaboration

FIGURE 10.2. The Future Supply Network.

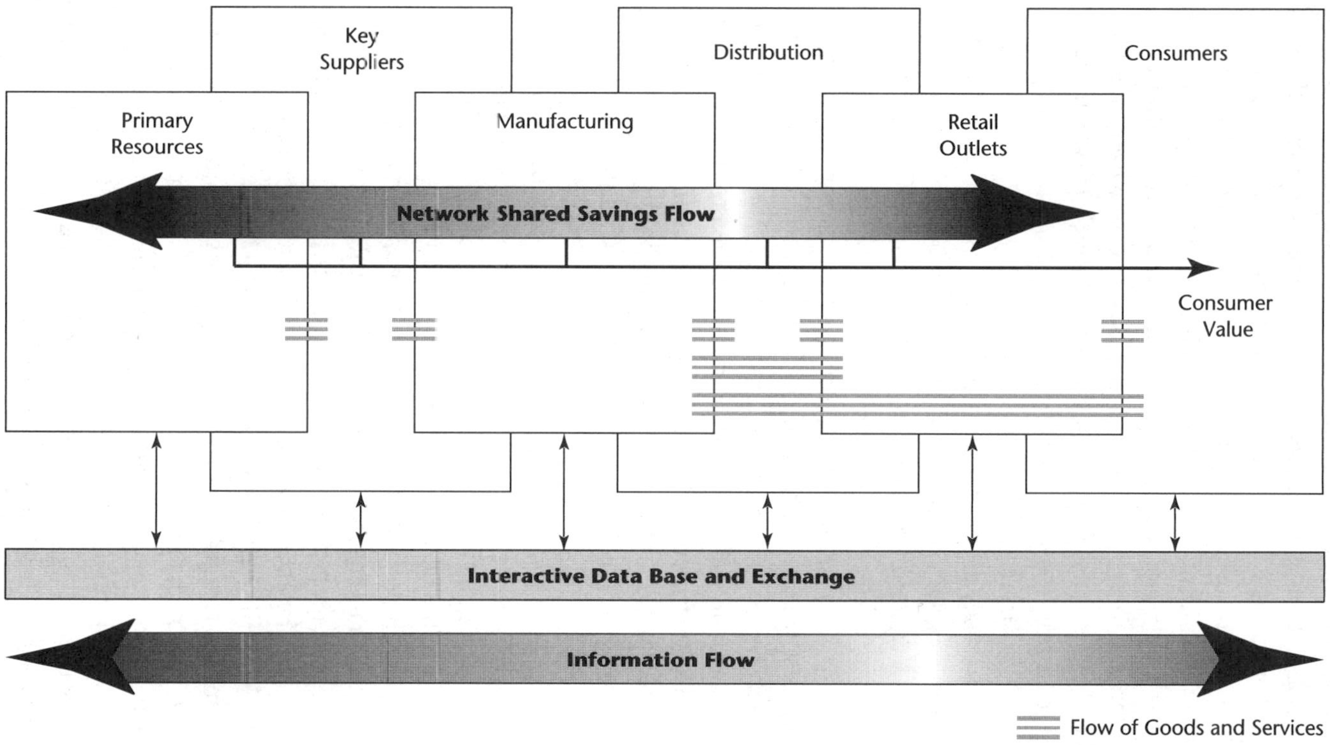

Consumers

Consumer Value

Retail Outlets

Distribution

Manufacturing

Key Suppliers

Primary Resources

Network Shared Savings Flow

Interactive Data Base and Exchange

Information Flow

▤ Flow of Goods and Services

of the interenterprise solution presented earlier. We believe that existing two- and three-step improvement efforts will be greatly extended as more successes are recorded and firms realize the value of full supply chain assessment. In a sense, such extensions will most likely continue until a chain is created for a network that starts with extraction from the earth and finishes after consumption and return to the earth. Our purpose, however, is not to draw out the extensiveness of a potential model. It is to indicate that ample opportunities exist for savings across the supply chain we have illustrated.

From key primary resources, as basic as grain and ores extracted from the earth, a flow of ingredients will move to suppliers that have a major impact on the costs of a particular manufacturer or converter. These suppliers will deliver goods and services that make the manufacture possible. From the manufacturing and converting process will come a flow of goods and services that either move directly to consumers, move directly to retail outlets, or continue to move through distribution entities and then to the retail outlets.

The distribution channel that is chosen will undoubtedly be affected by the dramatic shift under way in digitized information transmission and the innovative logistic solutions being developed. The key enabler of success will be the interactive data base that is used to exchange information about what is happening in the network. In successful networks, a flow of shared savings will be realized by the participating firms, with a significant portion going to the ultimate consumer to guarantee customer loyalty. An equally important portion will be reinvested in the network infrastructure to ensure continuance and build future viability.

To attain prosperity and strength in the network, all constituents will be actively involved in continuous process improvement, seeking all the enhancements that can ensure customer satisfaction in a virtually error-free environment. From the beginning to the end of the process flow, the network will be seamless; all extraneous activities, time, and cost will have substantially been removed. Supporting inventories will be as close to actual needs as possible, so working capital is at minimum levels. Business strategies will have been worked out for this network in a cooperative manner, providing all partners with the necessary information and required systems to get the right products and services to market in the highest-quality, most effective, and profitable manner possible with the current levels of technology. Customer feedback will be sought and meticulously analyzed to verify that the results are consumer-oriented. Optimization may still be a small step away, but the combined effort will have brought the network closer to that elusive goal than any competing system. A sustainable competitive advantage will be the reward.

Action Study: The Computer Products Corporation
···

For our final example, we have chosen a global study that spans most of the elements of supply chain optimization we have covered. It illustrates how a major organization took the time and effort to seek and implement significant improvement across a global network of activities.

The Computer Products Corporation (CPC) (a fictitious name and identity) is a global producer of computer products, with annual sales over twenty billion dollars. The firm is active on all continents through a network of sixty companies, with over 100,000 employees. Our story involves the North American representative of CPC. This segment of the company has over $5 billion in sales and is organized in five operating divisions that cover North America. This service division of this segment includes accounting and logistics and contains purchasing—core groups for finding supply chain enhancements.

The improvement effort began when CPC and other leading computer product companies were redefining how to gain a competitive advantage through innovative management of supply chains. The first determination by CPC was that current supply chain performance measures were not responsive or adequate for future market conditions. A few examples illustrate this point. Order lead times were considered an important measure, with the time defined as receipt of order to shipment to the distribution center. Most companies worked on a three- to four-day cycle. The future requirement was determined to be four to twenty-four hours. A quantum improvement would be necessary to meet this target.

Order completeness was important to eliminate the need for back orders. The traditional definition was 100 percent completion of the order, but the current reality was in the range of 70 to 95 percent. The service division of CPC knew that in the future the need was going to be in a tighter range: 97 to 100 percent. On-time delivery was defined as hours or days late after the customer due date, but most firms only calculated on-time shipments. The future requirement was to be on-time and just-in-time as defined by the customer.

To pursue the changes needed to meet these and other future requirements, the service group took a look at successful firms. The first conclusion was that these leaders had a definite focus on customer-driven strategies that made them preferred suppliers. This conclusion created a strategy with three requirements for the group:

1. *It would need a customer focus that included adjusting the supply chain (resources and technology) to respond more effectively to changing consumer needs.*
2. *It would need to align and link internal and external resources to create fast and seamless operations.*
3. *Service and cost optimization would have to become drivers to create cost-effective and innovative solutions for world-class distribution in the supply chain.*

Since the environment was a truly global one, additional constraints would be put on the improvement effort. Sourcing and routing would have to be more effectively conducted across many boundaries, cultures, and languages. Currency differences, foreign language documents, metric conversions, and multiple customer and agent needs would need accommodation. Special quality and compliance with trade regulations and custom controls would further complicate the solutions. These factors were worked into the improvement effort, with an added requirement that would affect the quality focus of the effort. There was to be a total network dissemination of information for all partners in the supply chain. This meant that any partner would know accurately when an order arrived, when it left, how it was coming, where it might be at any time, and why it might be late. Shipment and cycle-time tracking were to be ingrained features of the redesigned system.

Figure 10.3 describes the international supply chain in condensed - format. The infrastructure that supported this chain included an information system with data for replenishment, procurement, manufacturing,

FIGURE 10.3. CPC's Supply Chain.

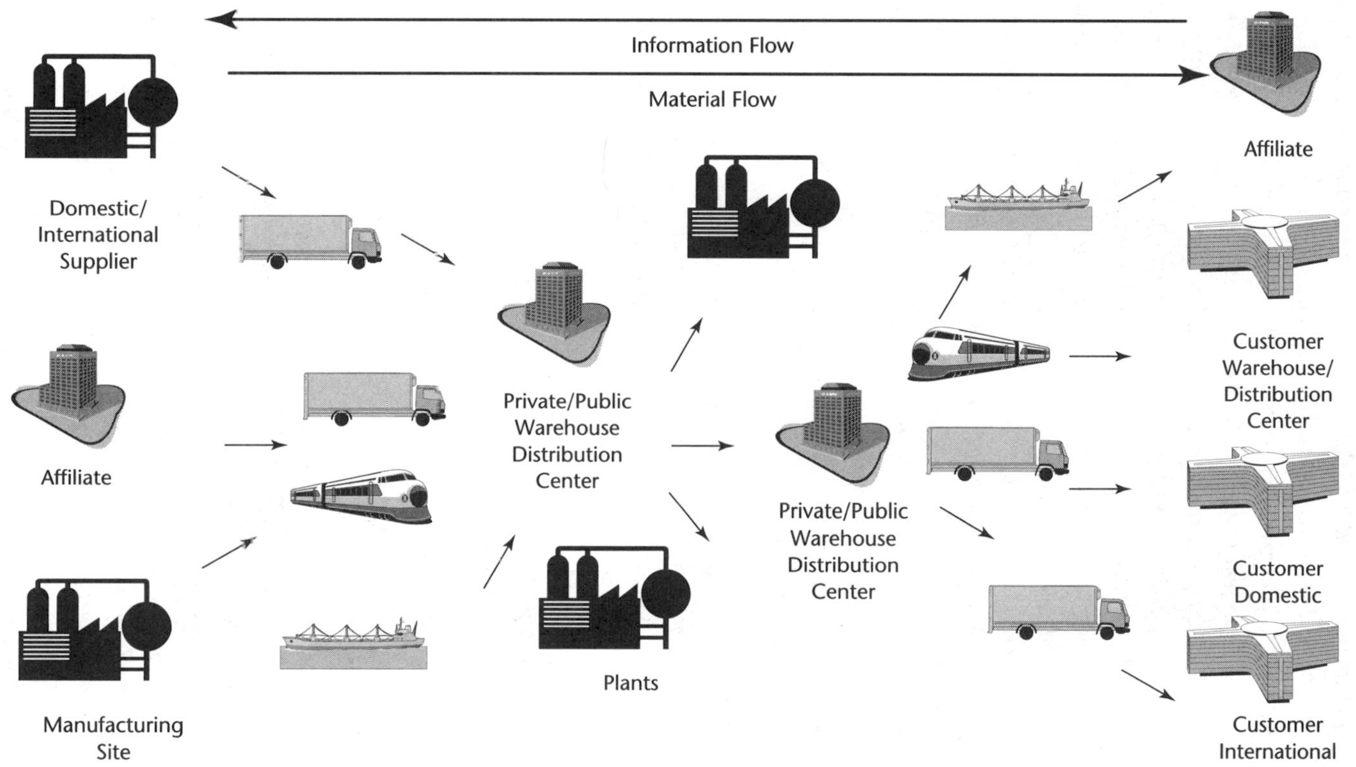

inventory management, distribution, sales order fulfillment, and transportation. These cross-company functions each took a look at planning, scheduling, and execution to determine the areas of improvement opportunity. Representatives from each function joined forces in a team effort to analyze their portion of the supply chain activities and to identify, with the help of their internal partners, the areas offering the greatest opportunity for effective change. Following many meetings, assessment reviews, and development of alternative solutions, specific areas were selected for improvement actions. (See Figure 10.4.)

Customers and suppliers were next brought into the effort, to help create the improvements being sought and to make certain that the right things were being changed. Supply chain integration and optimization teams were formed with both customers and suppliers. The purpose was to link up participants in the supply chain via processes and systems to better manage supply and demand between customers, CPC, and suppliers. The key ingredients were to be:

- *Insistence on horizontal process improvements rather than silo-type management concern for local turf issues*
- *Formation of sales and operations planning teams that would use recommendations from the joint teams to make needed redesigns to existing processes*
- *Training and specific education in supply chain tools and techniques for participants once the new processes had been determined*

The paradigm shift was to be from a short-term, arm's-length, local-focus orientation to a long-term, partnering, information-sharing, global, on-time network. Such a shift, they knew, would require redesign and reengineering of processes and education and training on the new systems that would be developed. This global supply chain optimization and reengineering effort is characterized in Figure 10.5. The preliminary meetings and discussions in this three-part improvement effort led to the supply chain flowchart shown in Figure 10.6. The original data developed by the internal team were now matched with input from the external sources as the three-part effort went in search of significant improvements across the total supply network.

Many areas were studied and redesigned for enhanced values. A few examples will illustrate the depth of the work. The sales order fulfillment

FIGURE 10.4. Supply Chain Infrastructure.

	Replenishment	Procurement	Manufacturing	Inventory Management Distribution	Sales Order Fulfillment	Transportation
Planning	Demand Planning	Supply Planning/ Contracting	Bill of Material Capital Plan	DRP/Network Planning	Sales Plan	Resource Planning
Scheduling	Order/Forecast Schedule/ Production Plan	Delivery Scheduling	Production Schedule MRP	Inventory Deployment	Order Schedule/ Inventory Allocation	Carrier/Freight Optimization
Execution	Transfer Ordering	Receiving Payment	Batch Recording	Inventory Tracking/ Recording	Shipping	Routing Rating Bill of Lading

Customer Satisfaction

Note: DRP = distribution replenishment planning; MRP = materials resource planning.

FIGURE 10.5. Global Supply Chain Optimization and Reengineering.

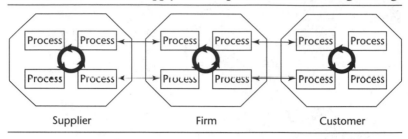

process was charted from beginning to end. Significant opportunities were found for inventory reduction, better routing, and better order tracking and replenishment. Replenishment-planning work flow was documented, with a positive impact being made on master production scheduling, materials planning and global procurement, and sales and operations planning. The conventional materials-purchasing process came under particular scrutiny to remove the nonvalue-adding tasks. The buyer's job was redesigned to become more that of a buyer and planner. The conventional process had an order entry function that verified product availability, then checked pricing and credit before sending a confirming order to procurement. Purchase orders were then issued to cover the needed materials. Under the existing system, such a sequence might or might not have met actual consumption demands.

The new replenishment process focused on a usage model that was developed by one of the teams. This model provided historical data that were compared with daily movement data, on a real-time basis, to create daily inventory replenishment needs for the customer stores. All the information on order entry, pricing, credit, and production needs, matched with current pull-through, now comes from the usage model. The buyer or planner then creates the flow of material necessary to keep inventories to a minimum and production at efficient levels. Features include EDI on a global basis from suppliers and customers, electronic order status updates, invoiceless processing, and electronic booking.

One example of the improvement that resulted occurred in the area of broker or customs clearance, the process of getting international goods through national borders and on their way to customers. The former process was characterized by:

FIGURE 10.6. Supply Chain Management at CPC.

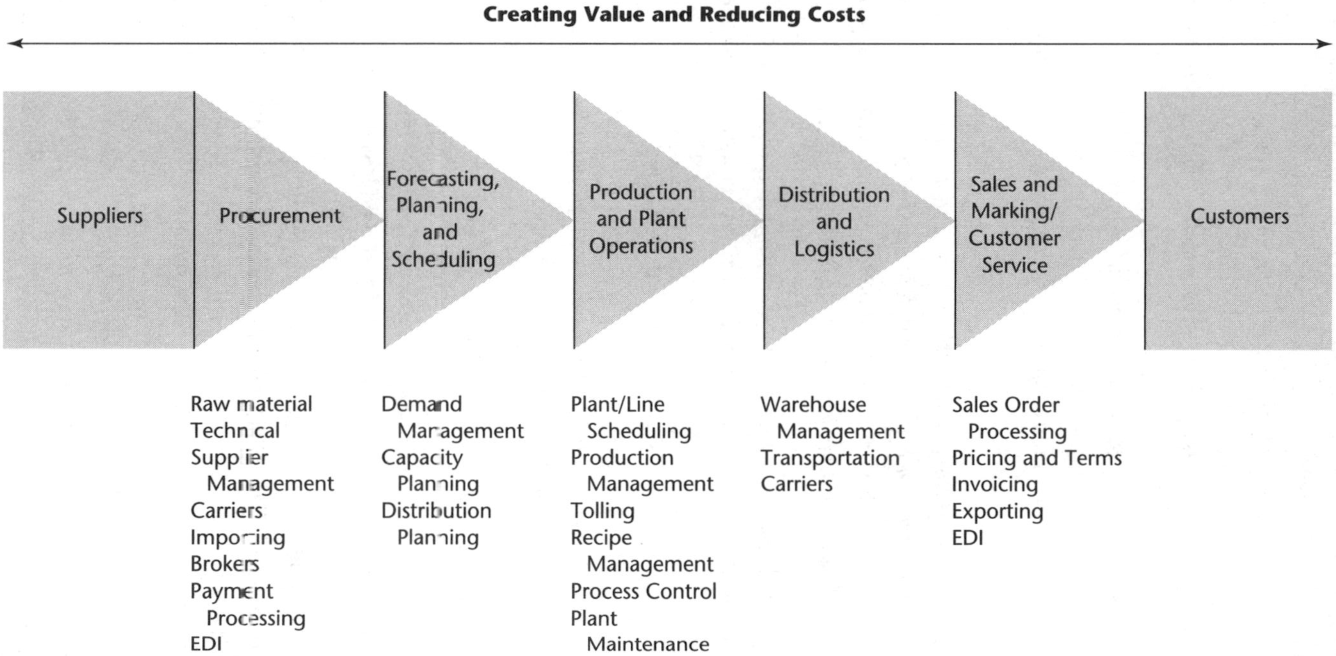

Creating Value and Reducing Costs

Suppliers	Procurement	Forecasting, Planning, and Scheduling	Production and Plant Operations	Distribution and Logistics	Sales and Marking/ Customer Service	Customers
	Raw material Technical Supplier Management Carriers Importing Brokers Payment Processing EDI	Demand Management Capacity Planning Distribution Planning	Plant/Line Scheduling Production Management Tolling Recipe Management Process Control Plant Maintenance	Warehouse Management Transportation Carriers	Sales Order Processing Pricing and Terms Invoicing Exporting EDI	

Note: EDI = electronic data interchange.

- *A massive paper chase to track products from many countries through many ports of entry*
- *The use of multiple brokers in the same port of entry to handle the required documentation, entry fees and duties, and transportation*
- *Many different processing techniques based on broker differences and local customs*
- *Huge back-office operations to rekey and process redundant data*
- *Constant telephone calls to check on shipment status*
- *Multiple process handoffs requiring tracking and introducing possible errors*

With the help of the partners, the improvement team redesigned this process. Their intention was to consolidate handling, outsource functions where it made sense to do so, and eliminate the manual features of the old system. The redesigned process bore these features:

- *The same broker was used for all processing in all ports in the United States, under an arrangement where the broker assumed responsibility for this function.*
- *One standard process was used for all transactions.*
- *Virtually no paper was needed to clear customs.*
- *Electronic communication was used to determine order status.*
- *One person handled an order from the beginning to the end of the transaction.*
- *Data were entered in one central location.*

In essence, CPC redesigned its customs clearance process to make it simpler and more effective. It then put the total process ownership into the hands of the broker to manage this noncore function, as the service group concentrated on the chemicals and products business. The savings in this one area were $200,000 annually. The division went on to establish notable gains in many other areas.

As the members of the service division review the results of their effort, they cite certain success factors in the new supply chain management system. Global partnering was a key ingredient in achieving improvement that had meaning across the network. Full-time resources were supplied by the participants, where and when they were needed, to attack the major redesigns that were deemed necessary. Cross-functional, cross-company empowered teams were the catalyst in achievement. State-of-the-art communications and information sharing made most changes possible and practical. The effort engendered a cultural change that now gets people out of their silo mentality to think outside the box and make the kind of changes that benefit the total organization and its supply network. The horizontal integration established as an early criterion was achieved, as were three types of documented benefits: strategic, measurable, and economic.

The strategic benefits include the development of a seamless procurement, manufacturing, and materials-distribution system. Groups within CPC as diverse as subassemblies, plastics, chips, and packaging have come together and pooled their resources to collectively focus on core common and mission critical solutions, that have an impact on attainment of the strategic plan. The measurable benefits had these documented savings: customer service levels, 95 to 99 percent; on-time delivery, at least 97 percent; invested inventory, down 30 percent; and administrative effort, down 50 percent. The economic benefits included significant cost improvements through reduced manpower, lower hardware and software costs, lower inventory-carrying costs, lower freight costs, and reduced warehousing and freight terminal costs.

CPC used its supply chain as an opportunity to combine the synergistic thinking that existed, from the source of supply to customer consumption, to reengineer a system far better suited to meeting the future needs of its markets. This is one more example of the opportunity awaiting any firm interested in getting ready for the next century.

Summary

There is an alternative to adversarial negotiating. It is the formation of sensible partnering arrangements across a full supply chain. The key elements are selection of the market leaders of the future, the best mode of distribution, the key suppliers, and the core strengths that have to be nurtured to create an unbeatable network advantage. Supported by leading-edge technology and communication systems, this type of network continuously improves itself as it works incessantly, with its customers, to find the means to sustain a competitive advantage.

References

Alter, A. E. "EDI Release 2.0." *CIO Magazine,* June 1993, pp. 63–66.

Bleakley, F. R. "Strange Bedfellows: Some Companies Let Suppliers Work On Site and Even Place Orders." *Wall Street Journal,* Jan. 13, 1995, p. A1.

Bowersox, D. J. "Best Practices in Global Logistics." Speech presented at the GMA Information Systems and Logistics/Distribution Conference, St. Petersburg, Florida, Apr. 5, 1995.

Csvany, H. "Where the Electron Meets the Road." *EDI World,* Dec. 1994, p. 4.

Fuller, J. B., O'Conor, J., and Rawlinson, R. "Tailored Logistics: The Next Advantage." *Harvard Business Review,* May–June 1993, pp. 87–98.

Hammer, M. "Reengineering Work: Don't Automate, Obliterate." *Harvard Business Review,* July–Aug. 1990, pp. 104–112.

Kearney, A. T. *Management Approaches to Supply Chain Integration.* Feedback Report to Research Participants. Chicago: A. T. Kearney, Feb. 1994.

Knorr, R., and Neuman, J. "Quick Response Technology: The Key to Outstanding Growth." *Journal of Business Strategy,* Sept.–Oct. 1993, pp. 61–64.

Kochersberger, R. "ECR? Don't Hold Your Breath!" *Supermarket Business,* Aug. 1993, p. 15.

McWilliams, G. "Putting a Shine on Shoe Operations." *Business Week,* June 14, 1993, p. 59.

Mathews, R. "Maximizing Individual Store Performance." *Grocery Marketing,* Aug. 1993a, pp. 16–20.

Mathews, R. "What Glory Price in the Brave New World of ECR?" *Grocery Marketing,* Aug. 1993b, p. 5.

Morehouse, J. E., and Bowersox, D. J. "Supply Chain Management: Logistics for the Future." Washington, D.C.: Food Marketing Institute, 1995.

Perry, L. "Quick Response to Nervous Tummies." *Information Week,* June 15, 1992, pp. 61–62.

Rouland, R. C. "Kmart's Got Flow." *Distribution Management,* May 1992, p. 42–44.

Salmon, Kurt, Associates. "Efficient Consumer Response: Enhancing Consumer Value in the Grocery Industry." Atlanta: 1993.

Salmon, Kurt, Associates. "Grocery Study." Report for Contributing Members. Atlanta: 1995.

Stewart, T. A. "Reengineering: The Hot New Managing Tool." *Fortune,* Aug. 28, 1993, pp. 41–48.

Tosh, M. "Spelling Out ECR." *Supermarket News,* May 10, 1993, pp. 14–15.

Tully, S. "Purchasing's New Muscle." *Fortune,* Feb. 20, 1995, pp. 75–83.

Warner, D. "Process of Continuous Replenishment Helps Mills Better Manage Inventories." *Pulp & Paper Magazine,* Oct. 1993, pp. 75–78.

Weber, J. "Just Get It to the Stores on Time." *Business Week,* Mar. 6, 1995, pp. 66–67.

Index

The Authors

●●●●●●●●●●●●●●●●●●●●●●●

Charles C. Poirier is a principal at the Chicago office of A. T. Kearney Consulting Services, a subsidiary of Electronic Data Systems Corporation (EDS). He has leadership responsibilities in the Consumer Products Group. Prior to joining EDS, Poirier was senior vice president of quality and productivity for Packaging Corporation of America (PCA). He was responsible for directing PCA's continuous improvement process and the company's drive for total customer satisfaction through quality performance. He was also a member of the firm's management committee. He served as senior vice president for manufacturing and senior vice president for corporate marketing and as group vice president of PCA's aluminum and plastics business.

With thirty-seven years' experience in various technical and management positions, Poirier is well known as a speaker and writer on industry topics. Prior to joining PCA, he was chief engineer, director of manufacturing, area general manager, and director of marketing and sales for the Container Division of St. Regis Paper Company.

Poirier received his B.S. degree (1958) in industrial management

300
· · · · ·

from Carnegie Mellon University and his MBA degree (1966) from the University of Pittsburgh.

Stephen E. Reiter is a principal with A. T. Kearney's Management Consulting Services in Chicago, responsible for the Office of the Chief Information Officer practice. In this capacity, he has assisted many worldwide corporations in achieving significant performance gains through application of Total Quality Management (TQM), process reengineering, and information technology (I/T). His education includes undergraduate work at Queens College–City of New York and graduate work at New York University's Stern School of Business.

Reiter has twenty-three years' experience in I/T leadership, serving the market in such positions as vice president and chief information officer for Tenneco's Packaging Corporation of America and Hillenbrand Industries, managing systems development, communications, research and development, TQM, purchasing, and customer service. His innovative use of I/T in support of manufacturing gained him selection by *CIO Magazine* as a Key Member of the Innovative 100.

Reiter has authored several articles and has been invited to speak at numerous business, university, and industry conferences. He has served on multiple graduate school advisory boards and computer industry and not-for-profit councils.